TYPICAL GIRLS? THE

TYPICAL GIRLS? THE STORY OF THE SLITS

ZOË STREET HOWE

OMNIBUS PRESS
LONDON / NEW YORK / PARIS / SYDNEY / COPENHAGEN / BERLIN / MADRID / TOKYO

Cover designed by Fresh Lemon
Picture research by Sarah Bacon & Zoë Street Howe

ISBN: 978.1.84772.780.0
Order No: OP52855

Exclusive Distributors
Music Sales Limited,
14/15 Berners Street,
London, W1T 3LJ.

Music Sales Corporation,
257 Park Avenue South,
New York, NY 10010, USA.

Macmillan Distribution Services,
56 Parkwest Drive
Derrimut, Vic 3030,
Australia.

Typeset by: Phoenix Photosetting, Chatham, Kent
Printed by: Gutenberg Press Ltd, Malta

A catalogue record for this book is available from the British Library.

Visit Omnibus Press on the web at www.omnibuspress.com

Contents

Introduction

The first time I heard The Slits was on a 'punk' compilation someone had given me as a birthday present. I put it on my CD walkman, holding it very carefully as I was being hurled down London's Holloway Road on a lurchy bus. I couldn't stop playing this one track, The Slits' version of 'I Heard It Through The Grapevine'. It was so much fun, and it had so much going on in it. Ari's quivering, stuttering voice was so mischievous, Viv and Tessa's backing vocals sounded so tough, basically the whole thing was just unlike anything else. These were atypical girls, and there was a definite resonance there for me. Why hadn't I heard about this group before?

My next step was to buy their debut album, *Cut*. I may have been discovering it years after its initial release, but this was a vital moment. The music and attitude were exhilarating, curious, funny and fresh, it was a relief in a way to have found it. Its potency clearly hadn't diminished, it changed something fundamental for me. The intense creativity and fearlessness that went into it practically hit me over the head with the concept they had lived and breathed: that anyone could do anything if they wanted to and live without limits. It was beyond gender and beyond punk.

I remember carrying a CD copy of *Cut* in my bag during my first year as a freelance journalist. Whenever I worked at a new place, I would often try to sneak something onto the office stereo. That would be my test – if they were open-minded enough to give *Cut* a chance, then I knew it probably wasn't a bad place to work for a while.

I wanted to know more about The Slits and their process, how they made this wonderful album, who they were singing about, and what moved *them*. Someone must have written a book about them, or so I thought. There were several on The Clash, plenty on punk in general, one on Riot Grrl even, but I wanted to read a book about The Slits in their own right. So, after a fruitless search, I decided I'd better get cracking on it myself. It became a dream and a mission that was several years in the making – and, serendipitously, the publication of it would coincide with the 30-year anniversary of *Cut* (and me).

Writing about The Slits and their work could never be done secondhand, as far as I was concerned; this involved speaking directly to all of them and the 'Slits Family', in Ari's words. (The Slits Family includes Don Letts, Keith Levene, Steve Beresford, Paul Rutherford, Vivien Goldman, The Pop Group, Budgie and others, all of whom are a part of this book.) This resulted in many hours of conversation, the airing of some fantastic anecdotes, the birth of some friendships, the receipt of some hefty transatlantic phone bills (worth it of course) and many, many cups of tea and the odd sugar rush. (Christmas cake, in Budgie's case. His visit was fortunately timed as I still had a few slabs of my mum's festive masterpiece in the cupboard. Keith Levene's interview, on the other hand, was powered by a sizeable bag of white chocolate rainbow drops he procured from the sweet shop below my flat.)

The Slits themselves have been there for this project from the word go, and have in different ways been incredibly helpful. Initial wariness from some quarters was understandable – no one had approached them in this way before and The Slits, sadly, were used to being exploited. But I was at pains to show that I wanted to do the opposite and shine a light on them and what they did, not to mention give them a platform to smash up some myths and share their own perspective of what was happening around them.

Tessa Pollitt was the first Slit I met on my adventure. Originally known as the quiet, mysterious one who rarely spoke in interviews, she has been an active part of the day-to-day making of this book. She connected me with different parts of the Slits jigsaw, as did Viv and Ari, calmly breaking down brick walls if need be. (Metaphorically speaking, of course. Although Tessa does do jujitsu.) I was also allowed to leaf through her vintage Slits scrapbook, into which she has pasted clippings and images, all surrounded by her own doodles and quirky illustrations. Her new cat, Jinxy, hid in my bag on one visit, and it was tempting to sneak it home and plead ignorance. But as I say, she does jujitsu.

Meeting Viv, whose cat also took great interest in the proceedings, was special too, particularly because, up to that point, Viv had not been especially keen to talk about punk. It was uncertain initially whether I would be able to speak to her at all. But she agreed to be involved and has been a generous and invaluable support throughout the entire process, which also saw her reconnect with Tessa and Ari and make a return to music in her own right. Ari, playing thoughtfully with her Rasta-Rapunzel locks, was passionate and witty as she unleashed free-form anecdotes and pin-sharp memories (in the unique accent Dennis Bovell describes with affection as 'Ger-maican') on a wet, windy November evening in Soho during a brief visit from Jamaica. Her enthusiasm has also been a vital force, and as she herself has expressed, The Slits' music, ideology and visual style should no longer be ignored.

The Slits were more than wild girl punks, and they ultimately proved that they *could* play, becoming innovative and exciting composers and mergers of musical genres in a way that hadn't been tried before. But they were hard to handle and impossible to categorise, which may explain why they have, in Tessa's words, "been written out of the history books - or the her-story books". However, the support for this project from every direction is testament to how respected The Slits and their timeless legacy actually are. It's a thrill to be able to say my first book is about this important group of individuals, who all continue to inspire me. I hope they, and you, enjoy it.

Zoë Street Howe
Soho
January 2009

Acknowledgements

I'd like to extend my heartfelt appreciation to the following people who have helped to make this book possible, and much more besides.

Very special thanks to Tessa Pollitt, Viv Albertine and Ari Up, for giving their time and trust and sharing their memories with grace, generosity and humour. Thanks also go to Slits founders Paloma 'Palmolive' McLardy and Kate Corris, and 'boy-Slits' Peter 'Budgie' Clarke, Steve Beresford and Bruce Smith for the good vibes and reminiscences.

Ann Needham and Frank Andrews at Ridge Farm studios allowed myself and my glamorous assistant (Dylan) to rifle through documents, take pictures, eat their jam and play with the cat, and for all of those things we are very grateful.

Communications with the music writer Vivien Goldman have been motivating and inspiring on many levels, as have those with Keith Levene, who has been kind, funny and candid. Producers Dennis Bovell and Adrian Sherwood and former Slits manager Christine Robertson were all incredibly helpful and supportive, as were Don Letts, Paul Rutherford, Dick O'Dell, Pauline Black and Raincoats Shirley O'Loughlin, Ana Da Silva and Gina Birch, who all spoke with genuine warmth about The Slits. Thanks also to Karen Walter at *NME*, Alex Ogg, Adam Blake, Lee Greenwood and Black Market Clash.

My husband, Dylan Howe, has been there for this project (and me) night and day. Joanne, Sean and Jemma Street, deepest thanks for the wonderful support. I shall always wear it. Gratitude also to Steve Cunningsworth – a true pal whose help and time has been very much appreciated.

Special thanks to Chris Charlesworth at Omnibus Press for taking on this project.

Timeline

1976

The year The Slits become The Slits, and …

January 10 – Howlin' Wolf dies.

January 21 – The first commercial Concorde flight takes off.

January 29 – IRA bombs explode in London's West End.

January 31 – Abba's 'Mamma Mia' is at number one in the UK singles chart.

March 16 – British Prime Minister Harold Wilson resigns, to be replaced by James Callaghan.

March 27 – The singles chart is topped by Brotherhood of Man's 'Save Your Kisses For Me' – the group then go on to win the Eurovision Song Contest with the song.

April 1 – Apple Computers is launched by Steve Jobs and Steve Wozniak.

April 23 – The Ramones release their eponymous debut album.

May 16 – Patti Smith performs at the Roundhouse in Camden, London. In the audience, Paloma Romero (Palmolive) and Kate Corris bump into Ariane Forster (Ari Up) with her mum, Nora. They invite Ari to be in a band with them, rehearsing the next day. The first incarnation of The Slits is born.

May 30 – Guitarist Keith Levene and Clash manager Bernie Rhodes discover Joe Strummer at a 101ers gig and invite him to join "a new band to rival the Pistols".

June 4 – At the invitation of Howard Devoto and Pete Shelley – soon to form Buzzcocks – The Sex Pistols perform to a small crowd at Manchester Lesser Free Trade Hall, sparking a second wave of punk bands to emerge from the North-West.

June 12 – The Wurzels top the chart with 'I've Got A Brand New Combine Harvester'.

July 3 – The famous 1976 heatwave reaches its zenith

July 4 – The Clash make their debut, supporting The Sex Pistols at the Black Swan in Sheffield.

July 6 – The Damned also make their debut supporting the Pistols.

August 5 – Big Ben's clock tower breaks down for nine months

August 30 – 100 police and 60 carnival-goers injured in Notting Hill Carnival riots

September 4 – 25,000 join Derry Peace March to call for end to violence in Northern Ireland

September 21 – The 'Punk Festival' at the 100 Club in Oxford Street, London, features The Clash, Siouxsie & The Banshees, The Sex Pistols and Subway Sect.

September 25 – U2 form in Dublin.

October 22 – The Damned release 'New Rose' – the first single marketed as 'punk'

November 13 – Chicago get to number one with 'If You Leave Me Now'.

November 26 – EMI releases Sex Pistols' debut single 'Anarchy In The UK'.

December 1 – The Sex Pistols swear on the seemingly drunk Bill Grundy's live TV show. This interview sees Grundy suspended from Thames Television.

December 3 – Bob Marley and his manager, Don Taylor, are shot in an assassination attempt in Kingston, Jamaica.

December 4 – Showaddywaddy hit the top of the charts with 'Under The Moon Of Love'.

December 6 – The Pistols' Anarchy Tour starts, featuring The Clash, The Damned and Johnny Thunders & The Heartbreakers, the band some claim are responsible for bringing heroin into the London punk scene.

December 8 – The Eagles release *Hotel California*.

December 10 – Community of Peace People co-founders Betty Williams and Mairead Corrigan win the Nobel Peace Prize.

1977

January 17 – Convicted murderer Gary Gilmore is executed by a firing squad in Utah – the first execution in the US since the reintroduction of the death penalty. He donates his eyeballs to science, prompting The Adverts to write the song 'Gary Gilmore's Eyes'.

January 25 – The Clash sign to major label CBS for £100,000, amid much consternation among punk fans. Mark Perry, the editor of punk zine *Sniffin' Glue*, declares 'punk died the day The Clash signed to CBS'.

January 27 – EMI Records drops The Sex Pistols.

February 4 – Fleetwood Mac release their multi-platinum album *Rumours*.

February 18 – Space shuttle Enterprise goes on its maiden "flight" on top of a Boeing 747. The longest-running UK comic, *2000AD*, is launched.

March 10 – The Sex Pistols sign to A&M Records outside Buckingham Palace, only for A&M to cancel the contract seven days later. The Pistols sign with Virgin.

April 3 – The Sex Pistols perform their first gig with Sid Vicious on bass at Islington's Screen On The Green.

April 8 – The Clash release their eponymous debut album on CBS.

April 11 – London Transport launches its Silver Jubilee buses.

May 17 – Queen Elizabeth II begins her Jubilee tour in Glasgow.

May 25 – *Star Wars* opens in cinemas, becoming the highest-grossing film of all time.

May 27 – The Sex Pistols release 'God Save The Queen'– which is promptly banned from being played on the BBC. John Peel, however, flouts the ban by including it in his Festive 50 later in the year.

June 3 – Bob Marley releases his album *Exodus*, name-checking The Slits in the track 'Punky Reggae Party'. Marley replaced their name with that of The Jam after learning they were female, according to Ari Up.

June 6-9 – Silver Jubilee celebrations are held throughout England.

June 11 – The Sex Pistols' 'God Save The Queen' peaks at number two in the charts amid claims from Virgin that the charts had been fixed to prevent them from reaching number one in the week of the Queen's Jubilee.

July 2 – Writer Vladimir Nabokov dies.

August 12 – The Adverts reach the Top 20 with their single 'Gary Gilmore's Eyes'.

August 16 – Elvis Presley dies. The Slits headline the Vortex Club with The Prefects and Tanya & The Tormentors in support.

September 16 – Talking Heads release their debut album, *Talking Heads: 77*, and Marc Bolan dies in a car accident.

September 19 – The Slits record their first Peel Session.

October 1 – Pele plays his final game of professional football.

October 14 – David Bowie releases *"Heroes"*.

October 28 – The Sex Pistols release *Never Mind The Bollocks Here's The Sex Pistols.*

December 5 – Jazz saxophonist Roland Kirk dies.

And The Slits film a scene for Derek Jarman's punk movie *Jubilee,* as a street gang who smash up a car.

1978

The Slits are signed by Island Records, Palmolive leaves and ...

January 26 – The Slits' *Live At The Gibus Club* is recorded in Paris under the temporary management of Malcolm McLaren. The tapes are given to Sex Pistols producer Dave Goodman in lieu of payment, and he keeps them for 25 years before they are released on Rough Trade.

February 13 – Anna Ford becomes the first female newsreader on ITN.

March 2 – The Slits head off on a UK tour supporting Buzzcocks to promote *Another Music In A Different Kitchen.*

March 8 – The first ever radio episode of *The Hitchhiker's Guide To The Galaxy*, by Douglas Adams, is transmitted on BBC Radio 4.

April 17 – The Slits record their second Peel Session.

August 26 – *Melody Maker* reports that the reggae artist Tappa Zukie was involved in a mysterious shooting accident in Kingston, in which his legs were injured.

September 7 – Who drummer Keith Moon is found dead after overdosing on a drug intended to combat alcoholism.

September 10 ˉ The first UK appearance of jazz musician Don Cherry at the Old Vic, Waterloo. The following year he would tour with The Slits on their promotional tour for debut album, *Cut.*

October 12 – Sid Vicious claims to have awoken in his room at New York's Chelsea Hotel to find girlfriend Nancy Spungen murdered.

November 1 – X-Ray Spex release their debut album, *Germ Free Adolescents*.

November 23 – Pollyanna's nightclub in Birmingham is forced to lift its ban on black and Chinese customers after an investigation by the Commission for Racial Equality concludes the entry policy is racist.

And Don Letts releases his debut film, *The Punk Rock Movie*, hailed by *Melody Maker* as the finest document of early punk so far. They write: "Derek Jarman's *Jubilee* was irresponsibly scabby, while Don Letts' homemade effort caught the early Roxy roustabout in all its rough 'n' ready gutter splendour…" The Slits appear in both.

1979

The Slits record and release *Cut*, and …

January 10 – British PM James Callaghan returns to the UK after an international summit to find the country in a state of industrial turmoil, prompting *The Sun*'s headline: 'Crisis? What Crisis?'

January 22 – Massive strikes kick off throughout Britain, sparking what becomes known as the Winter of Discontent.

January 27 – *Melody Maker* reports that John Lydon is in talks with Chris Blackwell to make a Blackwell-produced movie about sound-system music.

February 2 – Sid Vicious dies of a drug overdose.

February 7 – The Clash start their American debut tour at the Berkeley Community Theatre in California, opening with the song 'I'm So Bored With The USA'.

February 15 – Disco fever reigns as The Bee Gees scoop four Grammies for *Saturday Night Fever.*

April 10 – Jamaican reggae toasters Prince Far I and Prince Hammer head to Britain to tour with Creation Rebel and Bim Sherman, starting at Eric's in Liverpool.

April 20 – The Pop Group release their Dennis Bovell-produced debut album, *Y.*

April 23 – Violence erupts between the Anti-Nazi League and the Metropolitan Police, resulting in the death of left-wing activist Blair Peach. Linton Kwesi Johnson will later pay tribute to the protestor on his track 'Reggae Fi Peach' on the album *Bass Culture*, as will The Ruts in the song 'Jah War'.

April 27 – Patti Smith releases *Waves,* produced by Todd Rundgren.

April 27 – The Pop Group tour with Good Missionaries (formerly *Sniffin' Glue* editor Mark Perry's Alternative TV) to promote *Y.* Performing live with Mark Perry often ends up as a "complete Ornette Coleman-esque freak-out", with audience members joining in after being encouraged to bring their own instruments.

May 4 – The Conservatives win the general election and Margaret Thatcher becomes Prime Minister.

June – Janet Kay becomes the first British female to have a reggae song in the UK singles charts with Dennis Bovell's song 'Silly Games'. It reaches number two.

July - Authorities in California ban Roxy Music, Jackson Browne, Patti Smith and Todd Rundgren from performing at the Birbank Starlight amphitheatre for "moral" reasons, the latter two because they "attract a homosexual audience".

July 12 – Disco Demolition Night kicks off to promote a Chicago rock radio station, with activities that include blowing up disco records with a bomb.

September - Siouxsie & The Banshees lose two members when drummer Kenny Morris and guitarist John McKay walk out. Budgie later steps in as does The Cure's Robert Smith (a temporary arrangement at first).

September 7 – The Slits release *Cut* before heading off on an 11-date tour – entitled Simply What's Happening – around the country, with Don Cherry, Happy House (Lou Reed's backing band), Prince Hammer and Creation Rebel.

September 21 – The Slits release their single 'Typical Girls' /'I Heard It Through The Grapevine', which reaches number 60.

October 6 – The Clash movie *Rude Boy* is in final stages of production, with initial screenings scheduled in the New Year.

October 12 - PiL release a limited run of 50,000 copies of *Metal Box* at, in *Melody Maker's* words, the "staggeringly high price of £7.45". The limited edition albums consist of three 12-inch records that play at 45rpm, packaged in a metal canister.

October 21 – Buzzcocks embark on A Different Kind Of Tension tour – (until Nov 10) with Joy Division. *Cut* reaches 24 in Top 30.

October 26 – The Fall release their second album, *Dragnet*.

November – The Specials release their debut album, *Specials.*

November 23 – Public Image Limited release *Metal Box*.

1980

January 19 – The Pretenders top the UK singles chart with 'Brass In Pocket'.

February 2 – The Specials knock The Pretenders from the top spot in the charts with *The Specials Live EP* ('Too Much Too Young').

February 21 – The Slits play London's Electric Ballroom with the post-Palmolive Raincoats and This Heat.

March - The Slits and The Pop Group release their double A-side: 'In The Beginning There Was Rhythm' / 'Where There's A Will' on Dick O'Dell's label Y Records.

March 1 – Blondie's single 'Atomic' gets to number one in the UK.

March 17 – The Slits release their 'official' bootleg *Retrospective* on Y Records through Rough Trade.

April 10-15 – The Slits and The Pop Group play a string of dates in Scotland before touring Europe together in May.

April 26 – Blondie hit the top of the charts again with 'Call Me'.

May 18 – Joy Division singer Ian Curtis commits suicide.

June 13 – The Slits release 'Man Next Door', produced by Adrian Sherwood.

July 5 – Björn Borg wins his fifth consecutive Wimbledon men's title.

August 23 – David Bowie reaches number one with 'Ashes To Ashes'.

September 6 – The Police top the UK singles chart with 'Don't Stand So Close To Me'.

September 21 – First CND Rally at Greenham Common.

October 10 – Margaret Thatcher makes her "the lady's not for turning" speech at the Conservative Party conference.

October 26 – The Pop Group perform their final gig at a CND rally in Trafalgar Square.

November 7 – The Slits release 'Animal Space' on Human Records.

December 8 – John Lennon is shot dead by Mark Chapman in New York.

December 20 – Lennon's single '(Just Like) Starting Over' goes to number one.

December 27 – Lennon is knocked from the top spot in the singles chart by St Winifred's School Choir with 'There's No One Quite Like Grandma'.

1981

The Slits release *Return Of The Giant Slits*, and play their final gig...

February 24 – Prince Charles and Lady Diana Spencer announce their engagement.

March 6 – Buzzcocks split.

March 24 – Barbados police rescue Great Train Robber Ronnie Biggs after he was kidnapped in Brazil.

April 4 – Bucks Fizz win the Eurovision Song Contest for the UK with 'Making Your Mind Up'.

April 11 – Brixton is rocked by rioting.

May 5 – Irish Republican Bobby Sands dies in prison after 66-day hunger strike.

May 11 – Bob Marley dies of cancer.

July 5 – CS spray is used for the first time by British police in the Toxteth riots in Liverpool.

July 29 – Prince Charles and Lady Diana Spencer marry at St Paul's Cathedral.

August – The Slits release 'Earthbeat' / 'Begin Again Rhythm' as a 7" and 12" (also with 'Earthdub' on the B-side) on CBS.

August 1 – MTV debuts in the USA.

October – The Slits release *Return Of The Giant Slits* on CBS, and on the 12th record their final Peel Session with Neneh Cherry and Sean Oliver.

October 24 – London CND march attracts 250,000 people.

December – The Slits play their final gig at Hammersmith Palais.

Chapter 1

"There was no money, it was dreary, bleak – and then there was this circusy, glitzy glam rock stuff, you know, give the peasants something to shut them up." –Viv Albertine

It is 1976, and England is bristling with discontent. The nation is crippled by strikes and blackouts, and the air reeks as decaying rubbish piles up on street corners. Prejudice, chauvinism and boredom rule, dole queues snake round the block. And the soundtrack, up to now, has been pop, folk, metal, glam, soft rock and prog – out of reach and out of touch, as far as your average disaffected youth is concerned. Something volcanic is rumbling, and it's ready to explode.

At the Hammersmith & Chelsea School of Art in Lime Grove, Shepherd's Bush, North London teenager Viv Albertine meets West London upstart Mick Jones, pre-Clash, big-haired, big-eyed, spindly and channelling his inner New York Doll. "On the first day I saw Mick, he was wearing high heels and skinny red trousers with long hair," recalls Viv. "I just laughed because I knew there was no one in the whole art school whom I'd probably be friends with except for him."

Viv and Mick bonded over a mutual passion for music and a shared dissatisfaction with the mess it was in. To them, the only interesting figures, apart from David Bowie, seemed to be American – Patti Smith,

The New York Dolls, Iggy Pop, MC5 and The Ramones – and Mick wanted to change that, so in a quest to find like-minded people to create something similar closer to home, he set about organising jam sessions with different musicians wherever and whenever he could.

He wasn't the only one. There was one new band who, with the help of rogue entrepreneur Malcolm McLaren and fashion designer Vivienne Westwood, would show the way. Boasting a frontman who had already snubbed the mainstream and taken his influences from sources as diverse as Can, Ian Dury and Captain Beefheart, this group was about to explode a bomb under the British music scene.

Viv Albertine remembers: "About six months into art school, we heard The Sex Pistols were playing, just a little gig at Chelsea School Of Art. And that was it – it was like a light going on. It was the attitude more than the sound but it was like, my God, coming home at last. That was it… it changed everything."

"Before the Pistols, music was so bloody serious," remembers John Lydon, aka Rotten, in his autobiography, *Rotten: No Irish, No Blacks, No Dogs*. "It was merely images pertaining to something mystical, devoid of reality. How were we supposed to relate to that music when we lived in council flats? The Pistols projected that anger."

The Pistols are still projecting that anger at the time of writing, of course, but while they might not be taken as seriously now, whatever your take, if you weren't there the first time, be assured that what they were saying and doing back then was about as relevant and necessary as it could possibly get.

A seething London got its first breath of fresh Rotten air thanks to the Pistols' startling art school gigs during 1975 and 1976, and the motivating effect was immediate. The same thing happened in Manchester too. When the Pistols made it to Manchester's Lesser Free Trade Hall in June 1976, there were only 30-40 people present (actually a tiny fraction of the number who claim to have been there) but all of them went off to form bands, among them Buzzcocks, The Fall, Slaughter & The Dogs, Joy Division and The Smiths. Joy Division's Peter Hook famously summed it up: "It was like being in a darkened room for 20 years and someone showing you a way out," even if the feeling was, in Fall frontman Mark E Smith's opinion, that they could do a darn sight better than that rubbish on the stage. The point was that it was motivating. It wasn't all about London, and the very ethos of what would soon be widely referred to as 'punk' was what made most regional bands feel proud to stay put instead of feeling resigned to head for the capital for any chance of success.

The all-encompassing nature of punk, this assumption that anyone and everyone could form a band and get on up stage to perform, appealed just as much to girls as it did to boys. Until the emergence of the Pistols, life in Seventies Britain wasn't exactly the land of opportunity if you were a woman, and things were even less promising if you lived outside of London.

Christine Robertson, who would become the manager of The Slits, lived in Luton. "It was a cultural void," she says. "The world was quite boring at that time and although women got equal pay in '72, really the roles for women were still like this: you're going to be married, have children and be a housewife, if you're clever enough you might be a teacher or something. I wasn't really into that."

For women like Christine, the energy that drove punk turned dissatisfaction into action. It simply wasn't enough to settle back into the role that was expected of you while silently gritting your teeth as you watched your dreams disappear. Punk put fire in people's bellies, and inspired them to grab life with both hands. And maybe give it a shake too while they were at it.

"I lived my life in a punk ethic way," says Christine. "Not that anybody had told me what that was, but I had decided that anything was possible, and I was definitely not going to do what my mother did – definitely. My mum had five children, and every day I came back from school she was standing over an ironing board. To this day I don't iron. She was a wonderful woman with so much talent, but she was tied to that. It was a symbol. I thought, 'There have to be other possibilities out there.' In the mid Seventies I went to art school, it was one of my ways out. Punk came up in '76 and I came to London – this new direction was so energetic, and very anti-establishment ... I was thinking along those lines anyway."

This first wave of punk nihilism was having a primitive, far-reaching effect, stoking thought and prodding people awake, not to mention leaving a trail of ferocious new bands in its wake, joining the revolution, annihilating everything that had gone before with just three chords. It was Year One.

"I'd never played a musical instrument in my life," says Viv, "but fuck it, nothing mattered. Suddenly there was this little crack, this door opened for this very short period and you could just shoot through it. It was about having the nerve to say, 'I'm going out and I'm going to buy myself a fuck-off electric guitar'. My granny died and left me about £150 so I bought a Les Paul Junior."

Viv was fortunate to have two gifted guitar teachers on hand: Mick Jones, her boyfriend at this point, and long-time best mate Keith Levene, a precociously talented musician and fan of Yes guitarist Steve Howe, despite the perceived mindset that punk was hell-bent on destroying progressive rock bands. Levene has since been hailed as one of the brightest lights to emerge from the post-punk scene, and his playing would be widely imitated, influencing U2 guitarist The Edge among others. Levene has always been gracious about other musicians copying his style, humorously insisting that it simply points to their excellent taste.

Keith was a particular mentor to Viv, and her style, while very personal, bears his jagged, broken-glass hallmarks. Viv, on the other hand, was instrumental in bringing Keith into the first wave of punk as it crackled into life in the rough, multi-cultural neighbourhoods around Ladbroke Grove in West London: "Viv was the one who made me aware of the Pistols when they were more a myth than an actual band," recalls Keith. "The next thing I knew I was hanging out with her and Mick Jones. We were all living in West London and the punk scene was emerging, and as it emerged The Slits just happened. Viv said, 'I want to play guitar', and it made sense that it was me to be the one to show her something, she kind of ended up being a pupil, and a really great one. If anything, I taught Viv what *not* to play like."

Viv: "Keith was the most beautiful guitarist. He's a very sensitive, wide-minded, creative player. I was so lucky, he saw me through dark times when I could barely play."

Levene was a founding member of The Clash (and he would later join

John Lydon and Jah Wobble in Public Image Ltd) but by all accounts there was an element of tension between him and Mick Jones. Mick was a sensitive soul with a bit of an ego – Joe Strummer was once quoted as saying that on a bad day Mick could rival Elizabeth Taylor in a filthy mood – and he didn't take kindly to Keith teaching Viv to play. In fact he apparently didn't take too kindly to him full-stop, especially when he discovered, to his horror, that Levene was three years younger than him. "After that, he was a total bitch-cunt to me," Keith growled in Pat Gilbert's Clash book, *Passion Is A Fashion*. "There wasn't a single thing I could do right." Levene was eventually edged out of The Clash, while Viv and Mick's relationship was often peppered with rows.

"They were always bloody fighting," remembers filmmaker and DJ Don Letts. "[It was a] very passionate, fiery relationship. They have a very particular type of personality, Viv and Mick. Bloody-minded. Although I think nice people aren't always the ones who come up with the good ideas."

Between the aggro, Keith was quietly helping Viv expand her thinking and playing during the initial struggles between euphoria and frustration – and blistered fingertips – when anyone picks up the guitar for the first time. "I'd show her what Dave Gilmour would do on the one hand, and then what I would do, and she'd say, 'Well, I can't do either,' and I'd say 'That's OK, I don't want you to do either, I just want you to know about it'.

"The stuff Viv started coming out with was out there enough for me! I was like, 'I don't get how that's a tune, but that's great.' So that's how it works. Have this lesson, then I'll go away for a few weeks and come back and you're going to say, 'Keith, I'm fucking useless at guitar', and then you'll get better and say, 'I'm wicked at guitar!' and then that won't be enough.

"I taught her about plateauing, and how she could apply it to her life, not just the guitar. It wasn't all about guitar-playing, it was about approach. On all counts, hopefully, I was the right person at the right time for her."

While Viv was getting some skills under her belt, another guiding light appeared on her radar, albeit one from a bit further away: Patti Smith, the proto-punk poetess and singer from New York. In many ways

Smith was a more appropriate role model for Viv than the Pistols, not just because of her sex but because she was conquering the rock scene as a female very much on her own terms. Unlike countless women in rock and pop before her and many who would follow, Smith wasn't trying to be sexy or promoting herself with sexual imagery, yet, conversely, she wasn't adopting a masculine pose either – and as a result she had gained the respect of male and female music fans alike, at least those with open minds. "I felt it was my duty to wake people up," she said. "I thought poetry was asleep. I thought rock 'n' roll was asleep."

For Viv, the realisation that this approach was possible was worth its weight in gold. "That was a massive moment, Patti Smith's album *Horses* coming out," she says. "I remember seeing Mick on Oxford Street and we'd both just come out of HMV to get *Horses* – couldn't wait for it to come out, literally counting the days. When I got that home and put it on, my God, this was like the first woman in my life who had the same feelings about anything in the world that I had. Thank God I heard it, and to hear the passion of her and the sexiness of her without her being all tits and arse."

Paloma Romero was born in Franco's Spain in 1955. She was a restless soul, bright and independent, a square peg in a very restrictive round hole. She abandoned Spain for London in 1972, accompanied by her sister Esperanza.

Soon Paloma and Esperanza were living a far more relaxed, liberated life in West London, smoking dope, going to gigs and dodging the system in a series of mouldy hippy squats. Squatting was the order of the day and surprisingly easy since there were plenty of abandoned, bomb-damaged houses in this part of town just waiting to be broken into and adopted. These squats, formerly family houses, might not have looked like much – art student Gina Birch, later to play bass in The Raincoats, had an impressive collection of mushrooms growing in her toilet – but as well as being a fertile breeding ground for fungi, they were also hotbeds of creativity. Young artists full of vision but light on cash would come together and collectives would be formed. Why spend money on rent when you need it for paints, beer, charity shop threads, dope, guitar strings and gigs? This lot had their priorities firmly in place.

It was in one of these squats – at 101 Walterton Terrace – that Paloma met a charismatic musician who at the time called himself Woody. He was a chameleon, changing his persona as he saw fit, and in a matter of months would be known as Joe Strummer. But for now he was Woody, in homage to his obsession with the American folk singer Woody Guthrie, who wrote the song 'This Land Is Your Land' as a political response to Irving Berlin's 'God Bless America'. Paloma and Woody quickly became an item.

Woody was already in The 101ers, a popular pub-rock band who were making a name for themselves locally. Woody's perspective on life might have seemed fairly conventional at this point, but his blossoming romance with Paloma had a profound effect on him, and would mark the beginning of a lifelong fascination with Spanish culture.

Paloma and Esperanza spent their nights dancing at 101ers gigs at Acklam Hall, occasionally helping out with food and drink at the now legendary W10 punk venue. Seeing her boyfriend make waves on the scene was inspiring and frustrating in equal measure for Paloma, particularly when he started to distance himself from her and their hippy friends.

He had already been approached (some might say poached) by Keith Levene and manager Bernie Rhodes, who spotted Woody at a gig and wanted him to front the group that was becoming The Clash. This sparked a major change of identity for him. A rockabilly quiff replaced his droopy mane. He ditched his hippy dropout look in favour of tight jeans and a swagger. And he would now respond only to the name Joe Strummer.

Strummer's life and outlook were shifting in fundamental ways; he didn't want to be associated with his past and was already shedding his skin. At the same time Paloma realised she needed to change too, so like her boyfriend she dropped the hippy lifestyle soon to be so despised by punks, chopped off her hair and started looking for a creative outlet of her own.

Her name changed too, of course: "It was (Clash bassist) Paul Simonon," she says. "We were just hanging around somewhere, just joking: 'What's your name?' 'My name is Paloma.' Because it was a Spanish name and he couldn't pronounce it, he was just being wise and said, 'Palmolive?' I thought that was funny so I kept it."

With a new name, fierce image and a healthy dose of courage, Palmolive was ready to take on the world. While Joe may have largely left her to her own devices, his initial encouragement was all she needed to begin the next chapter and start making history as the founder of one of the most notorious groups of the punk era… although she didn't know that yet.

Chapter 2

"No one has ever loved an adventurous woman as they have loved adventurous men." – Anaïs Nin

Apathy had turned to urgency. Palmolive was more than ready to embrace something different. It didn't matter whether it was practical or sensible, or whether it was something her parents would approve of. It mattered more to let go of the shackles of other people's expectations and do something extraordinary – and potentially see something magical emerge from it.

"A lot of it was to do with Joe Strummer," says Palmolive. "We'd been living together for about two years at the time and he was really into [punk]. I was curious and I was really tired of the hippy scene, and I wanted a change, rather than necessarily *that* change. I thought, yeah, it sounds fun, I didn't really give it too much thought – I was crazy enough to want to do it! I didn't really care too much, and it was exciting."

Though Palmolive would become known for playing the drums, this wasn't her first choice. Initially she wanted to become a mime artist. The problem was that the mime troupe with whom she wanted to work was more interested in finding someone who could play drums to accompany their performances. Simply in a bid to get involved, Palmolive went with the flow and took the job. "I thought I wanted to do acting, so I joined this group," she explains. "We didn't really gel, but by now I was getting into the drums and forgetting about mime, and of course everybody was starting a band, Joe was in The Clash and it was all happening around me.

"I'd never thought of playing the drums before, I liked dancing. I'm more of a physical person so when I wanted to form a group, the idea of moving my fingers up a fret board didn't attract me. I like the drums, I liked rhythm, it was an instrument I was at home with. Melody wasn't my strong point."

When Palmolive started to play the drums, she came into her own, and while she wouldn't record with The Slits on arguably their finest hour – *Cut* – several years on, her powerful live performances and fluctuating rhythms proved unforgettable, and she would be credited for creating a unique style.

"Palmolive was something to behold!" says Don Letts. "She was like a punk rock John Bonham. She was heavy on the drums, furious."

Palmolive's first band was The Flowers Of Romance, now legendary even though they played very little and, by their own admission, not very well. Sid Vicious and Viv Albertine were also in the group alongside Jo Faull and Sarah Hall, the girlfriends of Sex Pistols Steve Jones and Paul Cook respectively. The group might not have been up to much, but like many early punk bands it was all about the concept, and The Flowers Of Romance was a statement against sentimentality, sensuality and romantic love. The image of rock'n'roll was saturated with sex, and punks, in the main, felt this should change.

"John (Lydon) called us The Flowers Of Romance," explains Viv. "It was a cynical take on it all, we are the flowers, the result of romantic love. It was a cynical time, it was the Seventies, a no-frills, strict way of looking at life. Not believing what you were told. It was against romance, the whole romantic love thing was cooked up, and punk was very aware of that, and derided it.

"This pissed off Mick Jones, who was a very romantic guy. When we were boyfriend and girlfriend – you know, we were each other's first loves – I wouldn't hold his hand, I wouldn't be seen to be all kissy with him, it was against what we believed in. But he wanted to be himself, a romantic and loving person. It was ridiculous, but he was really more of an individual in that sense than me."

The group rehearsed in the basement of Joe's squat in Walterton Terrace during the sweltering summer of 1976. "I remember lugging that guitar that weighed a ton on the Tube over to the squat," says Viv. "The band was all girls and then Sid, and we thought that was quite cool. He was on saxophone and jumping up and down, and I was on guitar, Palmolive on drums and Sarah bass. But we didn't really know what we were doing – none of us could play, we didn't really know how to write a song."

Working with Sid Vicious was far from conducive to getting anything serious done. Having one boy in an otherwise all-girl band was a nice gimmick, but in reality Sid's uneasy personality got the better of any creativity or progress. "Sid was so awkward to be around," remembers Viv. "He was so edgy that you couldn't really relax enough to write a song together."

Keith Levene also joined the line-up – for a week – but the group collapsed when Palmolive refused to succumb to Sid's charms, a snub that bruised his fragile ego to the point that the entire band imploded. Palmolive remains incredulous to this day. "Sid Vicious kicked everyone out of the group!" she laughs. "We had a practice in the squat where I lived with Joe, and everybody left and he was there, it was just the two of us.

"He was hanging around, trying to flirt with me. I did not like him at all, and I was with Joe, I just didn't like him in that way. He was obviously wanting something, and I was so naïve, I was thinking, 'Why doesn't he just go?' Then my friend Tymon (Dogg, from The 101ers) came in and the conversation changed."

Sid's seduction technique was unconventional to say the least. Perhaps not surprisingly, attempts to shock were the best he could do to hold Palmolive's attention: "In the conversation, he'd suddenly make remarks like, 'I hate blacks!' So I'd go, 'Well, I hate people that hate blacks!' Obviously we didn't gel, not that I thought you had to agree with people to be in a band. I didn't think anything of it.

"But the next practice we had, he said, 'You're out of the band!' And I said, 'What do you mean, I'm out of the band? Who do you think you are?' And he goes, 'You're not right...' Charming."

The off-the-wall sacking seems in hindsight like a punk version of what goes on in work situations around the world – female employee snubs male employer's advances and is suddenly 'not right' and booted out – and it extended to all of the other members of the band too, which came as a shock but had positive results in the long term. The ill wind that pushed Palmolive – and Viv – out of the band led to their branching out, becoming independent, working with others and writing their own material.

"I'm kind of upset and I'm thinking, 'This guy's a jerk'," remembers Palmolive. "But [then I thought] 'I really like the drums now. I'll make my own band!'"

Viv adds: "Sid dumped us but it was just as well, really. When that finished, I could write songs much more easily. The Heartbreakers came over from the US around that time – and brought drugs into the scene. I played with Johnny Thunders for a bit, but again, I didn't feel relaxed enough."

The Heartbreakers, of course, also brought with them the infamous Nancy Spungen, who quickly got her hooks into soft, soppy Sid. While Sid was busy falling under Nancy's spell, Viv was trying hard to progress musically. The Heartbreakers were exciting but very male, and she found that stifling. There was something about being able to write songs as a girl, without being expected to do things in a 'boy' way, or in a gratuitous way, that was absolutely necessary for Viv and Palmolive. They would soon be working together again, this time with another girl steeped in the spirit of punk who went under the unlikely name of Ari Up.

Ariane Forster, aka Ari Up, was born in 1962 in Munich, West Germany, into a life of music and bohemia, thanks to her flamboyant, well-connected mother. An heiress to the German newspaper *Der Spiegel*, Ari's mother, Nora, who was also quite a bombshell, played an important role in the music industry – and in the future of The Slits. In her earlier years Nora would put her wealth and freedom to good use, and became a music promoter in Germany, promoting tours and concerts by bands such as Wishbone Ash and Taste.

By the mid Seventies, Nora decided she'd had enough of Germany.

She took Ariane out of boarding school aged 13 and moved to Bloemfontain Road in Shepherds Bush – just a mile from Ladbroke Grove – to a house that would soon become legendary for its open-door policy for struggling musicians. Pick any punk star from around that era and it's likely they would've eaten and slept at Nora's. The guitarist Chris Spedding stuck around for three years. Ari witnessed plenty of coming and going but this was nothing new – she recalls her mother's friendships with everyone from Jimi Hendrix to Jon Anderson and Barry Gibb when they were living in Germany.

Being around musicians from such an early age made a huge impression on Ari, and it wasn't long before she ditched Holland Park Comprehensive in favour of a life in music herself. She actually returned to the school to perform a gig with The Slits later on – a show that ended in an egg-and-flour-chucking riot. The band gave as good as they got.

Ari was already naturally musical. She was learning to play the piano (much to Spedding's chagrin – apparently it put him off his song-writing) and had her first guitar lesson with Joe Strummer, who was a frequent guest at Nora's Shepherd's Bush sanctuary, as were the Pistols, John Lydon in particular, who would eventually become Nora's husband.

"I wasn't interested in John when we first met," Nora admits in Lydon's autobiography, *Rotten: No Irish, No Blacks, No Dogs*. "I came to notice John because Ariane was a fan. Ariane jumped on the stage at a Pistols concert in Soho, kissed him and said, 'You are the greatest'.

"John used to come around the house with (Jah) Wobble, Sid and the others. It was so wild. Some of the girls started to cut up the curtains, the kitchen was black and burnt out, it looked horrible. We had some terrible scenes there."

To be fair, they weren't everyone's favourite neighbours – on one occasion the man next door was apparently driven to the point of bursting in wielding a knife. (This probably wasn't the reason The Slits would later be inspired to cover the reggae classic 'Man Next Door', but you never know. Ari's wails of *'I've got to get away from here…'* on the track do sound quite sincere.) But violent neighbours and moments of punk madness aside, Nora's hospitality created an important haven for musicians to go when the rest of society treated them like criminals.

Ari's life rocketed into fast-forward when she and her mother went to a Patti Smith concert at the cavernous Roundhouse in Camden, North London, in May 1976. Everyone who was anyone on the early London punk scene was there, and it was a powerful gig.

Raincoats guitarist Ana Da Silva: "It was really inspirational, she (Patti) was doing something I wasn't used to, being really feisty with this band, all guys, but she was in the front and just giving everything – both a physical presence and an 'I'm not taking shit from anybody' kind of attitude. She came onstage with a flower, she put it into her mouth and she spat it, it was like the end of flower power, spitting it out. I will never forget that until I die."

Patti was all very well, but another young woman was making her presence felt on ground level too. Ari was throwing a tantrum at Nora in her soon-to-be trademark screech and the disturbance caught the attention of Palmolive, who was attending the show with her guitarist friend Kate Corris, then the girlfriend of John 'Boogie' Tiberi, a roadie for The 101ers.

Filled with her new passion for drumming, Palmolive was bursting to start a new band, an all-female one this time, no doubt to guard against any more Sid-style sexual tension issues, apart from anything else. One look at Ari convinced her she'd found the perfect frontwoman. She'd already stolen the show without even meaning to.

Palmolive: "She was being funny with her mum, throwing her hair around, and I thought, that's great! I asked her if she wanted to be in a band."

Ari was equally intrigued by Palmolive, if nothing else because she was wearing pig-shaped earrings, which she was rather taken with. This had to be a kindred spirit, even if Kate felt a divide because of the age difference: "I was a lot older than Ari," she remembers. "We really didn't get each other. I wasn't, however, old enough to know how to bridge that gap to a very strong-minded teenager."

But Palmolive was convinced. Ari may have barely been in her mid-teens, but she was something special. "I was amused by her," Palmolive continues. "Because of the experience with The 101ers, I knew I wanted a group but I knew we needed someone with no inhibitions as a front-person, and I thought she definitely doesn't have inhibitions! I thought she was funny and I liked her.

"We also had this girl on bass, Suzy Gutsy. She came to live with me in the squat where I was living but I have no clue where she came from!"

And so the first incarnation of The Slits was born – the line-up: Palmolive on drums; Kate Corris (sometimes spelt 'Korus' or 'Chorus') on guitar; the mysterious, hard-drinking Suzy Gutsy on bass; and Ari – at this point still a schoolgirl – on vocals.

The name 'The Slits' was sparked by an idea of Kate's – it was sharp, cutting, memorable and rather biological, but like everything they were to go on and achieve, open to interpretation. Was it a reference to female genitalia? Was it a reference to slashed-up punk fashion or aggression? The group didn't really mind which way it was translated, but most people, especially those generally unimpressed by punk rock and its practitioners, assumed it was sexual – and were duly outraged. This didn't do The Slits any favours.

Simon Reynolds, in his post-punk bible *Rip It Up And Start Again,* concludes that "The Slits' 'offensive' name… (was) the concave mirror to the convex phallic innuendo of Sex Pistols."

Ironic, then, that the word 'Slit' should hold them back and see them eventually swept under the carpet, when the more overt name 'Sex Pistol' was very much in the arsenal (no pun intended) of what made Malcolm McLaren's band of oikish ruffians potent, compelling and irresistible over the years.

Viv Albertine agrees in hindsight that the name was an obstacle to their progress, but there were other aspects of the band that proved far more difficult for the public to take: their gender, their bloody-mindedness, their wild behaviour and their ultimately avant garde 'anything is possible' musicality. They were written off by many as nothing more than a bunch of crazy women who were entertaining but musically incapable, a myth that dogs them to this day. But as Don Letts says: "Those who know, know."

Palmolive decided to strike while the iron was hot, and arranged their first rehearsal for the day after the Patti Smith gig. Once again,

Joe's squat was the venue, and anyone walking past the squat on their first day of rehearsals would have heard the fledgling group shrieking out a full-tilt rendering of The Ramones' 'Blitzkrieg Bop', a song from the group's first album, which, with its repeated call to arms of 'Hey ho let's go', was fantastically popular among the evolving punk scene in the UK.

Keith Levene enthused in an interview with *Perfect Sound Forever*: "That Ramones album was fucking *it*. What Roy Orbison or Buddy Holly were to rock 'n' roll, The Ramones were to us. They were fucking brilliant. It didn't influence the way I played though, not at all."

The Slits were just as determined to go their own way too and, armed with the Ramones as a blueprint and a room to practise in, they took their first steps, little knowing how influential and mind-expanding their own music would eventually become. In an unusual act of prescience, pioneering punk journalist Vivien Goldman braved their lair and summed up one of these early rehearsals in an article for *Sounds* magazine, dated December 11, 1976.

"As soon as you step into the squat, you're made forcibly aware of the presence of cats. Walk down a rickety staircase, avoiding planks missing from the floor if possible, and open the door with the loud noise coming from behind it.

"The Slits have formidable power and attack, even rehearsing in this ultra-gloomy basement. Palmolive is short and sturdy, with flashing Spanish good looks. She's a vicious drummer. Kate's shapely, with dashing grey/black hair, an elegantly be-Oxfammed American with a tingling line in rhythm guitar. Suzy, a tawny wild rose with a thick mop of dark waving hair, rosy cheeks, brown eyes, and rosebud-red lips, plays bass with dogged ferociousness.

"Suzy has been trying to form a women's band for years. She was in a woman band called Chaos, ''cos of all the trouble we had.'

"'You've got to learn that everything they're telling you is bullshit,' says Kate. 'It's really hard because you're a girl and you're expected to think in a silly way, not know how to put lights together, or carry heavy things.'

"Palmolive and Ariane are both wearing elaborate black weals of make-up slashed round their eyes, and the word 'SLIT' painted on their necks and cheeks. They'd only just decided on the name, and were justifiably excited about it."

This press attention – before The Slits had even played a note in front of an audience, by the way – was making its mark. Ana Da Silva remembers: "I remember very well this article that Vivien Goldman had written, she mentioned The Slits, which I thought was great, this band hadn't done anything but it was there in the papers and everything.

"She wrote about the heavy metal band Girlschool too. For me it was an important thing, it was like you could be in a girl band and like different styles of music I'd never heard done before by women. The Slits were part of my motivation for being in a band."

As a result of this early press interest, The Slits' reputation was already heading across to mainland Europe, sparking the imaginations of many burgeoning artists who, whether for environmental, political or personal reasons, felt trapped and frustrated. They caught the attention, of among others, German singer Nina Hagen, who was so inspired she left Germany and tracked down The Slits. The Slits embraced Nina as a like-minded spirit, as did John Lydon and other key members of the London punk scene.

Ari remembers, "Nina Hagen came from East Berlin, running away from that whole Russian oppression thing in East Germany. She came to our rehearsal room in 1976, because she already knew about The Slits as there was a revolution going on. Before we even hit the stage we already were known.

"When there's a revolution, it spreads like word of mouth to other artists. So other artists who needed to express themselves came in."

What was happening in London at this time was more than just another musical movement, it was vital, necessary, optimistic. Despite The Sex Pistols' cries of 'No Future', what many punks, The Slits in particular, were doing was creating a much better future from scratch, rejecting the past and the boundaries it supposedly set for them, and rejecting the future that society expected of them, the 'easy' option. The immediate future of the punk revolution would not be easy, but it would be worth it. A key element of The Slits' relative success was their unerring focus.

Raincoats bassist Gina Birch: "Ari said that being in the band, they had to be like being in the army, militant and focused. From the time they decided to have a band, they dressed as punks, lived this thing, and that's probably why Vivien Goldman was able to write about them, because they'd *envisaged* what they were going to do before they did it.

"And when they did eventually take to the stage, they just went for it completely."

Tessa Pollitt, born in London in 1959, was a fellow Patti Smith fan and an artistic teenager with a passion for music – absorbing everything from classical music to Billie Holiday, The Beatles, Nat King Cole, Ella Fitzgerald, T Rex and Dusty Springfield. Contemplative, creative and quietly independent, Tessa picked up a guitar in her early teens and taught herself, "basic chords to ease my teenage angst" from books. She grew up half in the country, with her dad, and half in the city with her mother. On leaving home at 16, Tessa headed off to study art in Chiswick, West London. It wasn't long before the *News Of The World* was on her case. She might not have said much, but she wasn't your everyday art student.

"I was at college playing a guitar, and this guy asked, 'Why have you got your legs apart?'" she recalls with amusement. "What does it matter? I'm not having sex with it. It was absurd, like you're not sitting in the correct position for a girl to play guitar.

"I started a group called The Castrators with two other girls called Budgie and Angie, but none of us could particularly play, it was just an idea. Suddenly the *News Of The World* was knocking at our door – they wanted to do a sensational article about punkesses. There's this classic line that says, 'These girls make The Sex Pistols look like choirboys!'"

In fact, the journalist behind the piece was none other than the same Vivien Goldman who'd written about The Slits in *Sounds*. She didn't normally write for the sensation-seeking tabloids, but had submitted her story in the hope of getting the concept of women in rock into the mainstream. Goldman was already a major supporter of punk, heralding it with genuine enthusiasm in *Sounds* and *Melody Maker*. And on this occasion, Britain's favourite Sunday red top.

"This was certainly the only time I wrote for the *News Of The World*," she says. "I remember I was living at 83a Cambridge Gardens and Tessa and Budgie came round to my place. Tessa was sitting on the bed with Budgie, who had this necklace with a pair of scissors because her group was called The Castrators. It was more of a conceptual thing. Put it this way – I don't remember the music but I remember the scissors!"

Thanks to Viv's articles, coupled with the tabloid editors putting their inevitable melodramatic spin on things, a big impression was created, far bigger than the reality of the situation, and certainly big enough for Tessa to get the silent treatment from her father. Well, it wouldn't be very punk if it hadn't ...

"This newspaper article was slapped on my dad's desk on a Monday morning," says Tessa. "Everyone was very curious! I don't think he knew anything about it. I rang him up and he didn't want to talk to me. You know what the papers are like, I was just taking the piss. They'd ask questions like, 'How would you deal with groupies?', so I'd just say, 'Well, I'd take them backstage and show them a good time.' I think he probably took it literally. But I was so naïve!"

Paternal disapproval aside, Goldman's article played a key role in assembling what would become the definitive line-up of The Slits. Suzy Gutsy's excessive boozing was alienating her from the others, who needed a bass guitarist who would take the group seriously, especially since the bass would become an increasingly important element of The Slits' sound once they had broadened their musical horizons beyond the punk thrash of their rehearsals.

"We couldn't do much with Suzy, she drank a lot," recalls Palmolive. "She used to just get loaded, and that was the reason it didn't work with her. We were trying to practise, we were more into it really. She was burnt out half of the time, while me and Ari were like, 'Let's do it!' So it wasn't right."

In contrast to the punk cliché of getting smashed and revelling in not knowing or caring how to play, even at this early stage The Slits, while untrained and wild, were taking their music and creative development very seriously. To this end Ari had placed an ad for a bass guitarist in the 'musicians wanted' classified section of *Melody Maker*, traditionally a place where bands found personnel. "A few guys rang up," Ari told another pioneering punk writer, Caroline Coon. "We asked them what kind of ideas they had, what music they listened to, and it was awful. They sounded as if they expected us to be wearing flowers on our shirts."

The problem was solved when Ari spotted Tessa in the *News Of The World* looking cool and striking ("a dead ringer for a young Liz Taylor," according to Kate Corris), and knew she had to track her down. She was a Slit if ever she'd seen one. The *NOTW* feature was also the first time The Slits' future bassist set eyes on them too – and a mutual interest was sparked. Tessa remembers: "I became aware of The Slits through that article, and Ari got in touch with me on the strength of it. It was right at the beginning of The Slits before they'd played any gigs."

Viv Goldman was naturally thrilled when, the next time she saw The Slits, she clocked Tessa adding her own schtick to their powerful image and sound. "Lo and behold there Tessa was again with this motley crew of wild and crazy chicks," she says. "But I didn't know the article had played such a role!"

So Suzy was out and Tessa was in, and asked to play bass – even though she had never played a bass in her life. "I just said, 'Yeah,' and decided to leave college and join them, this was far more exciting. I got on well with Suzy Gutsy, there was no ill feeling."

Suzy, by the way, was not seen again until she attended a Slits gig the following year at Cheltenham Art College. According to *ZigZag* journalist Kris Needs, she received a very special greeting: "The Slits grab all her limbs and cart her screaming to the front of the stage where she is unceremoniously dumped in an undignified heap." At least they didn't blank her.

Tessa had been living in a college hostel near to where she'd been studying, and since she was quitting college she had to find somewhere else to live, the obvious place being Nora and Ari's house in Shepherd's Bush. The whole band hung out there on a regular basis anyway, and they quickly became like sisters.

The bonding process wasn't the only thing that happened rapidly – within two weeks the band found themselves booked to play a gig at the rough and ready Harlesden Coliseum on Manor Park Road in North-West London (now a Wetherspoon's pub called the Misty Moon) alongside The Clash, Subway Sect and Buzzcocks, a killer punk line-up.

Headliners The Clash certainly had no qualms about having a female band on the bill. Instead of feeling emasculated or – heaven forbid – threatened, they took The Slits seriously as a potent punk group who, although in their embryonic stage, were worthy of support as much as any male group. In Ari's opinion, this early encouragement played a huge part in helping The Slits stick together and persevere with their aims, despite the barrage of negative attacks they suffered from both the public and the tabloid press.

"There was that window open that let girls be who they wanted to be," explains Ari. "[It happened] because of the support of our boys like The Clash. They were a huge part of it... Buzzcocks, all the boy groups, they were all part of it, they were a support system. Things weren't spoken a lot in the revolution, it was more an explosion and expression of a unified people who were all up against the world, striving to do what we wanted to do without being brutalised – physically surviving, not just mentally but physically surviving a day of walking in the street!

"So where the boys had to survive, we as girls were even more taboo, we had a harder time. But we had that automatic respect and admiration and freedom around the boys. Chrissie Hynde also got it from them, that's how she got through, she came from a different generation and different aspect, a little bit older and American of course.

"We had a strong unit, people just helping us getting stuff going. My mum helped with instruments, helped with the money for rehearsals. Everyone was our manager really – everyone can say they had a part in managing us. Keith Levene of PiL would help The Slits enormously by helping to mix sounds, helping to be a roadie at the live gigs, Joe Strummer too of course was a big part of building the group because of Palmolive. She had the vision of this girl band, she was the foundation of it.

"Palmolive and Joe Strummer were behind it, and Joe would be hanging out at my mum's place with his guitar – always had his guitar in his hand. [He] never really spoke, I remember him hardly ever talking – but he helped me with guitar, my first chords and stuff."

The Slits were now facing their first gig, put their way by Strummer. They were certainly unprepared from a musical standpoint but this didn't really matter because they were more than ready for it mentally.

The level of excitement and enthusiasm within the group was like a screeching kettle ready to boil over. "It was scary, and brave when I think back," says Tessa. "I had only just picked up the bass. But we just took risks then, we were driven to take on the world by whatever means necessary, but on our terms with no compromise."

Chapter 3

"It was when I found out I could make mistakes that I knew I was on to something." – Ornette Coleman

Chaotic rehearsals preceded chaotic gigs. The first, of course, was at the sticky-floored Harlesden Coliseum on March 10, 1977, with The Clash, Subway Sect and Buzzcocks. The crumbling red-velvet grandeur of the Coliseum usually played host to the screening of kung-fu movies to local West Indian audiences, but tonight it belonged to the punks from West London and, in the case of Buzzcocks, Manchester. It was an important gig, the first time in two months that The Clash had played live, which in punk terms was *ages,* a period of sufficient duration that The Clash's inactivity was described by Vivien Goldman as "near Garbo-like seclusion". What's more, The Clash and everyone else on the scene were treating the evening as a rehearsal for their forthcoming tour that May, in which The Slits had been invited to take part. Things were moving fast.

Film-maker, DJ and all-round scenester Don Letts had wisely brought his Super-8 camera to capture the proceedings, as he did at many seminal punk gigs. He was a veritable punk version of the photographer Arthur 'Weegee' Felig, always in the right place at the right time to capture the action. This gig was the first time he would see The Slits – and little did either party realise how influential each would be on the other. Over the course of the next few months Letts would introduce The Slits to reggae music, an influence that would change their musical direction, image and outlook, and see them transcend punk completely. The Slits, in turn, would soon take Letts on a trip he would never forget, a mind-expanding explosion of trouble and outrage.

But right now, as they contemplated the Clash tour, The Slits were a vital, compelling and quite mad punk band at the beginning of their journey. Palmolive, with help from Kate and Ari, had already been working on material – much of which would later turn up on their first album.

One of the songs was 'Shoplifting', a rapid-fire rollercoaster that nodded quite openly at what was often a necessary part of life for a skint squatter. Another was 'Drug Town' (later known as 'New Town'), Palmolive's thoughtful ode to the addictions of the terminally bored and uninspired.

Raincoat Gina Birch remembers Palmolive trying her hand at a bit of shoplifting herself, albeit not particularly successfully. "She used to go into the 24-hour supermarket at the end of our road. She had this big mac with holes in the pockets and she used to go in there and shoplift. The things would often fall out of the pockets and onto the floor, but she was so charming, they would just laugh and let her off. She did have a way with her that she could just get away with a lot of stuff – 'Do a runner, do a runner!' It's so funny because with Palmolive being Spanish and Ari being German, and Ana [da Silva] being Portuguese, they'd pick up these strange London colloquialisms and use them in quite interesting ways!"

As well as keeping a keen eye on what was happening in the world around her for a kind of anti-inspiration, Palmolive was working out rhythms, concepts and lyrics. Sometimes they were strange and elliptical ('FM' – 'my head is like a radio set...my nightmares don't project my dreams'), sometimes they were angry and outright confrontational ('Vindictive', 'Number One Enemy'), but they were always full of fire and earnestly meant. The bright and inventive Ari who, while she might not have talked about it much at the time, could also play piano, would also pluck ideas from her imagination and Kate would work out chord structures. Palmolive's drumming style was unlike any of the other drummers at that time, heavy on the toms, spare on the cymbals. Maureen Tucker, the Velvet Underground's quirky drummer who stood up to play and restricted herself largely to floor toms, would have been proud.

Palmolive remembers, "I started writing songs right at the beginning. I wanted to express how I felt. I used to like writing before, but not for a particular purpose, just for myself. So when I wrote it was more the lyrical side, expressing ideas. I come from a big family and we'd have big conversations. I used to like thinking about the purpose of life and things like that."

But in addition to the more high-minded, thoughtful themes, many early Slits songs had rather earthier inspirations – inspirations that were simpler, cheekier and reflective of The Slits' everyday life as teenage girls who were at once naïve and worldly.

Ari, Tessa and Palmolive offered some explanations of their songs to journalist Kris Needs in 1977:

Ari: "The first one is called '(Vindictive) Let's Do The Split'. It's about guys who split up with us. If he gives all the shit we will tell him to fuck off because we're not having that shit off guys. It's like a typical guy who wants to have the woman under his thumb like a housewife. We're not having it."

Palmolive: "We're not having it! 'Number One Enemy' is about all the people who tell you what to do all the time and you're just saying 'fuck off, we're not having it'!"

Ari: "'Slime' is about someone you want to have it off with. 'Shoplifting' is just about the shoplifting, that you usually do."

Tessa: "'Vaseline' is about coming on people ..."

Kate Corris would not remain a Slit for very long but she made a significant contribution to the early Slits' repertoire: "I helped to write 'New Town', 'Shoplifting', 'Let's Do The Split (Vindictive)', 'Number One Enemy'," she says. "I was the person who could figure out chords,

Palmolive or Ari would come in with a lyric, they were both really creative. Palmolive couldn't really carry a tune, and she couldn't keep a beat really, but I thought she was great, primal, great fun, but not reliable, and she didn't have a broad scope."

It appears that this feeling was in some ways mutual. No one can be certain whether various older members of the punk fraternity had a hand in influencing Palmolive on this, but the general opinion seems to be that Kate's days in The Slits were numbered as a result of not being 'cool' enough on stage. Some suspect Joe Strummer might have put the boot in about the laid-back guitarist behind her back, but no one knows for sure.

For now, though, Kate, Tessa, Ari and Palmolive would take to the stage together for what would later be described by Vivien Goldman in *Sounds* as "a big gig". Having embraced punk in its most immediate, energetic and defiantly untogether form, The Slits that night at the Harlesden Coliseum epitomised the chaos: Palmolive becoming increasingly infuriated with her shaky kit, an uncertain Tessa on a bass borrowed from Pistol Steve Jones (as Ari once said, if you put off starting a band because you have no equipment, you're not trying hard enough), Kate carving out chords and Ari stomping about like a brat and shrieking her head off.

Starting as they meant to carry on, they began the show before they had even reached the stage: just the way they walked into the room was memorable. Raincoats manager and photographer Shirley O'Loughlin recalls, "The Slits had a real gang feel, they would blaze into the room and people would just stand back. They had a huge presence. If they wanted to go from here to there it wouldn't matter if there was anybody in the way, they would just charge in a straight line, especially Palmolive and Ari. They really were an army, they were a gang."

It was not your run-of-the-mill gig. Different songs were played simultaneously and at various times instruments were discarded in favour of simply dancing around. Heckles from the audience led to The Slits challenging dissenters to get up and play the instruments themselves while they danced. Even more memorable was the girls' first onstage scrap.

Palmolive: "The main thing I remember is that we had a fight on the stage! The drums were going everywhere because I didn't know you had to secure the kit, so I'm hitting them really hard and they're going everywhere and I'm having to pull them back, and Ari's yelling because I'm going off the beat, and I just got so sick of it I threw the sticks at her. Everybody thought it was put on, part of the show, but we just had a genuine fight right there and then."

Tessa: "There is one picture where Palmolive is looking at me like, 'What the hell are you doing?!' I was playing a different song to what she was playing – and no one noticed!"

It didn't matter. Their rough vitality, style and power was everything at this early stage, and like The Sex Pistols had done before them, they were already spurring like-minded people into starting groups themselves.

Gina Birch, the founder of The Raincoats (later famed for being a favourite group of Kurt Cobain's), was also at that gig. She'd been to plenty of punk gigs before, and they had left a great impression and opened the way for a life in music, but seeing The Slits was the tipping point. "When I saw The Slits play, I just thought, 'I really want some of this!'," she says. "I'd seen The Sex Pistols, The Clash, Buzzcocks, Subway Sect – Vic Godard on the stage with a lyric sheet – and I'd never seen anybody in a band with the lyrics up on stage. You might think that's a small thing, but to me it was huge. It showed that things aren't perfect, you don't know the lyrics by heart. Or that you'd just written the song.

"There was an immediacy to it that was thrilling, but it was only when I saw The Slits play that I thought, 'This is the business. And it could have been me! It *could* be me!' They owned the stage, it didn't matter that, as all these journalists like to point out, they couldn't play – in fact that's such crap because they played in their own way. Palmolive played the drums like nobody else.

"As far as I could see the women and the girls in the audience suddenly felt this incredible liberation; we felt that we could do it, we hadn't had the guts to do it up to then." Gina had moved down from Nottingham to study at North London's Hornsey Art School, and she promptly made a point of booking The Slits for a college gig.

This night was also the first time Ana da Silva, Gina's future Raincoats consort, had seen The Slits. "They were so cheeky, and so free, especially Ari," Ana remembers. "She just did anything, she would pee on the stage if she felt like it! And Palmolive had this really happy look about her when she was playing, you couldn't take your eyes off her."

Running late, Vivien Goldman missed the onstage fight, but the urgency and sheer lunacy of the band was not lost on her when she sneaked in mid-set: "I was hot to see the first appearance of The Slits, even though I didn't catch most of it, they make my heart go brrr like a buzz-saw 'cos Arianna [sic] and Palmolive are so great," she wrote in *Sounds*. "Arianna sings lead in a black leather mini-skirt with de rigeur runs in her black fishnet tights. She's as winsome a brat onstage as she is offstage, stamping her foot and chiding us for bein' silly when we clap even though we don't understand the songs... For a first-ever gig, it was outstanding. Everyone knew it was An Event. People didn't want to leave. It was thrilling."

In his fanzine *Sniffin' Glue*, Mark Perry wrote: "The Slits played their first gig at The Harlesden Coliseum supporting The Clash in March. Their set was mad, noisy, brilliant. They were inspired but totally unrehearsed. Tessa knew very few of the songs while the singer, Ari Up, danced around screaming. I've got to admit, they scared the shit out of me."

There were some on the scene, however, including a few girls, who couldn't imagine that an all-girl group could actually operate within the punk environment, that the concept was too much of a 'statement' and too open to chauvinism, and that the whole adventure was plagued from the start by all those competing hormones.

American all-girl band The Runaways were super-popular of course, and their young age might have lumped them in with the punks, but their ethos wasn't the same. For all their adolescent aggression, their focus was ultimately on appealing to men, and they duly provoked randy responses like this one, from *NME*'s 'hip young gun-slinger' Tony Parsons: "Runaways brought the house down with some hot, hard, bitching rock and roll, the fact that they are young and extremely horny teenage females was a bonus."

The Slits were not like The Runaways – who wore hot pants, spandex and skin-tight T-shirts, all designed to excite teenage boys – and their music wasn't steeped in traditional pop or rock thinking, and as a result they sparked a different response. Indeed, Harlesden was not only their first show but the first night of many that saw the group begin to gradually change people's perceptions about the role of women, and prove even their own peers wrong.

Kate: "Chrissie Hynde always said she couldn't work with a bunch of girls, but The Slits were instrumental in changing people's tunes, big time. And after that first gig we did, Chrissie came up and said, 'Oh, I see what you mean now!'"

Not that they particularly cared what Chrissie Hynde thought – although she was soon to prove *them* wrong in her own right too. Kate adds, "At the time Chrissie was considered very uncool. She was full of it, but it turned out she wasn't. She was a loud-mouthed American girl who wore her hair the wrong way and bragged a lot as far as everyone else was concerned." Despite their antipathy towards "uncool" Chrissie, Viv Albertine – who was considered to be particularly cool – cited her in an interview at the time as the musician who first made her feel like a guitarist herself, not to mention the first girl she'd ever met "who played the guitar without looking like Joni Mitchell. It was great."

Viv was also impressed by The Slits' performance that night. The ever-developing guitarist was lurking in the audience, presumably to watch her boyfriend when The Clash came on. While Viv had turned down an offer to join The Slits at the very beginning, the energy of that first gig sparked her interest. "I rang them up the next day to say they were really good, and they said come over and that was that," she remembers. "I hadn't intended to be in them at first. But I went round there, we all back-combed our hair and suddenly we looked like a band!"

Viv's appearance set the seal on Kate's impending departure from the group. "Paloma said: 'You're out', or words to that effect," Kate explains. "She made it sound like it was a band decision, although the others tell me now that it was presented to them as a done deal. 'Someone' had told Paloma I was crap on stage, and that 'someone' has never been named. We all have our theories."

Some still speculate that the 'someone' might have been Joe Strummer, other theories point at journalists who reviewed the gig and supposedly weren't impressed by Kate's onstage presence, and these reviews may have been taken to heart by Palmolive, who was keen to see the band progress.

Kate continues: "Strummer was good. Any of his female friends who had bands he would try and get them a gig, because he was keen to be seen to be behind women in music. But it could have been him who said, 'She's crap, get rid of her,' because he did the same thing to me with Ramona in The Mo-Dettes (Kate's post-Slits band). But there are any number of people it could have been, and I doubt he would have wanted to take the whole blame.

"People would get you in a corner and go, 'You should get rid of so and so' ... The problem is that people listen, and then the problems start. But it may just have been that she [Palmolive] saw Viv as the more viable person and she thought she should get rid of me to get Viv in, I really don't know."

Though a shock to Kate, the change was ultimately the right thing all round. In a slightly surreal turn of events Kate was stunned when Palmolive offered her the position of manager after booting her out. Kate continues, "It was the right decision, even if for the wrong reasons. But directly after telling me I was sacked, Paloma asked me to manage the band. Whatever – I was not up for playing mummy to a bunch of crazy performers. And I don't have that single-minded mentality that it takes to actually break a band."

Palmolive, in hindsight, feels contrite about the sacking: "That was a hard decision, there was a sense of loyalty to Kate, so I feel divided about that. It wasn't nice to do that to Kate, but on the other hand I thought Viviane fitted the role better. That's just how we functioned. There were a lot of people who were thinking in the sense of getting it right, the right image. But that's what we did. I'm not proud of it."

Kate was, in all honesty, ready to move on herself. Outside of The Slits, she could see punk was already becoming a 'trend' that was attracting pretenders keen to jump on the bandwagon. Palmolive was ambitious on behalf of The Slits, but Kate ultimately wanted something different.

The post-Slit Kate later hooked up with drummer June Miles-Kingston, whom she met working on the set of Julien Temple's Sex Pistols film, *The Great Rock 'n' Roll Swindle*, and they recruited bass player Jane Crockford and singer/dancer Ramona Carlier to form The Mo-Dettes. She remembers, "June bought an old drumkit off Paul (Cook) and we started playing together. I remember playing with some guys at one point, thinking maybe all girls wasn't such a good idea after all, but none of them really took.

"Then I saw Jane playing with The Bank Of Dresden, and we decided to play together for fun. I think Jane brought Ramona in, and we played one gig for a party at the Chippenham [a pub in Maida Hill, West London]. It went down really well and we just kept going. We were determined to give it up when it stopped being fun."

The Mo-Dettes themselves weren't immune to meddling from outside forces – this time the knives were out for their lead singer – but Kate ignored it. "I remember Strummer telling me to get rid of Ramona, who at the beginning was a bit overweight and stood stock-still stage centre. As usual, I ignored his advice, and she became a great performer."

Chapter 4

"The only people for me are the mad ones, the ones who are mad to live, mad to talk, mad to be saved, desirous of everything at the same time, the ones who never yawn or say a commonplace thing, but burn, burn, burn like fabulous yellow roman candles exploding like spiders across the stars, and in the middle you see the blue centre-light pop and everybody goes, 'Awww!'"
– Jack Kerouac, *On The Road*

Viv Albertine quickly became the driving force in The Slits, organising rehearsals and keeping the band in check, and it wasn't long before she started writing material. Viv also introduced them to Keith Levene, who was 100 per cent supportive of the group and their process and was keen to see them succeed. "I could have just known Viv and not had anything to do with it, but I was involved with Viv teaching her guitar, not just for The Slits," he explains.

"Ari was an annoying person on the scene, but she also had juice. And I got on to Nora and said, 'I've seen this fucking purple drum kit, get it for Palmolive'. Viv was pushing, Ari wanted it, we ended up doing loads of gigs all over the fucking country. I'd do sound for them and stuff."

The age difference between Viv and Ari still felt significant, but Viv was fascinated by the free-spirited schoolgirl, and particularly inspired by her total lack of body consciousness – unusual for any woman, let alone a teenage girl.

"Ari was so young,"Viv remembers, "and the weird thing for me, as I was about five years older, was that you couldn't have a proper conversation because she was only 14. I tried to speak to her on the level of someone my age but she was a bit childlike – in a nice way, and it was partly because of the German thing – although she's quick with languages, she's got a good ear, and that's why she's so good musically. But that was weird."

Keith was similarly nonplussed, but impressed, by the super-confident teenager. "I didn't really take too much notice of Ari because she annoyed me," he says. "That's why her mum's called Nora. Ig-Nora. Sometimes you've just got to. But Ari's got a lot of power; let her play to her strengths and you've got a wicked person. She can't do anything about it. I appreciated her, I liked her, and I fucking like what she does. In the context of The Slits, it's great."

Nora was more than just a chaperone for her young daughter: she was putting her music industry nouse to good use and acting as a manager, as she did on and off throughout the band's career, especially when various unscrupulous parties took on the mantle of manager and tried to rip them off in the ensuing years.*

Palmolive: "Nora was a real manager all along. She cooked us meals, she was older and more together, she had a car, a phone, a home. We were, like, living in squats. She was into it herself, she liked the music, so whenever we had someone who didn't work out, she'd always fill in. In reality, she facilitated a lot of it."

While undoubtedly wild and eccentric herself, Nora seemed to be able to deal with normally frustrating situations in a relatively calm way, particularly if Ari started to kick off at her. "Ari used to insult and swear at her," says Palmolive, "but Nora used to just laugh at it, so we'd laugh along with it, everybody was happy. There was definitely the mother-daughter thing, but it was not your normal relationship."

"Ari was quite tantrumy but she was going through huge hormonal changes," explains Viv. "It must have been hard, living with her mother

* One 'manager' zoomed off on Palmolive's prized scooter and was never seen again.

who was partly involved in the band. No one gives her any credit for that, growing up in a punk band, her mother being part of the scene, no father on the scene. No one gave her any leeway because of that."

Nora's unconventional personality will have played a huge part in forming Ari's own uninhibited character, but Ari was very much going her own way. She might have been growing up with punk, finding her way, but she didn't care what anybody thought, or if she repelled 'typical boys' just because she didn't play by the rules or try to attract them. It wasn't about posing or posturing. She had better things to do, and she was having fun. Woe betide anyone who tried to stop her.

Viv: "I loved her style, and she had great attitude, and she was free. Ari was so free about her body, and in those days you didn't have to worry about having a perfect body like you do now.

"Now there's Girls Aloud and Sugababes, they're showing off their beautiful bodies all over the place. It was irrelevant back then – the guys didn't even look at you in that way. If you were huge maybe, or stick-thin, they might have noticed, but if you were just normal in-between, no one was like, 'She's got a great arse' like it is now, or 'She's fit'. There was none of that.

"So Ari was a bit like a child, she'd happily wear no clothes, or you know, pants over trousers, or pee on stage*. She was utterly relaxed in her skin, I think she probably still is."

That freedom and lack of self-consciousness, or sense of female competitiveness, was part of what made The Slits empowering role models for girls, and fearsome educators for boys – and they remain so now. They weren't trying to compete with male musicians, they weren't trying to use their 'feminine charms' to get ahead. All of those things went out of the window – although they would inspire the Viv-penned 'Typical Girls', later to be their ascerbically witty, skanking debut single.

While the girls had no trouble getting bigger and bigger audiences as the scene in London started to snowball, if you pan back, the light at the end of the tunnel still looked rather small.

Christine Robertson: "I remember seeing Loudon Wainwright. Not

* Ari explained later that she just couldn't get offstage in time, what's a girl to do?

my kind of music, but the thing that shocked me was that there were all these long-haired hippy students sitting on the floor, and I'd come from that Northern Soul background, and I just couldn't believe people would go to a concert and just sit there. I just thought, well, that really is the death of music."

Punk was growing but the mid-Seventies remained awash with acoustic-guitar-toting singer-songwriters as well as home-grown and transatlantic stadium rock and heavy metal, which was fine for playing air guitar to – and no one is denying that this is a noble pursuit – but what about if you wanted to dance? Well, where there's a will, there's a way.

One of the side-effects of the punk phenomenon was the way in which two separate but far from mutually exclusive music cultures gradually met in the middle, as restless white kids inspired by punk also began to sniff out Northern Soul clubs, blues dances and various hangovers from Mod culture, where they could dance out their frustrations and mix.

Christine remembers, "Where I'd been living in Luton, there was a West Indian population that brought with it blues and lots of soul, so there were one or two areas where you could go and dance."

In addition, the liberated, non-judgmental vibe at the West End's gay clubs was vital to the young alternative scene, not least because, as John Lydon maintains in his auto-biography, the music was simply better. Also, the chances of getting bothered for being different or, indeed, female, were considerably slashed. Soho's lesbian bar Louise's was a much-loved punk hangout, and offered a place to go that was free from bovver boys or dirty old men.

The Bali Hai club above Streatham Ice Rink in South London was another haunt, as was Dalston's Four Aces reggae mecca in East London. Ska and reggae clubs were hugely important – and while ska had been replaced by rocksteady in Jamaica because it had just become too hot and frenetic to dance to, in dreary England it was more than welcome.*

* As it happened England was starting to heat up too, not to Caribbean standards perhaps, but the sweltering summers of the late Seventies often saw young punks throwing themselves into the fountains at Tottenham Court Road's Centre Point after a night out.

But these were still dark times for live music – and those dark times inspired those desperate for inspiration to look further afield for influences – New York had already been spewing out fiery garage-punk such as The Ramones and The Stooges, and krautrock had its place, as did rockabilly, as The Clash would testify, but there had to be a way to freshen things up and bring something new to the table.

While The Slits might have bashed out Ramones songs in their early rehearsals, they were taking on a new influence that was to inform their songwriting for the rest of their career – dub reggae, in which guitar came second to a heavy bass sound and the mixing desk was king.

The Slits were by now hanging out regularly with Don Letts at his Chelsea treasure trove Acme Attractions, at which one of the attractions was Don's glamorous colleague Jeanette Lee, the future boss of Rough Trade, and the other was the eclectic music he would play.

Don: "At that time, popular music had lost the interest of the young people on the street, my mates anyway. I'm first generation British-born black so I already had music to ease my pain, and that was obviously reggae – very anti-establishment, and a lot of DIY aspects about it as well – the Jamaican punk rock. My white mates had to set about creating their own soundtrack."

And that soundtrack was influenced, definitely, by the sounds and rhythms drifting out of Don's shop. Buried under the Chelsea Antiques Market on the King's Road, Acme Attractions was a cheaper, more accessible answer to Vivienne Westwood and Malcolm McLaren's legendary boutique Sex up the road at World's End – and this annoyed Vivienne no end, of course. Acme Attractions was famous for its customised retro clothes and accessories, the scooter in the middle of the shop, the jukebox, and Don smoking moodily at the back.

"My shop was a lot more user-friendly, a lot more multicultural," explains Letts. "Vivienne and Malcolm's place was more Euro-centric, certainly a lot more expensive – you could come in my shop and spend £10; in Vivienne and Malcolm's shop you'd have to spend £50. But this was back in the day when shops were like clubs where like-minded, disaffected people hung out. It was in my shop that I became friendly with The Slits."

All the young punks hung out at Acme Attractions, if nothing else to listen to Don's music and ask Jeanette's opinion on their haircuts. (Well, Sid Vicious did, anyway. Girls like The Slits weren't likely to ask for anyone else's approval on their hair or anything else. In fact they'd have preferred it if you disapproved.) But on the subject of music, word got round that Don had a massive record collection that included some very rare reggae. He seemed to be able to get hold of anything. This didn't go unnoticed.

Don remembers, "A friend of mine, Andrew Czezowski, opened up the very first dedicated punk rock venue – the Roxy in the West End – and asked me to DJ there. He'd seen the reaction I'd got from playing reggae in the shop.

"I'd never DJ'd in my life, and this was so early in the punk scene there were no punk records to play. So what do I do? I play something I like – hardcore dub reggae. Luckily the young white potential punk rockers dug it too, they dug the fact that it was anti-establishment, the lyrics were about something, they liked the bass lines, and they didn't mind the weed either. So there was a serious cultural exchange."

While DJ-ing at the Roxy on Neal Street, Covent Garden, Don spotted a lucrative gap in the market. He was playing all that soporific dub between the bands that were on, but all the punks were on speed. Not right at all. So he invited his Rasta mates to the club to roll spliffs for the white kids so they would slow down during his sets. It balanced everything out, and Roxy founders Czezowski, Susan Carrington and Barry Jones were more than happy with how things were turning out in their new punk haven.

The Roxy opened in what used to be an old gay club called Chagaramas. With bench seats, mirrored walls and a subterranean stage and dance floor, it had just the trashy intimacy the burgeoning punk scene needed.

Quickly tiring of the initially motivating chaos and 'destroy' themes peddled by the earliest wave of punk, The Slits were absorbing Don's sounds like sponges, and spent many evenings after hours at his place in Forest Hill "amid clouds of ganja, shaking the foundations with heavy dub", says Tessa. "Once me, Ari and Chrissie [Hynde] got locked in a room upstairs for what seemed like hours. To this day I've no idea why! Funny things used to happen in Forest Hill."

Nobody wanted to leave the Roxy at the end of the night, and it made sense just to take the party back to Don's place, and that was where the reggae education continued. Tessa: "We were flooded with reggae. It was just more interesting than punk music, basically. The tunes I used to hear are still my favourites."

Though Don Letts probably didn't realise it at the time, the records he played by Big Youth, Burning Spear, Bob Marley and Prince Far-I sparked the expanding imaginations of The Slits and others, and helped steer the group in a new direction. While their early recordings might be pure punk – '(Vindictive) Let's Do The Split', 'Shoplifting' and 'Vaseline' thrashed, spat and intimidated with the best of them – a major shift slowly now occurred in their writing and arranging. Thanks to Don, they started incorporating the offbeat skanking guitar-chop, echoes, sound effects and much heavier bass lines.

"We all used to go to sound-system dances together," says Tessa, "We used to go to a lot of shebeens, blues parties: people used to take over an old house for the night, and just hold sound-system dances all night. I really miss that in Ladbroke Grove. At night-time now, it's dead in comparison."

Don would take them to hardcore reggae parties and clubs, from house parties to the Hammersmith Palais (prompting Joe Strummer to write 'White Man In Hammersmith Palais'). But while John Lydon and Strummer were happy to skulk in the shadows, taking it all in with a spliff and a can of cheap lager and trying not to attract too much attention, Ari threw herself into the thick of it: "Ari we took to a lot of places. She was fearless, unbelievable," says Don. "She'd go into places where sometimes I would look in and say, 'I don't know about this place, it's dodgy, I don't like the vibe,' and she'd say, 'Come on,' and just walk in there.

"You get Ariane to a club and within five minutes she is the centre of attention. If there were a spotlight in the house, it would be on her. In fact the psychological spotlight was always on her. And they weren't laughing at this crazy white woman, they were digging the fact that she knew her shit. She could out-dance anybody. She's never changed, this girl. She's lived in parts of Jamaica I won't go."

Ari remembers this with justifiable pride: "I could walk into any blues party. You'd hear dub bass on every corner. If you wanted to go to a basement party, you'd just listen and follow the sound.

"You might pay 50p to go in, then you were in total darkness and a cloud of weed, and huge speaker boxes from floor to ceiling in a tiny little ghetto apartment. The bass doesn't even go into your ears at that stage, it's in your belly and chest. Some were sound-system dances in the town hall or the club, then later on after it closed we'd go to the after-party in a basement. They looked at us with curiosity, not scorn."

A core of young punks earned a reputation for being open, creative and embracing of black culture, as well as other cultures from around the globe too, but black music was the presiding influence at that time. And as Ari recalls, a lot of black teenagers found they could identify more with people like The Slits than other black kids who were more in tune with soul and disco.

"We, coming out of not being able to relate to anything as girls, found a way to express ourselves in punk," she explains, "and we found a lot in common with the urban kids. People talk about outcasts, but we were the outcasts of the outcasts. So the outcasts of the outcasts got together with the outcasts of the outcasts! There were lots of black kids into soul, versus the reggae kids.

"They used to call the soul kids 'Sticksmen', after the reggae band. They couldn't understand black kids who didn't educate themselves about identification, things to identify with, like Rastafarianism, Haile Selassie, Martin Luther King and Marcus Garvey, and Garvey's philosophy.

"The Rasta and reggae kids were thinking about it but a lot of kids couldn't understand the culture. Sticksmen had big afros, slick outfits, lots of gold, the pimp look. The Caribbean reggae kids over here couldn't understand how the soul kids were acting, they had more in common with us, and punk – even with us as girls, that's why they didn't take offence when we walked into parties."

The white punks' obsession with reggae and dub struck producer Dennis 'Blackbeard' Bovell - Matumbi-member and the man who would later go on to produce The Slits' debut album, *Cut* – as particularly interesting. "Young punk kids were getting into what a lot of young

West Indian kids should have been getting into," says Bovell, "but they were getting into R&B, and it was the older generation that was into ska and reggae.

"There was a section of my generation that was heavily into Lover's Rock; by then, Janet Kay would be starting her climb up the charts. So that was on the one hand, and then all these punk kids started grooving, not to the British side of reggae but the Jamaican side of reggae, Prince Jazzbo or Tappa Zukie, more of the DJ kind of sound-system reggae, quite hardcore. Interesting that they picked up on that."

What was especially intriguing was that, unlike in many other movements, there was an embracing of differences, as opposed to an attempt to homogenise. There was a mutual respect; the white youths didn't expect their black contemporaries to morph into them, nor vice versa, but their fascination with each other's style and sounds would alter everything. And it all came from a place of genuine interest and respect, which is more than can be said for what was happening elsewhere on the streets and in UK society as a whole.

Don Letts: "Understanding our differences made us closer. It wasn't by trying to be the same. I didn't want to have a Mohican, Joe Strummer didn't want to have dreadlocks, although Ari did. Ari is particularly chameleon-like – she's about as international a human being as they come. Can't speak Spanish though." Well, nobody's perfect.

Don's standing as a general mover and shaker attracted the attention of Bob Marley when he visited London during this time, although initially he was outraged by Don's rebellious demeanour, which didn't comply with his Rastafarian culture. In Bob's eyes, Don was hanging out with some questionable characters.

Ari remembers, "Bob Marley said to Don: 'What you doing wearing bondage, and leather jackets and with your locks out?' Don was one of the first Rastas who also got shit from people because he had his locks not always in a hat, and he had a leather jacket instead of a khaki suit … I mean, Rastas look crazy and rebellious anyway, they look nuts, so they already have that style, but Don had that punk look, which he mixed with the Rasta look.

"Bob Marley was really offended, he was very sceptical. But because Don really knows how to persuade and talk, he has that talent to represent and show what's going on, he'd say, 'No, that's the ting now, it's the 'in ting' now – there's a revolution going on and everyone's into reggae.'"

This was evidently enough to persuade Marley to embrace the London punk scene and even write a song about the coming together of these two cultures, 'Punky Reggae Party'. It was Marley who coined the term, according to Ari, and he was so taken with what Letts was telling him about these fantastic, exciting, rebellious bands who shared his love of reggae, he name-checked them, largely on Letts' recommendation.

Ari: "Next thing you know, Bob Marley does a demo, a pre-recording of the recording he will put out eventually, of 'Punky Reggae Party'. We never called ourselves punky reggae, we weren't even thinking of labels.

"Anyway, he sings, 'The Clash, The Damned, The Slits...' He put The Slits in there. I heard the demo he gave Don Letts, and I was like, 'Wow!' But when he found out we were girls he took the name of The Slits out, and suddenly it was another punk band in there*.

"This is a true story... he was a chauvinist. He was a Rasta from Jamaica and when he sees girls looking like us, it was like, 'Oh my GOD', he flipped out. So he took the name out. It's a typical Slits story – his story is just one of many."

Vivien Goldman, also a cohort of Marley's, must have heard that original demo, because she quoted the original line, boasting The Slits' name, in an article in 1977. Free-thinking and peace-loving he might have been, but that 'freedom' of thought was conditional, for him at least. After gracing The Slits with a tribute at this early stage in their career, ripping it straight back out once he realised their gender was a major disappointment, which made it hard to respect him in quite the same way.

Whatever rebellious spirit is embodied in the cult from a Western perspective, Rastafarianism has a deeply held tradition of chauvinism, but Don Letts never subscribed to this and was very much onside right the way through for The Slits. Indeed, the rebel dread was soon to be kept very busy by the band, who appointed him their manager, a position that

* The Jam – zsh.

The Slits in 1977: Palmolive, Viv Albertine, Tessa Pollitt (seated) and Ari Up. (LILIANE VITTORI)

A pre-punk Viv Albertine, Keith Levene and Mick Jones outside Viv's squat in Davis Road, Acton, West London, 1976. (COURTESY OF VIV ALBERTINE)

Tessa, Viv and Ari put their best feet forward. (COURTESY OF VIV ALBERTINE)

Laura Ashley as you've never seen it before - Viv Albertine and Paul Simonon, posing for a Laura Ashley calendar in 1976. (JANE ASHLEY)

Viv Albertine, in full punk glory, making tea in her squat, 1977. (COURTESY OF VIV ALBERTINE)

The Slits (pre Viv) - Tessa Pollitt, Palmolive, Ari Up and Kate Korus - at their first gig, Harlesden Coliseum, 1977. (IAN DICKSON/REDFERNS)

Ari Up and Kate Korus live onstage at the Roxy Club, London, March 1977.
(ERICA ECHENBERG/REDFERNS)

The Slits stage, 1977. (SHIRLEY O'LOUGHLIN)

Spitfire Boys – a pre-Slits (and Banshees) Budgie and pre-Frankie Goes To Hollywood Paul Rutherford, 1977. (COURTESY OF VIV ALBERTINE)

Ari Up, 1977. (CHRISTINE ROBERTSON)

Tessa Pollitt and the White Riot tour bus, Manchester, May 8, 1977. (LEE GREENWOOD)

Steel Pulse with The Slits, 1977. (RAY STEVENSON/REX FEATURES)

Viv Albertine, backstage, 1977.
(RAY STEVENSON/REX FEATURES)

Ari Up, live at the 2nd Mont De Marson Punk Rock Festival, France, 1977.
(IAN DICKSON/REDFERNS)

Tessa Pollitt (RAY STEVENSON/REX FEATURES)

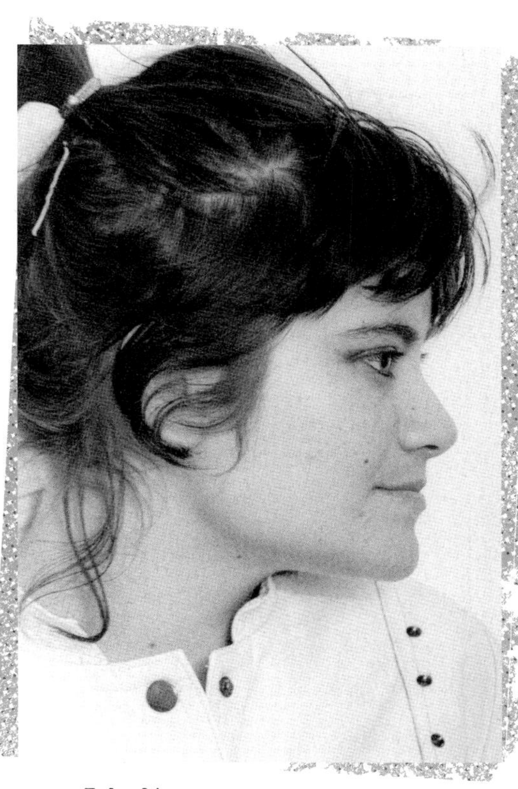

Palmolive (RAY STEVENSON/REX FEATURES)

Ari Up (RAY STEVENSON/REX FEATURES)

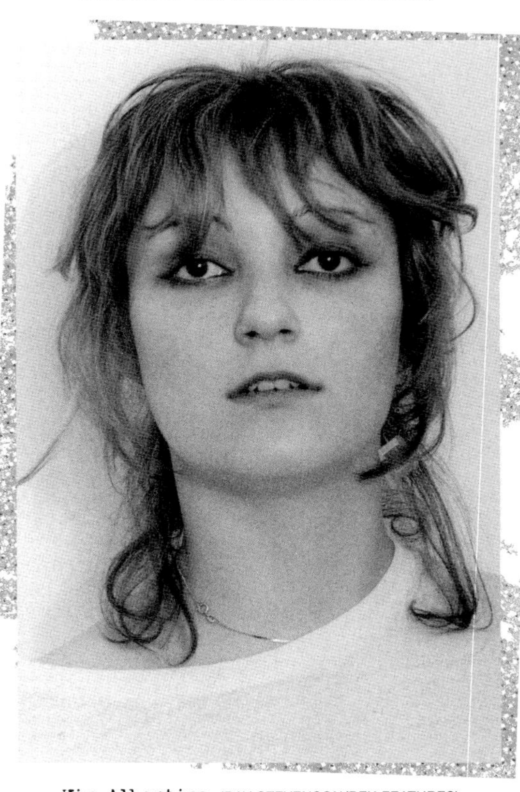

Viv Albertine (RAY STEVENSON/REX FEATURES)

The Slits, 1977. (RAY STEVENSON/REX FEATURES)

was simultaneously enviable and unenviable, so he could take care of them while they toured with The Clash, Subway Sect and Buzzcocks. However, with the exception of the ever-reliable Nora, he'd be just the first of many managers.

Tessa: "When it came to managers, Don was more of a friend, it was a temporary thing. We went through so many managers I can't tell you! Christine Robertson was brilliant but that was much later. We'd have these brief encounters with people who attempted to be managers... but initially we had to book a lot of the gigs ourselves. From being teenagers, we grew up very quickly."

It's quite likely that one of the reasons for wanting Don Letts on board during the tour was because The Slits and The Clash were angling for some on-tour bus inspiration in the form of mix-tapes, mix-tapes and more mix-tapes, which could be provided by Don, so they could take the sound of the Roxy with them. But while The Clash were the ones to be hailed as the punks who created that irresistible hybrid of punk and reggae, it was The Slits who really mixed it up, shaking off the mantle of reggae tourists and crossing the breeds, before taking the result above and beyond anything anyone had tried before – and the adventure had already started.

C90s and attitudes at the ready, the White Riot tour was poised for lift-off. And while no one said it was going to be easy, everyone knew it was going to be a blast.

Chapter 5

"The writer of originality, unless dead, is always shocking, scandalous; novelty disturbs and repels." – Simone De Beauvoir

May 1 rolled around and the month-long White Riot tour began, kicking off at Guildford's Civic Hall. In the same month X Ray Spex appeared at the first major Rock Against Racism gig. It was an important time for making a stand and ensuring a high-profile chasm between punk rock and prejudice.

The White Riot tour, which would later be described by journalist Jon Savage as the "last great punk rock tour", was funded entirely by The Clash, and this was typical of their philanthropic stance when it came to supporting up-and-coming groups, a stance now immortalised in Strummer's posthumous music charity Strummerville.

The Jam also joined the line-up, but soon turned on their Cuban heels after falling out with Bernie Rhodes. The Slits were not particularly bothered by The Jam's absence: to Viv at least, Paul Weller was disappointingly old-fashioned at the time. "Someone introduced me and said, 'She's a guitarist' and he'd say, 'Oh yeah, we could do with some crumpet in our band.'

"It's funny, he's seen as such a sensitive musician but there were very old-school types within the scene as well." After experiencing respect and a sense of equal footing among most of her punk peers, Weller's comment seemed rather unevolved. But The Slits had bigger things to concern them.

The Palmolive-penned 'Number One Enemy' seemed to be a self-fulfilling prophecy, in the eyes of the public at least. Because they stood out from the crowd the early punks in London and elsewhere were often looked upon with distaste and treated with caution, or aggression, but The Slits, being girls, were regarded as particularly dangerous and unpredictable. This was partly because they *were* unpredictable, but a myriad of deeply ingrained Seventies prejudices didn't help their cause. Palmolive at the time admitted her strength and power on the drums came from "thinking of people that I hate" – and there were understandably no shortage of candidates.

Still, the prospects for this particular tour were somewhat more promising than those of The Sex Pistols' earlier Anarchy tour, much of which had been abandoned, and the vibe was lighter, like a "school trip", as Tessa remembers. "It was St Trinian's meets the Bash Street Boys," she says. "Punk was like being caught in a comic." But it was hard work too – every single night they played a gig, and the tour took them everywhere from the Edinburgh Playhouse to the De Montfort Hall in Leicester to the California Ballroom, Dunstable. They even squeezed in a date at the Brakke Grand in Amsterdam.

Buzzcocks' Pete Shelley told Pat Gilbert: "(White Riot) was the first proper road show. The Anarchy tour hadn't managed to do that. Its notoriety went ahead of it like a leper's bell. The Clash played everywhere with The Slits, Subway Sect and us. It was great, it was actually working."

What helped it work, from The Slits' point of view, was the fact that the male punk groups continued to be very supportive of them. It wasn't just an initial show of kindness that wore off once the 'girl band' novelty had dissolved. Despite help from Don and Nora, for the first few years of the punk revolution, The Slits felt largely alone – but it would be friendships with The Clash, Buzzcocks and many other groups that got them through.

Ari: "From 1976-78, we were wheeling and dealing, doing all our own shit basically, without the help of the industry. The only support we had was from our guy friends who were all in groups, all of our peers like

The Clash and Pistols and other groups like Eater and Subway Sect, Slaughter & The Dogs, Buzzcocks of course.

"People like Siouxsie & The Banshees, X Ray Spex, Adverts, Talking Heads, they were the only other bands that had girls in them, punk girls with the same type of vibe: 'Fuck everything, I can't relate to anyone, no one in my family, none of my friends, none of my future, none of my past, got no one to look up to. I'm just going to believe in me and do my own stuff and jump on the stage'."

All in all, on this tour, it *was* working, but it was hard work – The Slits were hard work, between themselves and for other people. Personalities on tour are always magnified and every moment, positive or negative, is more intense. It was easy to feel lonely sometimes, even within the bosom of the punk family.

Viv: "Tessa was very close to Palmolive, she and Palmolive were a bit like naughty girls together. Palmolive was the outgoing one and Tessa was the sort of sidekick. It was a bit excluding, you know, band dynamics and all that. And Tessa was very quiet, always known as 'the quiet one' – it was probably a couple of years before we had a proper conversation or I saw her cry or anything.

"So there was the bass and drums dynamic, and then there was Ari on her own, completely confident and doing her own thing, and me on my own. So me and Ari were both on our own, but Ari didn't mind."

One mutual foe they could easily unite against was the rest of the world, most notably the (generally) thick, scared and bigoted red-top-reading public, and it has gone down in punk folklore that on the White Riot tour itself The Slits became officially enshrined as public enemy number one. Depending on one's point of view it was a fantastic compliment, but it served to make life difficult for them, and for the man who was supposed to be smoothing the way, Don Letts, who was "mis-managing them", as he often quips, at the time.

Most hotels banned the girls on sight, and then rang all of the other hotels in the area to ensure no others took in these terrifying liabilities either. Tessa remembers arriving at one hotel and, just because she had 'The Slits' graffitied on her guitar case, they were thrown out immediately. The provocative name was enough, and that notoriety was flaring up angrily wherever this lawless girl band happened to be.

Stories of friction between the tour-bus driver, Norman, and the girls, Ari in particular, are legendary. Confronted with the loud-mouthed, free-spirited and generally scantily clad 15-year-old, he decided he would lay down the law and simply not let The Slits on the bus. Never mind The Clash or Subway Sect – these bright, attractive, confusing young women were far more of a threat.

The Slits, therefore, were unable to even board the tour bus unless Don bribed Norman, which he did on a daily basis, but the uptight driver still made it very clear he couldn't bear them. They would turn up in tiny micro-skirts, slashed-up tops and fishnets, and to make matters worse Ari was working on those dreads, which at this early stage resembled an unwashed, matted bird's nest. These were definitely not the sort of girls a man of Norman's conservative outlook had ever encountered before, and every move they made wound him up. All this aggro, and they hadn't even played any tour dates yet.

"People didn't do this to The Clash, nor Buzzcocks, nor Subway Sect – just us," says Viv. "It was like apartheid. Ari would be shouting and laughing too loud and singing, and Norman couldn't stand it, it would make him cringe, he couldn't stand this young woman showing all her legs and half her arse, shouting and laughing and enjoying herself on the bus.

"She was dressed like you wouldn't have minded fucking her, he just couldn't stand it, that's what it was... that dichotomy of 'you want to fuck them, and you want to kill them'."

The Clash and Subway Sect didn't need to be bribed (neither would Buzzcocks, but they were travelling separately) and the shabby treatment from Norman and Normankind simply made the boys on the tour more protective of the girls. Joe Strummer memorably substituted the lyric 'What a liar' for 'What a Norman' during The Clash's song 'Deny' at their Leicester gig. Never mind gender differences, they saw Norman and his like as the enemy and The Slits as equals. They never lost sight of the fact they were girls too – but no one got "corrupted".

"The Clash were real boys," remembers Viv. "I don't think they ever saw us as not girls, there was always that there, especially as I was going out with Mick and Palmolive had been with Joe, and Paul [Simonon] was quite sexually aware, not that I'm saying he wanted to do anything but there was always an awareness of boys and girls.

"Ari was at school at the very beginning. Would I let my daughter be in a proper band and go on tour at that age? No way! But Ari didn't get corrupted, it was such a strict ethos, people weren't into screwing, it wasn't a shag-fest. Punks weren't into that particularly. There were always one or two, but people at the top like Malcolm McLaren or Johnny Rotten were asexual in a way. You had your Steve Joneses of course, it was written all over him what he was about!

"We weren't treated like ladettes like it is now but there was a respect without any problem, and an appreciation. I'm sure they didn't think we were anything as good as them, but they never said it and it was cool. "

Another soon-to-be bosom pal and honorary 'boy-Slit' was future Frankie Goes To Hollywood star Paul Rutherford, who first saw The Slits when the White Riot tour hit Manchester's Electric Circus on May 8. They were playing the set they had first unleashed on Harlesden in March, which included 'Drug Town', 'Slime', 'Vindictive' and 'Vaseline'. Their ability was still on the rough side, but that didn't seem to put anyone off, least of all Paul. "That was the first time they'd played up north, and I just fell completely in love with them. I thought they were amazing, they were the best band of the night," says Paul.

"I was in The Spitfire Boys at that time, and when they later got their first gig just as themselves up north in Eric's in Liverpool, we got support as we were the only Liverpool punk band at the time. I'd come down to London to see them too and we became great friends, I was just in love with every one of them. They were really doing something. To me they were the biggest band in the world, still are." The Slits were just as fond of The Spitfire Boys, and were a vital support to them when audiences were scant or they had nowhere to sleep.

"We were playing a gig at The Rock Garden in Covent Garden, and The Slits came down to hang out," says Budgie, Spitfire Boys' drummer and a future Slit (and Banshee) himself. "There was nobody else there. We were really privileged to have The Slits in our audience because they were the only audience!

"I remember crashing at Ari's mum's place. There was a bit of fan-worship from Paul to Ari, and we were lucky to have a place to stay, we thought it was really cool. The really exciting part, coming from where we came from, was that suddenly you had this thread right to the centre of the London movement – Malcolm, Bernie Rhodes, later Nils Stevenson, the Banshees manager. The Banshees were an enigma, and so were The Slits, but if you were in the camp you were like a little gang."

The Slits were very appreciative of the friendship of their like-minded male counterparts, and the boys were equally grateful for the girls' time, interest and generosity. There was a healthy dose of awe thrown in too. And while on tour, their pals might have developed the odd crush, but they were respected as a group, not treated as dolly birds.

Don remembers, "Everyone on the scene liked The Slits. For a start it was four girls, and when you're on the road with a load of ugly geezers, any female is a delight, as long as she's feminine, and it can't be denied, those girls cut a fine form.

"I mean, we were young guys, let's be honest, we were teenagers. I mean, what the fuck? So there's all that going on. But primarily they were respected as The Slits the band. They weren't sexual objects, but obviously being female made it that much easier to get through the door."

Well, that particular door anyway. There were plenty of other doors that would be slammed in their faces for the same reason. But at least on tour they were among friends (and Norman). Rivalry wasn't as much a problem in the punk scene as it could be in other movements, as they were all in the same boat; it was more of a mutual support network than a dog-eat-dog minefield.

Don adds, "When you're young you move in circles of literal gangs or metaphorical gangs of like-minded people, but I don't remember any specific rivalry between bands – they were all distinctly different, they weren't really treading on anybody's turf. Because there were different wings to this movement...well, a movement can't be a movement with just one band. They all sort of needed each other so it could be a bona fide movement."

The cause aside, this was also a bunch of creative, funny teens having a ball. There were pillow fights, spontaneous jam sessions. Mick Jones would help to tune the girls' guitars, and the journeys between towns had that constant soundtrack of Don's mix-tapes. They were like an excited bunch of big kids. At one point while stopping for petrol, Don filmed a woman flying into a rage just because Topper [Headon, Clash drummer], Paul and Clash crony Robin Banks were bouncing up and down on a see-saw to pass the time.

After hooking up with Buzzcocks at the various venues, they'd settle in before the gig. On occasion would there be the odd cat fight, as Don remembers, or an alpha-male dispute in the green room, but generally nothing too dramatic. Buzzcocks guitarist Steve Diggle and Mick Jones initially regarded each other with grumpy suspicion before becoming the best of pals. "I'd much rather have been in The Clash anyway," admits Steve.

To many, particularly the justifiably angry feminists of the Seventies, the fact that The Slits were actually included in this tour, and making a lot of noise while they were at it, was to be taken very seriously. They were having fun and doing what they wanted. Many women were not even remotely having fun or doing what they wanted – they were either housewives or doing jobs they didn't like or that didn't stretch or inspire them, or they were despairing of a future that looked all too similar.

The Slits weren't particularly interested in Women's Lib, and their approach was ultimately more successful and less eroding on themselves: don't get angry, don't think about chauvinists, get on with what you want to do and as long as you don't think they have any power over you, they won't.

Ari explains: "We weren't political, we weren't feminists by label, but we were automatically women's rights by being who we were and making sure we were who we were and remaining who we were. Punk really started with equality of girls. There's a whole culture – the first looks of so-called punk, so many girls contributed to that. And of course Vivienne Westwood, there was a window for female expression in punk when it started. That's why The Slits were even able to survive and live it, and be born into that revolution and have a chance. Windows were opening for them, even like the fanzines – the first punk fanzines were made by girls."

This was also the case for female music writers, not just on fanzines but in the hitherto male-dominated world of weekly music magazines – *NME, Melody Maker* and *Sounds* – that catered to fans whose interest lay beyond chart fodder, be it punk or prog or all things in between. It wasn't easy, in fact it was very hard to get through unless you were quite tough and prepared to "outman the men, like Barbara Charone", as Vivien Goldman observes. But the opportunity was there if you were prepared to grab it and make the best of it without letting sexism get under your skin.

Vivien explains, "I can definitely say that the arrival of punk made people like me and Caroline (Coon) feel a lot less alone, that for the first time we could really be part of a community instead of being one of the lads, but not really one of the lads.

"I don't think you're wrong when you see that conflict, I don't think you're being paranoid. But you can't live in a state of siege. You just have to have a light laugh and not be surprised. If you let it define your reactions, of course sometimes you have a wobble and it does, but generally you can't. You lose your wholeness and you're coming from a place of negative response to a bad vibe instead of coming wholly from your centre."

As *Jolt* fanzine editor Lucy Toothpaste told Jon Savage in his book *England's Dreaming*: "I never got one punk woman in any of my interviews to say she was a feminist, because I think they thought the feminist label was too worthy. But the lyrics they were coming up with were very challenging, questioning the messages we'd been fed thru *Jackie* comics."

Writer and artist Caroline Coon, who spent time with The Slits on the White Riot tour and went on to manage The Clash, witnessed a fresh approach when she questioned The Slits on 'the Feminist Question'. The response was fiery, humorous, impatient and liberated in its sheer nonchalance.

She eulogised in *Melody Maker*: "The Slits are driving a coach and various guitars straight through a cornerstone of society – the concept of The Family and female domesticity – not, I hasten to add, that The Slits themselves will have anything to do with the Feminist Question ... While Ari groans at the very mention of the female gender, Viv warns me off.

"'All that chauvinism stuff doesn't matter a fuck to us. You either think chauvinism is shit or you don't. We think it's shit ... Girls shouldn't hang around with people who give them aggro about what they want to do. If they do they're idiots.'"

If only they had a pound for every assumption they must have been militant bra-burning feminists. An all-girl group is an all-girl group – an all-boy group is just a group. And an all-girl group that isn't demure, wistful and sporting the same frocks and hairdos like some Phil Spector concoction is definitely to be treated with suspicion. Even when people with good intentions said their 'hurrahs' for 'Women in Rock', this still went a long way to shoving said women into a pigeonhole. No one referred to 'Men in Rock'.

NME responded to a well-meaning reader request in 1976 that they do a 'Women in Rock' feature with the spiky riposte: "Great thinking – when we've done that we could follow it up with 'Black People of Rock, Jews of Rock, Blue-eyed People of Rock, Short People of Rock and achieve true liberation by categorising everybody in the world according to their gender, race, religion, colour, pigmentation or height. Let's get together and split up."

It remains a problem that any female in the music industry is lumped into the 'Women in Rock' category, something that The Raincoats and The Slits can appreciate more now, but at the time it was frustrating, simply because, other than sharing a gender, the groups were very different indeed.

Ana da Silva: "It's to do with people's character. I can't go onstage and be Ari because I'm not Ari, I didn't want to be Ari. I'm who I am, and that was the thing with The Slits, they were all very different people. Tessa's very quiet but she's amazing on stage, she looks so tough, and just as interesting as anybody else.

"They gave something, we gave something different, and that's why we didn't like to be all together, always the 'girl bands'. In retrospect we think it was more positive than that, but we didn't like to be seen as 'a girl band', we wanted to be seen as a band that writes these kind of songs, that plays like this on stage, that do this way of recording, all the different aspects of being in a band, we wanted that to be seen as something that was The Raincoats, and The Slits were The Slits.

"We didn't want to be in the papers only if there was an article on 'Women In Rock', that got on our nerves."

This form of 'acceptance' was often a barrier of its own kind that was difficult to ignore, and left The Slits in particular struggling to shake off any association with feminism in its more political, militant sense. They knew it wasn't going to do them any favours, and it wasn't where they were coming from.

Keith Levene: "I think it's better they didn't push the feminist side of things because it's in your face anyway, you don't need to do that. It goes without saying. If you do start saying it, you can fuck up a whole other aspect that you might miss out on, and then there's the whole 'oh poxy feminists, who gives a fuck?' you know? Not me, but some observers might think like that.

"It was weird, the punk thing. It mattered that they were girls, but it really mattered that it didn't matter that they were girls. It matters they were there. You had a few firsts going on."

Where The Slits stood in the great feminist debate was the last thing on Don Letts' mind; he was more concerned about transporting them from A to B without getting a serious headache. He was at his wit's end trying to keep everything under control, but once he got them on the bus and on the road, he was damned if he could get them into hotels. The determined young manager was using money from his latest Chelsea retail experiment, Boy, to fund The Slits. Their manager-band relationship was only six weeks long, but what a six weeks.

"Touring with The Slits, that was a trip. It was chaos," says Don. "Punk was a social pariah, wherever you went the spotlight was on you, and it would bring out all of the people who were anti-punk, but it would also bring out a lot of people who just wanted to jump on the bandwagon, who didn't really have any ideology.

"It was potential madness. In fact it was guaranteed. Doing anything with The Slits was madness, you didn't have to be on tour! Just going down the street with them was mayhem. Ari was like a whirlwind, still is.

"Sometimes they'd be fighting before, during and after the gig. Entertaining for onlookers but for me it was a total pain in the arse. I remember them always having a go at Tessa for some reason. But I have to say that when they hit the stage, they really brought their shit together. And they weren't just The Slits on stage, they were The Slits 24/7, it wasn't an act.

"I remember trying to get them signed in to a hotel and Ari was behind me wrecking the place before we'd actually got signed in, so of course they'd then say, 'We can't have you here.' It was a really hard time.

I remember checking out of a hotel and I hear the hotel manager giving us a bill, and it was for like, drinks, food, dinner, and then I heard 'One door' – and I was like, 'There's a bill for a door?' and he said, 'Yes, there's a door missing'.

"It was fun too, I ain't complaining, but at the end of the tour I remember standing at the back of the hall next to Bernie Rhodes, manager of The Clash, and I looked at him, and I looked at The Clash, and I thought, 'I don't want to be this side of the fence, I don't want to be a manager any more.' Maybe if I'd have tried to stay their manager we wouldn't have been friends any more."

Indeed, friendships and futures were at stake all round where punk was concerned. Beneath the fearsome image lay discipline and passion, and anyone who lacked it, in the case of The Slits at least, was in danger of being left behind.

"I almost didn't make it to the White Riot tour," chuckles Tessa. "We were all rehearsing in the basement of this squat in Angel, I was having an off day and I'd taken a pill someone had offered me. I started to rehearse and then I got in a mood and threw the bass down and walked out. And you can see on Don Letts' *Punk Rock Movie* everyone's going, 'Tessa's useless, we bought her equipment, we did this for her, we did that, why can't she get her shit together?'

"I knew they were just about to throw me out of the group, so every single day after that I was in the basement practising the bass! Ari wanted me to stay in the group and I was determined to make up for my ways and pulled myself together.

"It was real fun, the White Riot tour, Subway Sect were one of my favourite groups at the time. Your playing gets better when you go on tour, it's good for your musicianship."

Life on the road was heady – and while the band generally lived healthily and avoided drinking too much, their high-octane personalities and general defiance ensured an unforgettable trip. They were also showered with more spit than they ever thought possible (there was much finger-pointing as to who started off this almost universally unpopular punk tradition – some say the Pistols, some say The Damned – all say they hated it, although this clearly didn't transmit to the enthusiastic gobbers in the audience).

Thankfully, the spitting wouldn't last forever. A few years down the line The Slits would find themselves being pelted with roses (as well as phlegm) on the promotional tour for their first album, *Cut*, particularly in Italy. Which is a bit more civilised. But right now, The Slits felt it was way too early to be making their own records. While they were writing songs all the time, they knew how raw they were, and they were serious about getting their songs just right before they rushed into the studio. Good decision.

As we know, there was at least one couple on board the bus, and tensions ran high when Viv started to get close to Subway Sect guitarist Rob Marche. According to Viv some "unpleasant scenes" ensued between her and Mick Jones as a result. What's more, Palmolive had just split up with Joe Strummer, which led to a month and a half of the pair trying to avoid each other while on the same bus. Love and romance? It was never that simple.

"The White Riot tour was awful for me," admits Palmolive. "I'd just broken up with Joe, so I did not like that. It was a mutual thing, but it was still hard. In the van it wasn't too great. I don't remember it being a fun trip but you find other people to talk to. It wasn't comfortable, but at the same time it was very exciting, we were playing all these different places, and that took my mind off it."

Tensions aside, the bands generally stuck together, as all punks – not just The Slits – were under fire from the outside world most of the time. But the girls learnt how to handle situations quicker than most. "Whenever there was trouble it was usually The Slits that would save our arses," laughs Don. "They were like howling banshees, oh man..."

If the mood took them, of course, anyone could be a target for The Slits' aggression. On one occasion, Tessa let off steam at the Roxy club in the direction of Pistols drummer Paul Cook. Without rhyme or reason, the 'quiet one' ran at him and ripped a hole in the back of his jacket. He'd stolen it from Malcolm McLaren that day though, so he must have anticipated at least some kind of karma.*

* A slightly different version of this story appears in Nils Stevenson's published diaries, *Vacant,* featuring Ari as the perpetrator of the jacket-ripping crime, but Tessa insists his memory clearly failed him on this anecdote. Credit where it's due.

Musically, The Slits were improving all the time; the cliché of how 'they couldn't play' was already becoming a memory to those on the scene. Their rawness and exuberant musical innocence led them into experimenting in ways The Clash and Buzzcocks did not, and as a result of Palmolive's background they started to become curious about African music, which they would later explore in greater depth, and which certainly affected how Palmolive approached the drums. A tribalism was coming into play that would, even after she left the group, leave a stamp on The Slits that would be echoed in the notorious topless, muddy and defiant cover of *Cut*.

The spirit of punk was supposedly all about trying something new, rejecting what went before, though admittedly most of the male groups still referenced the past whether they meant to or not. Those old, albeit very valid, influences of rockabilly, blues, mod culture and rock 'n' roll still cast a retro shadow over the music of The Clash, Jonathan Richman & The Modern Lovers, The Lurkers and the Pistols – but The Slits didn't have those references simply because they hadn't paid them any attention. So they really did have to go a new way.

Palmolive laughs, "The public always seemed so amused by us, they were like, 'I can't believe these girls are doing that!' There was definitely something about us because we were girls, and in some way we were also very naïve. We were very raw, so that was not normal.

"The Clash were punk but they had that background, like Joe had The 101ers background, I didn't have that at all, none of us had. I grew up with flamenco music, I like African music, I had never really followed rock 'n' roll. So even when I played the drums, I didn't like playing the hi-hat, or the cymbals like normal bands did, I liked the toms much better, so I'd always experiment with those sounds much more, I was curious.

"It was almost like when you give a little kid paint – it always comes out different because they don't have a preconceived idea about what they are supposed to do, and we didn't know. Some of it was an advantage and some of it was a disadvantage."

It was around this creatively charged period that The Slits started really thinking outside the box and experimenting on stage. Numbers such as 'Vaseline' featured one section of the song with just voice and drums, the next section with drums and bass, the next with guitar and bass, then voice and guitar and so on. While they may have seemed chaotic, some of the original ideas they had clearly practised and thought about were executed truly effectively. As with art, it's easy for the ignorant to say, 'My six-year-old could do that', but it's the idea that matters. And The Slits were full of ideas.

Chapter 6

"The Slits are one in the eye for the rock'n'roll rulemakers who judge everything on how fast you can play and what sex you are. They're raw and can only get better – they know they've got to and will." – Kris Needs, *ZigZag*, 1977

Once the White Riot tour had hurtled to a close, The Slits threw themselves into rehearsing in the dingy basement of a squat at the Angel, Islington in North London, which had been found for them by Sarah and Crystal, the girls behind the punk fanzine *More On*. After soundproofing the cellar with old blankets, they would practise with military discipline for their next strike.

"We rehearsed like crazy," Tessa remembers. "We really worked hard at the squat in Angel, it was free. We didn't have money, we were signing on, Palmolive had a cleaning job. Viv was the most together of the band. She was the hardest worker. She was the most articulate and responsible one, she was sharp, in a good way, with words."

Viv's verbals were certainly an asset, and not only during their famously spiky interviews. They were now penning new songs based on their own lives and relationships, songs full of vitality and perception such as 'Typical Girls' and 'Love And Romance'; still vibrant, sarky and energising but a step forward from the sheer aggression of before.

Palmolive, however, was more thoughtful in her writing as her search for fulfilment deepened. Two of her songs, 'FM' and 'Adventures Close To Home', were full of hazy, melancholic atmospheres and strange, troubled lyrics, such as this one, from 'FM': 'Thousand nights of confusion wedged in my mind, breaking down another illusion/ Today's transmission will give me the solution …'

While many of their contemporaries were already releasing records and keeping the studio engineers busy, The Slits were careful not to head to the studio before they all felt absolutely ready, although the songs that would appear on The Slits' first album were being imagined, shaped and constructed all the time. Palmolive played a significant part in the material that would eventually be used, even though she was starting to slowly pull away from the group and look towards the next phase in her life.

But for now, she was still very much a Slit, soaking up and utilising influences from African music, children's songs, punk and reggae. One aspect of the band's learning curve that both mystified and frustrated them in equal measure was that certain individuals from cultures that had inspired them found it impossible to accept what they were doing.

Tessa remembers one particularly uncomfortable occasion: "In a lot of different cultures it's forbidden for women to play the drums. We once went to a 12 Tribes house in South London with Don, and Ari started playing the bongos, and they threw us out of the house because it is forbidden for women to play the drums. It must be really deep-rooted from the past. For a woman to play drums, it's taboo. But then I go back to Palmolive, the way she played was so inspiring. She's so animated, just like Animal from The Muppets! It's good to have broken some of those taboos.

"Women do play musical instruments in a very different way from men, if they have the confidence to, in a very childlike way and then it really works, it's coming from the heart, totally honest. The White Stripes drummer Meg White is incredible, she's one of my favourites."

When they weren't rehearsing and absorbing music and ideas, The Slits continued to do a pretty good job of frightening people – and not just your dyed-in-the-wool Rastafarians. The tabloid press' knee-jerk reaction to The Sex Pistols and their friends in the Bromley Contingent eating Bill Grundy for breakfast on live TV simply lit the touchpaper for a public reaction of shock and horror at punks in general. The reality of this for those on the ground in Notting Hill and elsewhere was actually quite dangerous, with an increasing number of cowardly vigilante attacks, which the real enemy – the mainstream establishment, the so-called 'Babylon' – did little to prevent.

"Minor things were blown up out of all proportion," says Tessa. "People were scared of punk at that time. The reputation grew bigger than the actual facts."

The Slits managed to alarm people before they'd even said or done anything, largely because of their unique visual style. It was full of humour, they were just having as much fun as they could with clothes and their hair. We're not talking Farrah Fawcett hairdos or regulation late Seventies 'Purdey' haircuts (a national obsession – for women anyway – thanks to Joanna Lumley's glossy pudding-basin style in *The New Avengers*), we're not even necessarily talking about Vivienne Westwood. In the same way that they created something new in music by combining their influences, these girls started something new fashion-wise by combining everything they liked, everything that inspired and provoked thought. They did it their own way and fashion copied them – it was not the other way around.

Tessa often wore androgynous outfits, a shirt, tie and leather jacket, skinny trousers, biker boots, eyes ringed with kohl and her black hair messy and unadorned, or with sections tied up into smaller ponytails with wraps and rags. Viv wore girly frocks, ribbons, rags, even socks trailing from her blonde hair, and sneakers on her feet (a look referenced by Lily Allen). Ari would sport anything from her famous Silver Jubilee knickers-over-trouser combo – Superman-style – micro-skirts and fishnets or dresses and boots, an oversized man's mac and a bees-nest of matted hair. Palmolive sported artfully ripped charity-shop togs with lace gloves, silver Doc Martens, clashing colours and hair back-combed within an inch of its life – and of course, no razor had been near those armpits, and she would flaunt her furriness at any opportunity.

Ana da Silva: "Palmolive was the first woman I ever saw in a newspaper or magazine showing her armpit hair – she held her arm all the way up. Still today if somebody shows a bit of hair there it's a big thing, but she was there showing it, 'I've got it and it's here!' It sounds like a little detail but it was so inspiring."

Gina Birch: "Ari and Palmolive both wore these big raincoats. Everybody thinks we wore raincoats, but it was them really. We wore big baggy jumpers and funny shoes, pyjamas and our hair all messy, definitely grungy – Chicks On Speed say we were the precursors to that grunge look. But Viv had her tutus, necklaces with teeth on, Palmolive would wear bin-liners, silver lamé, stripy trousers, Tessa had her big Harlequin jumper that she had for years ..."

Those impressed by The Slits' visual explosion were at this stage in the minority. Their look would see them spat at, attacked, barred, and, in Ari's case, even knifed. This occurred after the famous 1976 Sex Pistols gig at the Screen On The Green in Islington, when a man sneaked up behind Ari and stabbed her in the backside, snarling, "There's a slit for you." Thankfully Ari's famous flasher's mac absorbed most of the damage.

Don Letts: "They used to take a lot of shit, people would attack them on the streets and hurl abuse at them, they were the witches of West London. They didn't fit that stereotype of what a woman should be – but that was their strength. They looked at what was on offer for girls in those days and said 'No thank you. We'll decide what we want to do, we'll decide how we want to be and how we want to look.'"

Punk peer Paul Rutherford remembers the riots The Slits could cause simply by walking on stage: "One time we supported them at this mad club in Bristol. All these beer boys just went nuts when The Slits came on and [they] started throwing beer glasses at them. It was really heavy, *really* heavy.

"There used to be a lot of that. They're a bunch of girls and you'd get these big angry dudes going after them. They were like mini-Boadiceas though, they were fantastic, and they got quite heavy with them. They looked like warriors, Ari with the flailing hair. Even though they were really peaceable, they weren't daft. But it was quite tough for them, it was the dark ages.

"Back then people thought the world was falling apart because people were putting safety pins through their noses. 'The end is nigh!' But it was very peaceful in comparison with the way the world is now. And within the punk scene, it felt like you were in a very nice gang, which wasn't really a gang."

The culture of narrow-mindedness was at the root of the problem – but if you looked as unusual as Ari, trouble could kick off at any time simply because it was so difficult for people to know how to cope with her. She says, "At that time, I was just like an alien to anyone that ever met me. The minute I decided to have my locks and be the way I am in my life, I knew that with it comes the package of tribulation and scorn. These memories are so imprinted on us.

"It sounds like I am over-dramatising, but actually I am under-dramatising. People do have made-up memories over time, especially if they have taken a degree of drugs, which I have not. Then the memory goes, or sometimes you can't move on with life if you have too many of those memories, but we [The Slits] all remember different parts of the puzzle.

"The world was a different planet. It was like a witch-hunt at first for us. I'd been stabbed of course, so it was a constant phobia thing, how can we make our lives the way we want to be without society telling us what to do, how can we remain like that without being attacked or without giving up spiritually and just go with society's flow?"

Even at the blues parties they attended, where they at least felt more accepted than on the street, they could rile onlookers. On one occasion someone tried to push a massive bass-speaker stack onto them. The Slits managed to get out of the way just in time.

In the oppressive society that had suffocated England since the Fifties, it was somehow terrifying for the vast majority of men to observe women looking and behaving like these four girls. This was an age when most female 'role models' were designed to appeal to men's salacious instincts: dolly birds showing lots of leg, leather-clad rock'n'roll clichés like Suzi Quatro, or cleavage-focused sex bombs sucking in their cheeks.

The Slits weren't taking themselves too seriously but they knew they didn't want to be like any of these. They were learning all the time, taking music seriously and living creatively without inhibition or feeling the need for permission to do so from anyone else. This captured imaginations and inspired action, and the advent of The Slits sparked a small but significant rush of female musicians with their own musical and visual style, including Swiss post-punk group Kleenex (later to be renamed Liliput when the tissue manufacturer threatened to sue), saxophonist Lora Logic, The Mo-Dettes, The Gymslips, Delta 5, The Au Pairs and The Raincoats.

Although The Slits were acting in a liberated, feminist-without-using-the-feminist-label kind of way, they still were feminine in their own unique way, which was confusing, not only for men, but also for plenty of die-hard Women's Libbers. But as Vivienne Westwood once said: "Feminists wish women to seem like men. They're not men."

At least these young renegades had decided that what their families had simply accepted before was not good enough for them. Suddenly there was an opportunity for people to be themselves, and, contrary to what the daily papers might imply, this wasn't tied up with violent or intimidating behaviour. It was about freedom, creativity, acceptance or improvement of the self and thinking in different ways. It was about taking art and fashion and music seriously, and most importantly, doing it yourself.

One person who fell hook, line and sinker for The Slits' fashion sense was *NME* writer Nick Kent, who later wrote in their first feature in the weekly in 1978: "The Slits may well have the most disorientatingly bedazzling collective visual of any group going right now … the full sense-swerving visual impact was only truly forced home to me when one day last spring I chanced to witness the foursome walking down Oxford Street, causing all pedestrians to step back in a heated display of awe, disgust and fear.

"I stood unobserved, entranced by the spectacle as the four of them, all wild bedraggled hair and heavy duty duds – made their majestic promenade down London's main shopping centre, putting the transient straights crossing their path under well heavy manners.

"The Slits – with their colours aloft - imperiously blazing a trail of chaotic collective resolve, immaculately bedraggled in the territory of Lipstick Vogue agogo, temps, secretaries, cheese-cloth blouses and simpering femininity in full facile bloom. Girls, you won my heart that day."

Punks had to be able to stand up for their look, so a lot of thought went into it – and there was no sign of a Mohican, by the way. 'Punk' wasters hanging around on the King's Road and outside Camden Town

Tube seemed to be missing the point, almost wearing their own uniform, which was not quite in the same spirit.

Future Slits manager and multimedia artist Christine Robertson says, "I was involved in punk as an audience member and a promoter in the regions – if you went outside of London you were in extreme danger as a punk, although I don't think I actually dressed up as a punk, I just had my own style, which was made up of charity-shop stuff and some period pieces that you could find in charity shops, a mixture of things, anything you could put together that would express your own style.

"I always laugh when I see pictures of 'punks' with the Mohican, and people think that was punk – it wasn't really. But it was enough to get spat on to wear a short kilt skirt, fishnets, maybe DMs, a Fifties jacket, ripped T-shirt, or a shirt you'd written something on, that was very punk. So yeah, I always laugh when that 'Mohican' look is what people think is punk. And the Seditionaries look, nobody could afford that."

If you weren't a punk, among the accessories deemed attractive for women at the time as advertised in the back of the music papers, were customised guitar picks bearing the words 'pick me' on necklaces, to be nestled in the cleavage. For the man in your life, T-shirts featuring cheery catchphrases such as 'Happiness is a tight pussy' were resplendent amid ads for ELO, Eagles and AC/DC merchandise. Easy to see why people started writing on their shirts instead.

Punk professor and reggae guru Vivien Goldman wrote an epic '77 article in *Sounds*, in which she noted, from the DIY anti-fashion to the rebel stance, "punks and dreads are on the same side of the fence". And thankfully, as her interviewee Bob Marley had obviously by now had the Don Letts treatment, the reggae legend wholeheartedly agreed.

Vivien wrote: "Bluntly, who gets picked up in the street by the police? Answer: those natty dreads and baldheads.

"Bob Marley and Lee Perry both said it, sitting in the thick white carpeted luxury of Basing Street (then Island Records): 'The punks are the outcasts from society. So are the Rastas. So they are bound to defend what we defend,' Marley paused, flexing his arms. He's wearing a bright blue tracksuit, and he'd just finished telling us why he wears just tracksuits and faded denims onstage. It's because he doesn't want to wear flash clothes that the youth will admire, envy, and feel frustrated 'cos they can't have.

"Remember all those declarations in the early days of punk that echo his sentiments? Anti-chic, poor people's fashions, dustbin liner chic ..."

Visually The Slits seemed to have no reference points. It's natural to draw on past heroes and icons to piece together your own unique look, whether it's rockabilly, mod, skinhead or maybe, in the style of the uber-glam Roxy Music, an essence of the Thirties – but this was not the way of The Slits. So how did they create something from nothing? Picking up signals from space, suggests Vivien Goldman. Why not? Most people treated them as if they'd come from another planet anyway.

"It was an adrenaline rush just to see them as they had developed this visual code," explains Goldman. "It was profoundly influential. They were stylish girls who picked up the mysterious signals that create fashion in people's minds at the same time, like signals from outer space, or from deep within the core, like an 'Earthbeat', as The Slits would say.

"It was a look I would define as cognitive dissonance. Everything they wore contradicted the received understanding of everything else. Lily Allen does it now, all those people who adopted it, Courtney Love, any funky, 'edgy' girl who came out after The Slits, unless they just wear nothing in particular, like those bland American pop stars."

"Walking down the street we looked like we'd just stepped out of a fetish movie," says Viv Albertine. "I might be in rubber stockings and high heels, a little tutu and a ripped T-shirt, hair all back-combed and blonde and black all round my eyes. There were no reference points for any man to look at and say, oh she's a mixture of things from a Ridley Scott film or whatever. I looked like I'd stepped off some sick porn movie set, and they were utterly freaked out and threatened.

"We were four girls, walking down the street, ripped clothes, showing our bras – no Madonna! Nothing to reference it. The clothes we bought were from Sex or in real sex shops hidden away in Battersea and places like that, proper stuff. Once me and Sid went round bondaged together."

The intention behind the look wasn't to just shock and horrify though, not for The Slits anyway; it was more a case of sticking it to the man – literally – by taking something close to the heart to maybe a lower echelon of male and turning it inside out, which may go some way to explain the extreme reactions they prompted. "At the time we were wearing the porn stuff, we were turning it on its head," says Viv. "We were saying, 'You think this is sexy? Well, is it so sexy when it's on a woman who'll give you shit?'

"We were subverting it. It was one of the things they only saw when they went to prostitutes. They understood when it was there or in *Playboy* magazine, they didn't understand when it was actually in front of them with crazy hair and strong eyes, they didn't know what to do with it. It was like we took their language and fucked it up for them. 'That was ours!' We ruined it for them. It was fun."

People were either threatened or they were inspired to copy them. Understandably, with The Slits' image as well as their music, less imaginative but perhaps in some way like-minded culture magpies would do their utmost to look the same and, inevitably, be hailed as the originators themselves. That early Eighties Madonna-Cyndi Lauper look with the ribbons, tutus and lace gloves? Pure Viv Albertine.

Don Letts is more than happy to speak up for The Slits. He could see for himself that people were later passing off their ideas as their own, not just visually, but artistically as well. "The pioneers never reap the rewards. It's the ones who come later to reinterpret – they're the ones who collect. That's the life of creative, avant-garde people. You've got people today who think they're outrageous and pushing the parameters, but when you look at what The Slits did with the limited funds they had, it's incredible."

Only once would you have seen any of these spiky, startling wild things looking a bit frilly and romantic, and that was only because they needed the money – yes, Viv and Paul Simonon were actually persuaded to pose in Laura Ashley clobber for a photo shoot run by the designer's daughter Jane.

Viv had been sharing a flat with Jane Ashley, with whom she went to art school alongside Mick Jones and Simonon. Surrounded by these angular, naturally stylish youths, Jane decided to bring together her love of punk with her mother's designs and offered them £30 to take part in a shoot. While it didn't take much to persuade the penniless punks, stepping into a long, floaty dress for Viv was breaking some serious rules. For a punk to wear Laura Ashley, was brave. But she secretly quite liked it, and, as Viv wistfully recalls, "Mick (Jones) said I looked lovely."

So much for how lovely they looked, even in the eyes of a normally convention-snubbing member of The Clash. Laura Ashley herself refused to use the images in her shops, although they were used in her yearly calendar. But the pictures were more than just another shoot to Jane: "These extraordinarily creative times in our lives are also full of drama and conflict. Those pictures of Viv and The Clash helped me resolve conflicts about my identity. Isn't that what creativity is for?"

All the same, Jane Ashley ended up with her own conflict with Viv to resolve – or rather, the rest of The Slits resolved it for her. With the usual gusto reserved for people they weren't too keen on, they confronted Jane team-handed at Don's *Punk Rock Movie* screening at London's ICA after she had evicted Viv. The landlord had apparently disapproved of the increasing number of punks hanging out at their flat and was leaning on Jane to do something about it. So Viv got the boot.

The Slits might have got on each other's nerves at times, but their loyalty to each other in times of strife always overrode any internal friction. "We were like sisters," remembers Viv. "Sometimes it would get nasty, it would get personal, we would get fed-up or irritated, but at the same time, if anyone would threaten any of us, we would all want to kill that person. We were very protective of each other."

While the intentions of punks, for want of a better word, were to break boundaries and force the old school to change their perceptions whether they wanted to or not, Keith Levene admits they didn't change as much as they thought they would when it came to attitudes against image, youth, and women. Not for want of trying, of course. "There's a lot of wankers around now," he says. "It's like so much of this shit never happened. There are so many guys who are still like that, chauvinist twats, it's nearly 2010 and it's like we're in the Seventies still.

"The only reason I know the difference is because I was a kid in the Sixties, otherwise I don't even think I'd be hip to it, I wouldn't even get it. I was brought up when kids were seen and not heard and men did… well, it was horrible, black and white, Sixties and smelly and wrong. Which is why I left school at 15, I couldn't take it, all these male teachers, fucking twats. I'm just as bad, I used to fancy all my (female) teachers! I guess that's hormones, and I didn't treat them like sexual objects, I kept it to myself."

In its own weird and wonderful way, punk was offering an alternative to cock rock, sex kittens and pigeonholing, which is why it gave women like The Slits, X Ray Spex singer Poly Styrene, saxophonist and jazz freak Lora Logic, The Mo-Dettes and The Raincoats the confidence to explore their own ideas, and fight for them if they had to. But sooner or later punk itself would become a pigeonhole too, another label, another box into which narrow-minded, lazy observers could package The Slits – or try to.

Multi-instrumentalist Steve Beresford, a member of the experimental minimalist band The Flying Lizards, would later collaborate with The Slits on tour and on their final album, *Return Of The Giant Slits*, and he agrees that people need to view them in a broader way than simply as a female punk band. "This is a problem with people who have one-track minds," he explains. "The thing with The Slits is not only were they the first all-woman punk band, they were the first punk band to go, 'You know what, let's not do that any more. Let's look at dub music and soul and see what we can do with that.' People can't hold those two ideas in their heads at the same time.

"The Slits get put down as just being mad girl punks – which they were, and still are – but they made some fantastically great musical decisions."

Like many bands around that time, The Slits hated the term 'punk'. Its first usage in describing a style of music was in *Creem* magazine in 1971, by the US critic Dave Marsh, and British writers, led by Caroline Coon, were quick to pick up on it. The Slits, however, were known to rip the word out of posters if they saw it. Palmolive told Kris Needs at the time: "We are not punks. We're The Slits," with Ari adding, "And we make Slits music."

Another cliché that irritated the group was the assumption that Ari was the star of the show – they all agreed that everyone's personality in the group was unique and vital. For once it was not all about the front-person; Tessa, Viv and Palmolive were no backing band.

Gina Birch: "With The Slits there was a complete rejection of the status quo. With The Sex Pistols, Johnny Rotten was just so incredible in his rejection of what a performer should be like, he was stunning – the whole band was interesting but it was John who was the focus. But The Slits did it completely across the board for female stereotypes, there was nothing typical about them."

Though they would unfortunately spring back into place once punk was dead and buried, the rock'n'roll clichés of yore were abhorred and irrelevant. "Punk was sexless," explains Keith Levene. "We were so fucking tired of the old, 'Oh, he plays guitar, he must have a huge libido' thing. The Sex Pistols were actually like the last rock'n'roll band. There's no myth with Steve (Jones), he perpetuated all that, and he's got no problem about it. But I used to have all these guys in glasses watching me, they were my groupies! And I used to think, 'Well, that's funny.' And I used to think, 'That's really punk.'

"I don't remember any guys hanging around The Slits getting anywhere, you know? I don't remember guys even thinking like that; once you were at a Slits gig, if you were thinking like that you weren't watching the band, you were just there for no reason."

Heartening stuff, but plenty of punks, from Don Letts to Pete Wylie, have since admitted to harbouring carnal twinges for members of The Slits, but they were wise enough to keep quiet about it at the time. Plus, perhaps the reason any bloke would fancy one of The Slits in the first place was not because of their hair-twirling, flirting attempts at being sex symbols. So maybe they'd be let off.

While on the streets they continued to spark all sorts of repressed feelings of rage and sexuality, musically their vitality and originality was attracting attention and respect, notably from one man who would be instrumental, and largely alone, in championing punk on the radio. BBC radio no less. He may have played records at the wrong speed now and again, but he would also play your track twice in a row if he really liked it. He'd include it in his Festive 50. And he'd immortalise you live in one of his already legendary sessions.

Capturing the attention of John Peel was an important coup for The Slits, and they didn't do it by halves.

Chapter 7

"I always feel that the music I genuinely like, the stuff I play on the radio, is my own way of going out on the street and righting the wrongs that I think should be righted." – John Peel

Like The Slits, John Peel was never particularly troubled by the idea of the mainstream, and throughout his long career as a BBC legend he remained devoted to alternative music. He was accompanied on this mission to find the new and exciting by his open-minded, good-humoured producer, John Walters, and this team was more than ready to give The Slits a push.

Former hippy Peel embraced punk wholeheartedly, which prompted cynics to wonder out loud whether he was merely trying to appear edgy, particularly as he wasn't getting any younger. But Peel explained that this new explosion of music sparked feelings in his core, echoing how he reacted when he first heard rock 'n' roll. "It wasn't a deliberate kind of refusal to grow old gracefully," he told *Melody Maker* in 1978. "The first records that moved me strongly were things like Little Richard and Elvis Presley records, and Gene Vincent records. They were very basic and very direct.

"I was moved again by the idealism of the hippies, which I passionately believed in. I genuinely believed we were going to change the world and that society was going to be altered by what we did. With the new wave came a combination of these two things. It was back to basics, to very simple direct music, and at the same time they seemed to be hoping, like the hippies, that they could make some sort of changes in society that would make for a better way of life. The two things together I found very exciting."

Walters would scour the capital and its outskirts every week to go to punk gigs, searching for raw talent. It had to be Walters instead of Peel because Peel was too recognisable and would be immediately deluged by a mountain of cassettes from hopeful musos. And who could blame them?

On August 16, 1977, the day that Elvis Presley died, The Slits were playing at the Vortex. Peel had already expressed in his *Sounds* column that year how his "heart was heavy" that he hadn't seen them yet, and he was already determined to get them in for a session. So Walters sneaked Peel down to the show.

The ready-for-anything producer knew they would be in for quite a night of it when they sought out The Slits, particularly as their live sets were becoming legendary. Forget the concept of an ordinary gig. Keith Levene, who would faithfully pitch up to man the sound-desk, remembers every concert was a one-off. "Slits gigs were events," he says. "I was just going along to do the sound, half dragged along and half wanting to be there! But they were events, as much as a little gig could be. They were all fucking different.

"I don't even know if they had set-lists – they were so fucking mental, it didn't matter. It seemed like they just said, 'What shall we do now?' They'd stop in the middle of things, but it was wicked. Because they were girls they might bump into each other on stage and say 'Sorry', but that had nothing to do with anything.

"There was this whole excitement. They really were events, they didn't do a gig every day, they did one this week, three that week, one a month later. I just found them really exciting. It was great going round with them, and it was great watching them get better."

Walters was not on top form when he first saw The Slits, but he could see why Peel was so excited by them. He told *Melody Maker* the following year: "We'd just done a recording and I was a bit smashed by then.

But I thought, 'This is a girls' Clash. And not only that, there are about EIGHT of them. Most unusual...' That was a joke by the way."

Peel added: "Technically they were all over the place. I thought, 'If we get them in, is it only because they're women, or what?' But we got them in to do a session feeling there was something there which could be good."

Peel's first meeting with Palmolive was typically memorable, at least according to the DJ's semi-autobiographical book *Margrave Of The Marshes*, which was completed after his death in 2004: "Palmolive greeted John [Peel] in the Vortex club by banging his head against the head of the man with whom, until that moment, he had been engaged in polite conversation. John reported: 'Being a well-bred gent, I merely smiled and continued my conversation. Come to think of it, we are shortly to record these Slits for Radio 1. I think I will take several of my friends and lie in wait for the brazen creature outside the studio."

The Slits' pre-*Cut* Peel Sessions in 1977 and '78 were often remembered as favourites of Peel's – at the very least they didn't behave like their mates The Clash, who, in the broadcaster's words, "did half a session and then wandered off – unbearably pretentious – they said the studios weren't good enough. Not a very punk attitude."

Joe Strummer added a final 'up yours' to this by saying that "listening to John Peel was like a dog being sick in your face." Well, it was that or maintain a dignified silence. Which was also not very punk.

Anyway, back to The Slits and Peel – the beloved broadcaster adored them, but, as Ari has pointed out, he rather unhelpfully paid them the back-handed compliment that his favourite thing about the band was their inability to play coupled with their absolute determination to play – an affectionate dig that, as an obvious result of his influence, entered the public's consciousness, became legend and has dogged the band to this day.

As a matter of fact, anyone who has heard those sessions will know that not only can the band play just fine, they are truly exciting, interesting recordings, even by today's standards, from the strident backing vocals of 'FM' underneath the sound of a radio being tuned, to the cacophony of squeals, gasps and purrs in 'Love And Romance', to the mature funk-driven beauty and sparkling energy of their later sessions for Peel in 1981.

Ari: "When people said we couldn't play in the early days, when we had that raw punky sound with the heavy bass – if you listen back to those Peel Sessions now, you can tell that's rubbish, we obviously could play.

"Now when boys try to play it, because I have so many solo groups that I play with and I rehearse Slits stuff with about three, four different bands, they have such a hard time learning it. They get confused with the feeling and emotions of it, because our musical approach is spontaneous and emotional. It's not as mathematical as the boys' stuff, it's more wavy, like an ocean wave, in and out – and weird chords of course... At the time we made song structures that no one could really fathom yet, it hadn't been put into the world."

To take the point of view of a male punk who was particularly close to The Slits' cause, the response is similar. Keith Levene is almost as exasperated as Ari on this tired but persistent subject. "'They couldn't play'... well, they could, couldn't they? They couldn't when they started, then they could and they just got better.

"Tess could play. Viv could play. Take on board they're an early punk band, they're possibly one of the only other actually creative bands that came out. I always liked groups like Subway Sect but my thing with them was – don't do something to be different, do something different if you've got something different. With The Slits, I don't think they were *trying* to do anything different, they *were* different, unique."

The first Peel Session with the group was recorded on September 19, 1977 at Maida Vale Studios, presided over by producer Tony Wilson, and they hurtled through 'Love And Romance' (not yet officially known as 'Love Und Romance'), a reverb-soaked version of the exhilarating and venomous 'Vindictive', a brooding, bass-heavy 'New Town' and a fearsome yet profanity-free – ie, radio-friendly – rendition of 'Shoplifting'. It hit the airwaves eight days later.

Viv: "That was the first time we'd been in a studio. Lots of people thought the result was better than the album *(Cut)*. 'Vindictive' is not on any LP, and 'New Town' was very different when re-recorded. It was also the only recording we made with Palmolive, as an all-girl band. The energy and the aggression and the speed, I can't even believe I ever felt like that, who is that girl? And have you ever heard a girl like that since?"

Peel was hooked, proclaiming the session as "just magical" – even *NME*, which had previously branded The Slits 'puerile', duly noted that their sessions for Peel boasted "a riveting maverick form and momentum".

Peel said in an interview at the time: "In the end they did what is genuinely one of our first classic sessions. The first session was bootlegged. We've had letters from people in America asking for a tape of it."

They recorded their second session the following April, in which they performed 'FM', the thunderous 'So Tough' and 'Instant Hit', the last two dedicated to two of the Slits' troubled friends. Ari recalls, "'Instant Hit', about Keith Levene, is lyrically similar to 'So Tough'. They're both about some of our peers taking junk, taking heroin. In the Peel Session version of 'So Tough', about Sid Vicious and John Lydon, we actually sang the names too, 'John, don't take it serious, Sid is only curious.'

"John didn't like heroin. The biggest break-up between John and Sid was that Sid took heroin. That whole heroin romance, that naïve romanticising of the heroin mentality was so not The Slits, was so not the rest of our friends, and [for] the few people who did get hooked on it, it was just a very sad situation. The song was written as we saw it happening around us."

The Slits' first Peel Session performances are all completely different from the eventual album versions for *Cut*, but nevertheless, the vitality is addictive. They took the sessions seriously and concentrated intently, particularly as it was the first time they'd performed without an audience, an aspect of the session that threw them off-balance at first.

Palmolive remembers, "The recordings for John Peel were very interesting but they were hard for our band because we rely a lot on the response from the audience, which was always very extreme and got us going. To suddenly play in this sterile environment was kind of intimidating in a way. It was like, 'OK, go back and do it again.' That's normal for most musicians but we were used to just doing our thing, you know, 'That's how I play it!'

"But to me, from the music point of view, that's the best of The Slits, those sessions. I thought they were very strong. I'm glad we did that."

Nevertheless, despite her enthusiasm for the results, not to mention the head-banging-together incident, Palmolive admits she doesn't really remember Peel himself very well – which makes you realise just how many people's heads she must have banged together in her time …

It will come as no surprise to learn that in the studio the engineers were somewhat flustered by the group. They thought Ari was a "maniac", according to Ken Garner's book *In Session Tonight,* and took every opportunity to re-tune their instruments. They may as well not have bothered, which was also the case with the well-meaning Mick Jones when he attempted to tune their guitars on tour. Guitar mentor Keith Levene wanted to impress upon his protégées that there was more to it than simply being in tune, encouraging them to embrace the concept that 'mistakes' would generate new sounds and ideas if paid due attention, and also that being slightly out of tune never stopped Jimi Hendrix.

"I was kind of showing them what not to play too," says Keith. "This is how people play guitar, but this is how I view it, like an atonal droning instrument without tuning it, just as is. You don't have to do this, you don't have to do that. There's an E, there's an A, and it's the same fucking progression – it could all be the same note, it could be no note – it could be discrete frequencies. What are they? Well, let's not go there. I'm actually getting to know what they are, but I don't go to those places because I know them, I don't need to go back to them.

"It's when I play something I don't know, that's when I repeat it – a lot of people will perceive that as a mistake, but if they hear a mistake 15 times running, it ain't a mistake. They're going to have to take it on board as it is. It's neither the right thing nor the wrong thing, it's just a fucking note."

Keith may have given Viv the confidence to play freely, without worrying about getting it wrong, but in Tessa's case, teaching herself and gaining confidence was an ongoing process. "I was never formally taught," says Tessa. "It gives you a very different quality to your playing, drawing, the way I paint too. You always feel technically inadequate, but there are so many ways to learn, and there is value in all of them. I have to work on disciplining myself. It's a bit of a weakness, maybe due to being a daydreamer!"

But something magical happened whenever The Slits had a chance to show their mettle, and maybe it was partly because they were initially given so few chances to do so. The urgency and fire that were trademarks of their earlier performances are especially arresting in those first Peel Sessions, rushing like a tidal wave out of the speakers and over the unsuspecting listener in a way that ensures they are unforgettable. And the so-called mistakes obviously didn't bother Peel.

Viv: "John was one of the only men in the industry, plus being that bit older, who was utterly unthreatened by us. He totally got us, and was absolutely supportive – not in a jokey, 'aren't they funny?' way, he just got it.

"We felt relaxed with him and he rated us, thank God, he kept us in the public eye in many ways. Even after his death we've been mentioned because of him and I'm so grateful for that. Also at the time I would say he was the only man, apart from John Walters and a couple of journalists who were a bit older, who could handle us mentally.

"We were banned from mainstream radio because of our name. And we thought, 'Well, do we change the name so we can get radio play?' but then we thought, 'No, we've come this far, this is who we are.' Now it wouldn't be a problem, but that's what we were kicking against. No Slits record would be played on the radio because of our name, no PR guy would sign us because we were too much trouble or too in your face."

Of course, this lily-livered mainstream media ban was not directed solely at The Slits. The BBC above all was determined to pretend it didn't exist in order to protect the sensitive emotions of their audience.* The tabloid press adopted a different policy but with the same goal in mind – ending this terrible musical and cultural outburst that was supposedly so threatening to their readers, the ordinary people on the street. Tessa still has a clipping from a red top that hysterically reported that when its journalist approached the band outside their rehearsal studio, one of the girls squirted washing-up liquid at them, "claiming it was acid".

Sensational stories, true or not, sell newspapers, so in many ways punk was a godsend to the traditionally hypocritical tabloids, enabling them to

* Amusingly, a decade or so later, artists such as Cliff Richard would be met with a radio ban for the opposite reasons.

preach from their pulpits about the breakdown of society while at the same time report on the punk phenomenon in as much lurid detail as they could conjure up. An easy recipe for sensationalism was the practice of deliberately assuming the literal meaning for cynical, off-the-cuff responses to interviewer's questions, which of course seemed all the more shocking when the answers came from young girls. Had the interviewee been a male musician, the public would probably have thought, 'How rock 'n' roll!', as one does. But throwaway sarcasm from playful, confrontational girls was met with horror – and would ultimately make everyday life very difficult for them.

Mo-Dette Kate Corris: "The point was, as far as I was concerned, that we were girls who just did it, we had no affiliations or axes to grind, and somehow that was more radical than climbing on one or another platform. Lester Bangs once said to me, 'It's not enough to be girls any more.' Lester was a great writer, but he was also often full of it."

It *was* enough to be girls, of course. Indeed, it was more than enough from the point of view of the marketing departments at most record labels where the very fact that a singer or group happened to be female was something – everything, in some cases – to exploit from a sexual angle. But The Slits didn't see it this way and this ensured that while many others from the punk scene, including plenty of no-hopers, got snapped up, they were left without a label during the initial punk explosion. It is ironic that while The Slits were celebrated and admired by their peers for supposedly thumbing their noses at commercialism, in reality the group were crying out for the support and guidance of a record label.

"We had a hard time getting a deal," admits Ari. "Most groups were signed in 1977. I remember Joe Strummer walked up to me and said, 'Respect The Slits, respect, you're the only guys who didn't sell out.' He used that word, I remember clearly, 'You didn't sell out'.

"I didn't really know what he was talking about, but he felt like as soon as [The Clash] had to make a deal, they had to make some sort of compromise. It was at a club when he told me that, so maybe he was drunk, but he did feel that all these groups had signed and he respected that we hadn't. But I didn't respect that we didn't get signed! We wanted to be."

Their situation wasn't helped by an element of self-sabotage going on from various members of The Slits. "There was a time that every label called us in the space of one week," recalls Ari. "Every day the phone was ringing, every single label, and Viv, I think, or Palmolive, made a tape, and taped all the phone calls, and took the piss, laughing at them.

"We didn't take them seriously because, even though it was these hot-shot labels that we should have maybe negotiated with, if we were more mature and older and had a management that was dealing with us properly, we would have been negotiating. But we couldn't at the time, our management was us, basically. We had a new manager every week but that wasn't real management.

"We didn't like how they approached us, they were like: 'Cash in on your image!' you know, to make us look really trashy, corny – and they weren't offering good money, a good foundation."

So, The Slits, and, as far as the mainstream was concerned, punk in general, remained frustratingly under the radar. Aside from its superficial image as dangerous, nihilistic and anarchic, punk's real, empowering value remained hidden from the masses, which is regrettable, especially given how keen everyone is to relive the 'triumph' of punk today, not to mention how so many young people at the time would have benefited from being shown another way.

No, unless, like the Pistols, Buzzcocks and Joy Division, you were fortunate enough to be given some exposure by Granada's Tony Wilson on *So It Goes* (or you were fortunate enough to have been in the North West at that time and seen it on the telly), punk bands were largely ignored as far as TV was concerned, and potential fans, so desperate for an anti-hero, were deprived.

"There was a bar," says Christine Robertson. "The BBC doesn't have any archive footage of The Slits because they didn't consider them important enough to film. I remember a few years ago seeing Joe Strummer coming out of Paul Simonon's exhibition, and a camera team from BBC London hustled him for an interview. He had a right go, saying, 'You're pointing a camera at me now. You couldn't be fucking bothered back then though, could you?'"

Within the closed society of punk, away from the TV cameras and tabloid press, something else was happening that had nothing whatsoever to do with the public's perception of boys with spiked hair and safety-pinned cheeks. The Clash, and Paul Simonon in particular, were becoming increasingly fascinated by roots reggae, as were the likes of Keith Levene, The Pop Group, who also embraced free improv, John Lydon and, of course, The Slits. They weren't just buying the records from Rough Trade in Portobello Road (at the time the main outlet for punk and reggae records), or listening to it with a spliff in their hands in the Roxy. Well, they'd been doing that too, but they were taking it further than that, and it didn't take long for this coming together of sub-cultures to be positively exploited by music impresario Chris Blackwell.

"It was a very interesting marriage, it seemed like an acceptance of the white population, albeit the rebel section," says Dennis Bovell. "Chris was at the helm of this."

Blackwell, the founder of Island Records, was born in London, raised in Jamaica and zig-zagged between the two countries for years. He brought to London licensed tapes, initially selling them to London's black communities from the boot of his car. Soon he was getting bombarded by white teenagers eager to part with their money for obscure Jamaican cassettes.

The young entrepreneur formed Island Records in Jamaica in 1959 at the age of 22, and had his first real success with 'My Boy Lollipop', sung by Millie Small, which reached number two in the UK singles charts in March 1964. Licensed by Blackwell to the Fontana label, this was the first ever UK crossover ska hit and for most people in England it was the first time they had ever heard the infectious rhythms from the Caribbean. But Blackwell would not limit himself to the music of the island he loved so much. Unusually for the time, he was open-minded with a diverse outlook, which assured Island was perpetually in the thick of whatever was new and exciting, which was perfect when punk came knocking. In the meantime he'd signed Fairport Convention, Traffic, Cat Stevens, Free, Bob Marley, Linton Kwesi Johnson, Robert Palmer and Grace Jones. The man had serious taste.

Producer Dennis Bovell was well aware of Blackwell's liking for reggae and still keen to encourage women to start making waves in reggae themselves, even though the Rastafarian culture was notoriously misogynistic and seemingly fearful of women.* The most obvious way to get Jamaican girls who up until then had been restricted to singing back-up vocals pushed forward was through the softer, sugar-coated style of reggae known as Lover's Rock.

"It had come to the middle-of-the-road thing, that's what was happening – Abba, Brotherhood Of Man," Dennis remembers. "So it was fantastic that there were women like The Slits doing music – well, soon-to-be women anyway! Girls, really.

"On the reggae side of things, I'd been involved in Lover's Rock, and the theme of Lover's Rock was to get young girls up front, singing. Reggae was saturated with men, hardcore Rastafari. So we thought, let's inject some love into this thing, for all those girls who want to sing and get up front but who find the Rasta thing a bit too hardcore and fundamentalist.

"So it was like, let's get Louisa Mark, she was someone I did a record for – 'Caught You In A Lie'. That all started things. And then Brown Sugar did a song called 'I'm In Love With The Dreadlocks', and of course, later there was 'Silly Games', the song I wrote for Janet Kay."

Ari Up was very aware of Lover's Rock, and respected the fact that Louisa Mark at least erred on the slightly earthier side of the genre. But it was clear this was not where The Slits were going. "Lover's Rock was huge, and Louisa Mark was an amazing Lover's Rock girl who really gave birth to it," she explains. "She was huge in Jamaica but she was English too. And she was more rootsy. Not like reggae music for the dentist's office. Not slimy, smoochy Lover's Rock where you want to just throw up – more rootsy reggae."

While Lover's Rock was an important step, it would take a bit of punk attitude to really push things forward for girls and do something genuinely exciting, and Dennis would soon play a huge part in the album that would take on this very mission.

* A female music journalist was apparently once thrown out of a well-known reggae musician's car when he sensed she was starting her period.

Chapter 8

"The noise bothered me, so I started wearing earplugs." – The beginning of the end for Palmolive's tenure in The Slits.

Having clicked with Buzzcocks on the White Riot Tour the year before, the Slits would embark on another tour of the UK supporting the Manchester group throughout March 1978. Buzzcocks were promoting their now-classic album *Another Music In A Different Kitchen* and beginning to explore the art and ideas of Paul Klee and Marcel Duchamps, with singer Pete Shelley describing aspects of their direction at this point as "surreal and Dada". Steve Diggle, however, remembers them all having big tour-bus singalongs and making up cheeky new lyrics to Althea and Donna's reggae hit 'Uptown Top Ranking', however, so it obviously didn't get too serious. The wild spirit of the White Riot Tour lingered on too - it was on this tour that Tessa had to spend a night in a police cell after being caught spraying 'The Slits' onto a wall opposite Manchester's Electric Circus venue.

By this time The Slits finally felt ready to record their own album, and thankfully, although they didn't know it yet, they were closer than ever to being signed to a label where respect was mutual. Rightly or wrongly, they had deliberately declined the early offers that came their way, believing it better to wait until they knew that the time was right. This was partly through their own resolve but also, as Don Letts points out, because they weren't the easiest band to approach, and they were unwilling to tolerate industry dinosaurs who couldn't handle them, or worse, tried to exploit them.

"What terrified the A&R men," says Letts, "was that The Slits thrilled not only the guys but more importantly the girls. Back in those days, up until that point, girls were doing backing vocals for some male cock-rocker. People like The Slits, Siouxsie Sioux and Poly Styrene were strong women taking no shit, standing centre-stage. That was very inspiring and empowering for women up and down the country, tremendously important stuff."

Whoever signed The Slits was therefore going to have to tread very carefully. Island Records could see how important they were and were taking an interest in the group, but something was going to have to change before The Slits could move forward. Island or anyone else would have to make sure the group knew they weren't going to be exploited. The Slits knew what they *didn't* want.

"We were the first girl band that wasn't put together as a gimmick or by a man," says Ari. "There were The Runaways of course, but they were made to feel they had to compete with guys, holding their guitars on their crotches, gimmicky and sexualised. Again, a guy* was behind them. Granted they played their own instruments, but that's about it."

The Slits were accruing material for their first album all the time, and there was no shortage of possible album tracks. But this was a period of renewal in many ways, with the driving raw sound of their early punk days giving way to something new, and as a result they turned their back on a few old favourites in a bid to shed their skin.

Tessa: "We were choosy about the songs we wanted to use. Everyone contributed with lyrics. I had slowly started to. I didn't initially because when I'd just joined the group they already had songs, but sometimes someone else would write a bass line, someone else would write a melody, or someone would just come up with a whole song, but everyone contributed, which is what makes it interesting."

Viv adds, "'New Town', 'FM', half of them were already written when

* Kim Fowley

I joined, the other half were written afterwards. I would write with Ari. I'd write mostly lyrics and she'd write music, or we'd write the music together. One or two Tessa wrote."

"Some of our old songs were dropped completely," remembers Ari. "I think we should have kept 'Number One Enemy', and 'Vindictive'. They were great songs, but at the time we were probably so sick of them. We were teenagers anyway, every few months you change.

"'Shoplifting' we kept, because it was something we all related to for so many years, everyone did it – just from big corporations, the big supermarkets, Babylon! Now I look at it differently of course."

Palmolive's song 'New Town' was everyone's favourite track within The Slits at that time, and it would probably be the one that would go through the greatest metamorphosis. "I restructured it," says Viv. "It was originally known as 'Drug Town', of course, all about drugs and I had this mad mate called Matt Collibeck who lived in Crawley, and he was at a rehearsal one day and he said, 'It's too literal, it's not poetic, everyone's taking drugs and the mood of it all, it's like these new towns like Crawley and Milton Keynes,' so that's how we gave it that title, because those new towns were springing up in the Seventies."

From the start, Viv had chosen personal themes ('Ping Pong Affair', 'Instant Hit' and 'So Tough') that reflected her own feelings about life or her close friendships, or wit-laden observations scrutinising relationships with a dose of sarcasm. 'Love And Romance' celebrated the punk ethos of shunning conventional notions of sentimentality. Musically, it was a strident riot of shouting, dissonant melody, jangling guitar, girl-gang backing vocals, with lyrics flipping deftly between saccharine and startling: "Call you every day on the telephone, break your neck if you ain't home." It was one of the few Slits songs on which you would hear a cymbal crash, and while all of their older tracks would be reworked, The Slits were keen to keep the essence of this song intact.

Viv remembers, "In those days it was very rigorous, you couldn't hold hands with your boyfriend, you couldn't look smoochy, everyone would take the piss out of you, 'squelchy' as they would call it. Romance was ridiculed as a conceit. So you couldn't do anything habitual. 'Love and Romance' was me getting a bit carried away with all the clichés of being in love."

'Love and Romance' and 'Typical Girls' both explored these themes with considerable spiky amusement. As Ari observes, their satirical take on how girls were seen, how they should behave and how they were manipulated by 'romance' is still every bit as relevant today.

"'Love and Romance' was an oldie but a goodie," says Ari. "The lyrics were cynical and sarcastic – we were so not 'love and romance'! To have a picket fence, the American dream with the pretty house and garden, to be a wife and have children with the husband, or be a model or a beauty queen – all of that stuff, we didn't want.

"We're still like that now. We might be into real love and relationships, but it's that thing of being free spirits, to be able to grow into who you are first before you have to belong to someone, that whole idea of ownership that goes with love and romance. Even now, guys are still possessive, and back then it was totally about losing your identity as soon as you were involved romantically."

'Typical Girls' would soon become one of their most famous and loved songs. On this track The Slits took the opportunity to poke fun at the clichés and difficulties that girls are brought up to consider so painstakingly once they hit adolescence – complexions, weight, wardrobe crises, magazines, and the wooing and manipulation of boys. It's funny, a piss-take, but also cautionary. The opening line, 'Don't create, don't rebel', is warning enough to kick any potential 'typical girls' into touch.

Viv: "I came across the term 'Typical Girls' in a sociology book and thought, what a fantastic title, so I wrote that down, and that's all the things you're supposed to be, worrying about this, worrying about that, being a girl, basically."

Ari adds, "'Typical Girls' was, again, a satire. We're so not typical, we're anything but typical, but in the end there's a twist. Yes we *are* really typical girls, but not by the standards of society, the magazines, the fashion industry, the media and the music industry.

"The song is to say, 'Look what they say about girls!' We're emotional, unpredictable, we can't drive well, we're sensitive, out of control, buying magazines, worried about spots and fat, which a lot of times we do, but we threw it back at the people who always insisted that those were the only things a girl would ever be. A typical girl who can't do shit, can't do nothing with her life, will always be dependent on a man and on society. We were also throwing it back at the women who defend those types – sometimes the women are actually worse."

It wouldn't have been punk without the addition of some not particularly subtle romantic sparring in the form of 'Ping Pong Affair', about Viv's frustrating relationship with Mick Jones. This track was also worked up for the record, provoking a response from Jones in the form of 'Train In Vain' on 1979's *London Calling*, the only ballad The Clash recorded.*

"Ah, Mick!" Viv laughs. "Yes, that's about Mick Jones. I don't know if he knows. Mick was living in West London and we'd have a row and I'd storm off in the middle of the night and I'd be in the street all scared, so it was all about that. He had magazine and record and comic collections, that's mentioned in there too. The lyric 'dreaming on a bus', I love the way Ari harmonises on that bit. I remember getting a postcard from Mick, written on the tour bus, and he quoted that bit to me."

Palmolive, meanwhile, was moving further into exploring wider themes as well as her own less satirical take on social issues. She remembers: "The track 'FM' was towards the end for me. When I look at the lyrics I wrote, I can totally see my walk through that. At the beginning, the songs were like, 'I'm gonna be your number one enemy', it was just like an explosion, and then it was like, 'Wait a minute, what's going on here?' With 'FM' and 'Adventures Close To Home', those two were more like the real me.

"'New Town' was also more like a criticism to what was around us, in your face, people working and for what? 'Shoplifting', you know, I'm going to do whatever I want, I don't care. By the end I was trying to make sense of what I was doing. 'FM' came first then 'Adventures Close To Home'. I wanted Tessa to sing that. I was closest to Tessa. To begin with I was closest to Ari, but the group evolved, and I felt Tessa had a sensitivity, and she could sing it better."

Palmolive remained one of the most popular members of the band, boasting a ferocious style – famously speeding up unpredictably, or

* There is much speculation that the 'Train In Vain' line, "You say you'd stand by your man", echoes Viv's line in 'Typical Girls': "Typical girls stand by their man…"

rather, predictably unpredictably. But Viv maintains this is a very female thing: "We didn't want to just bang out a 4/4 rhythm and blues rhythm. We kept saying to ourselves, 'How do we feel?' If a woman is making music, do we just do habitual copying of what men do, rock 'n' roll?

"It sounds a bit airy-fairy, but we naturally sped up and slowed down, we sometimes put a 3/8 rhythm in by mistake, we were untutored in music but we wanted to listen to who we were inside, not just copy other people. We couldn't play what men could do, those sort of 4/4 times, never speeding up, never slowing down, couldn't do it! I don't know if women really can.

"We thought about our menstrual cycles and our this and our that, and we tried so hard to play in rhythm and in time. We could do it when we had a male drummer. In the end, we shouldn't have bothered, we did try very hard not to fall into those clichés."

Palmolive's love of flamenco, which she heard and absorbed during her teens the way others would listen to British and American pop and rock music, may also have had an effect on her playing. Flamenco can suddenly accelerate into a frenzy after a measured beginning, stopping, starting and fluctuating, rarely maintaining a strict tempo throughout. But whether this was a factor or not, this erratic style was starting to hold the group back.

As much as everyone adored and respected Palmolive, the more the rest of the band developed musically, the more they felt the need for a steady heartbeat, one that would provide stability within the chaos, and also lighten up their sound. The band were reaching their creative peak and anything or anyone who hindered them, whether intentionally or not, had to go in order for them to progress.

Palmolive was seemingly losing interest in the group, and had started to search for personal fulfilment elsewhere, as well as a more experimental approach to music. She also felt the need to distance herself from the tensions between herself, Ari and Viv.

"There had been tour incidents," she explains. "We were having personal problems in the band. I was getting on well with Tessa but with Ari and Viviane, it wasn't working right. I started to get disillusioned. I had a lot of questions. I observed things, like I was observing people coming out of the gigs, and thinking there's something wrong here. I had a gap feeling, like an intuition. It wasn't what I'd hoped for."

Viv remembers: "It was while we were rehearsing songs to go on the album. Palmolive was very taken by a guy called Tymon Dogg. They were very close musically and she was very influenced by him, and I think it was a bit religious as well, it was going down that route."

Palmolive explained in an interview on the website Nstop: "I started getting into a spiritual thing, like astral travelling. I became very fascinated, I started throwing the I Ching, like divination. I started contacting spirits... I sound weird, but that's what was happening.

"I didn't have any control over it, but it was very powerful if you can imagine yourself going out of your body. And all that was happening with the gigs. We kept practising, we still functioned on that level, but my life started taking a turn. I started going to the gigs... the noise started bothering me, so I started putting in earplugs."

This detachment, physically and mentally, didn't go unnoticed. The writing was on the wall, as far as Viv was concerned. "I hope I'm not remembering this wrong about [Palmolive], but she would not appear at rehearsals, she was more interested in a much more experimental wing of music than we wanted to go down, and she was excited by the Tymon Dogg influence and not excited by us. I think we seemed a bit ploddy and rockish in comparison to what she was going into musically.

"Although you might say we said, 'That's it, you're not turning up to rehearsals and you're not into it.' I think in a way she steered it subconsciously. Often you bring about your own fate without realising it. That would be my take on it and I hope I'm not insulting anyone by saying that."

From what Palmolive says, it sounds as if Viv is right on the money: "Maybe I provoked it, I did start to lose interest."

Another problem affecting Palmolive was that she was getting seriously concerned about Tessa, who had started taking heroin. Palmolive and Viv first noticed this after The Slits' performance at Paris' Gibus Club in January 1978. Palmolive: "There was a guy called Geno. Tessa and he became an item. He was a really lively, nice guy. Then the next time I saw him he was, like, dead, he looked like a ghost. He had got into heroin, and I believe that's how Tessa got into it. We were living together in a squat, and when she was hooked on heroin I remember fighting with her about it. We were taking dope and stuff but nothing heavy, I remember going, 'Tessa, don't do it!' She was my friend and I could see that was not good. I was joking around but telling her to quit, and I dropped it [the drugs] through the crack in the floor.

"Usually Tessa is very easy-going and laid-back and she got so mad at me, she was furious! I didn't do it on purpose, it just fell through the crack."

Viv adds: "I remember Geno and Tessa getting into heroin. I felt very left out, I couldn't take it, I'd just been ill, but I was tempted just to be part of the gang, which is how heroin gets you. But my self-esteem crept up and said, 'Well, Viv, you've been ill...' and thank God I didn't take it. It was a spiral for Tess."

Tessa remembers first trying the drug two years earlier, although she didn't immediately become a regular user. But heroin doesn't let you get away that easily. It lurked in the background for Tessa ever since that first dalliance until she succumbed to its inevitable grip. "I'd had it on hold since I was 17," she explains. "I might have used it a couple of times along the way. We weren't a drug-taking group, but I've always had a hunger for mind-altering substances. I'm quite a dreamy, solitary person, it suited my character."

Yet another issue hanging over the group was the perennial problem of not having a real manager, or perhaps even having too many potential managers, and one more had appeared on the horizon, none other than punk svengali Malcolm McLaren, who was wooing them determinedly. On the surface this might have been an auspicious choice, and some bands might even have found his attention flattering, but Palmolive had a bad feeling about it.

"There was the thing with Malcolm," sighs Palmolive. "He wanted to be our manager. The three of them were into it, and I remember he invited us to this gay club, and I remember him talking to me because I had written a lot of the songs. I remember to this day, he said, 'I want to work with women, because I hate women and I hate music – and I thrive on hate.' Honest to God, that is the truth.

"So I'm going, like, 'You guys? Did you hear this?' I couldn't believe he had said this to me, but the others were into it at first. Malcolm

McLaren was like a big dude in our scene, but I put my brakes on and I said I do not want to work with him."

Tessa admits they were keen to move forward, and the idea of being managed by the established, notorious Malcolm and his 'Glitterbest Gestapo', in the words of writer Nick Kent, was tempting on one level, but they soon realised his game plan was at odds with their own ethos. They spent two weeks under his jurisdiction. It was Malcolm who took them to the Gibus Club where they even performed the Velvet Underground song 'Femme Fatale' with Nico, and Palmolive even got a lovely set of Pearl drums out of him. But the relationship was not meant to be.

"The problem with Malcolm was that he wanted to make us the female version of The Sex Pistols," Tessa explains. "But we were different, it would have been the biggest mistake. We weren't a guitar-based band. It would have been a disaster, it would have taken away the character of The Slits. But we thought we'd try him out, we needed some help." At least McLaren paid for a few rehearsals.

Don Letts was amused that Malcolm, his old rival from his retailing days on the King's Road, was trying to take on the most bloody-minded band in town: "No one could make The Slits do anything and they certainly weren't going to be Malcolm's puppets, nor were they going to be anyone else's.

"Don't get me wrong, I like Malcolm, I think he has a great way of looking at things. And he had a role to play, no two ways about it. Maybe not the role he says he had, but a role nonetheless. Plus he and Vivienne Westwood were ten years older than all of us so they could see it in the context of an ongoing counter-culture. And that was really important."

Better no help than the wrong help, and Palmolive's instinct was correct. McLaren was an expert puppeteer who expected his charges to do his bidding without question, and to be able to mould them in such ways he thought might best achieve whatever Machiavellian motives he might embrace. Subsequent whispers have it that Malcolm planned to sign them to the German disco label Hansa to become a four-piece 'subversive disco' vocal group, a sort of Angry Brigade Boney M. The fact that this would mean The Slits ditching everything they'd worked towards so far mattered not one iota to him, even if he realised this was the case. Even worse, he also harboured plans to make a titillating movie starring The Slits as a cute all-girl band who end up getting sold as sex slaves to a sleazy Mexican disco.

When Palmolive gave him the elbow, McLaren concentrated on trying to poach their younger and, he hoped, more impressionable singer. She says: "He was trying to just then get Ari, and not work with us when he saw the resistance, but Ari decided she did not want to part with us. People can say whatever, but that's what I remember and that made a strong impression on me."

They might have shunned McLaren, but The Slits were still friends with John Lydon and Sid Vicious, and they were aware of their troubled friendship. Viv, as we know, was inspired to write about it – and it seems that, certainly after the release of their debut album, *Cut,* listening to a Slits song is as close as you can get to understanding from the inside some of the close relationships within that scene.

"'So Tough', that's Sid and John," says Viv. "I remember talking to John on the phone, and he was saying, 'He thinks he's so tough,' about Sid, so I just went away and wrote that song." 'So Tough' was a strong, topical, vital song with honest, almost prophetic lyrics: "They say you're acting like a star, they say not everything's wunderbar / You want money, girls urgently, too much too soon you wait and see..."

Keith Levene remembers being impressed by the originality of what Viv had devised: "When she was writing 'So Tough', she showed me the guitar riff she'd come up with for that, and I thought that was wicked. I couldn't hear the timing it was in and I couldn't imagine how it was going to come out."

While the song's earliest guise was different from the *Cut* version, it boasted the now trademark Slits harmonies, spikiness and perceptive lyrics. At the time, it was intended to be the group's first single.

After Malcolm and his managerial overtures came the glamorous PR guru Magenta DeVine, who intended to help The Slits put 'So Tough' out as a single (with 'New Town' as a B-side) on Real Records. But Deaf School manager Frank Silver stepped in, putting the kibosh on it when it turned out that, with regard to money and the group's future output, the agreement was apparently not all it should have been. Luckily their ultimate label of choice, Island Records, had already been showing an interest.

It had taken The Slits a long time to reach this stage, and the press was becoming increasingly impatient with what they saw as a lack of progress, as in 'not delivering'. However, when he interviewed them for *NME* in November 1978, Nick Kent found that the fact they had already been a band for two years meant nothing to them and that only now were they ready for the next all-important stage. Songs had been written and honed, and musically they were far more confident.

"As far as they're concerned they've only just begun," wrote Kent, "and it's the future that's important, though God knows what may arise. And there's only 13 songs, but they're good songs."

The other reason behind the belief that they hadn't been particularly visible to the British music press in comparison with other groups was because they had been spending so much time honing their skills and gaining more live experience abroad. With her experience of promoting in Germany, Nora was able to keep The Slits busy as a live band, and she took them to mainland Europe to perform a few gigs at venues she had links with. With Nora at the wheel of a trusty white van, The Slits trundled across France and Germany, where they met free improviser and future Slits collaborator Steve Beresford and offended some nuns into the bargain.

"We went to visit Nora's old school in the mountains somewhere, probably in Bavaria," remembers Tessa. "There were nuns there, and Palmolive said something rude. Nora was like, 'Control yourself, these are my old teachers!' I can't remember what for the life of me it was she said, just some stupid little comment to the nuns, but Nora got a bit pissed off!"

In Munich The Slits were on the same bill as the pop duo Marshall Hain, who'd just had a hit with 'Dancing In The City', and it was through the collective struggle to find a vegetarian restaurant – always a problem in Germany – that they hooked up with Steve Beresford.

"We did this thing in Munich where we had the worst food ever," remembers Steve. "If you don't eat meat forget about it. We all went to Munich's most famous Bavarian restaurant protesting that most of us were vegetarian, I think we had fried eggs, scrambled eggs and boiled eggs. And perhaps a few slices of cucumber."

It was hard enough to find a vegetarian eatery at the best of times during the Seventies, and it would be a continual quest for The Slits over the years, but in the land of the bratwurst, where pork was considered an acceptable vegetarian option, it was often a fruitless (or veg-less) challenge. Tessa, one of the few meat eaters in the entourage, remembers, "Every meal in Germany that was supposed to be vegetarian had gravy and pork in it! They didn't realise that, like, pork is not a vegetable! I mean, I eat meat, so it didn't bother me..."

Racking up experience and developing their confidence, the future was looking bright for The Slits, but the end of an era was looming. After much gnashing of teeth, Ari and Viv urged Tessa, the member of the band who was closest to Palmolive, to take her aside and sack her, for want of a more sensitive term. While Tessa admires how Palmolive handled being given her marching orders, some of their fans were not impressed.

Tessa takes up the story: "We'd been waiting a long time to get the right kind of record deal. Palmolive's drum style was too wild, we needed a sharper drummer, which was extremely upsetting for me because I lived with Palmolive in a squat in Ladbroke Grove, Elgin Avenue.

"Then it was decided that I should be the one to tell Palmolive that she's not in the group any more. It was the most horrific thing I ever had to do. I never felt confident about my own playing, and it's not like she wasn't better than anyone else. Viv was very on the case regarding keeping the creative purity; if something wasn't right, or was compromising the creative side of The Slits, it had to go.

"I think we lost a lot of fans. I think Palmolive was a lot of people's favourite. She had her own style of drumming but when you're recording it wasn't bang on time. But how dare I criticise her playing when my playing was quite similar. I play by feel, not by knowledge.

"Who knows what would have happened if Palmolive would have stayed with us, we would have gone down a different avenue, I think. But it was a group decision and it was a really harsh one. A lot of people thought we were crazy to have done it.

"Then, Palmolive joined The Raincoats, which is good that she didn't give up, she fought back and carried on playing. We did stay friends for a bit but of course it went a bit funny and we did leave the squat we were living in. There was no ill feeling, she is a very forgiving person, but there were a lot of fans who didn't forgive us. And that is the sad story of what happened with Palmolive."

Palmolive accepted the decision. "It was like, 'It is not working with you, you can't keep the beat,'" she said in 2008. "Whatever, I wasn't great. They wanted to go in a certain direction and I really didn't want to, so I understand it."

She was quickly embraced by the Raincoats, who were practically family anyway, especially since Palmolive's brother-in-law, Richard Dudanski, had been playing drums with them. It was Richard who alerted them to the fact that Palmolive was no longer in The Slits, and he stepped down as drummer in The Raincoats as he felt it would be a good move for Palmolive. As a group they were earthy, thoughtful, less unpredictable, but shared The Slits' interest in jazz artists such as Ornette Coleman, Miles Davis and the more experimental, free side of the punk scene. And they were also huge admirers of hers.

"Palmolive was a gift to us," says Gina Birch. "We went on to make history thanks to her."

Ana da Silva adds: "God, it was better than winning the lottery, definitely! I had never given any attention to drums. That was totally alien to me, we weren't musicians so we didn't know about drumming. Looking at Palmolive was the first time I looked at a drummer and understood what they were doing, or felt what they were doing, which is even more important. And then when she was joining us, it was like, 'My God!'"

"We just thought she was the most amazing, brilliant, wonderful, fantastic person and the most extraordinary drummer," adds Gina Birch. "It was heavenly for us. She was in mourning, she was sad, but we could talk and it was a different kettle of fish."

Gina remembers that herself and Ana, despite their obvious joy at working with their favourite drummer, were very aware that this was a difficult time for Palmolive. "It was terribly sad. Palmolive was a thinker, and she had a lot of deep thoughts and deep feelings, and The Slits were her passion, but she wanted something more.

"Tymon Dogg was more from the hippy era and much more spiritual. She wanted to do a cover of one of his songs in The Slits, but they weren't so into the spiritual leanings and her interest in Tymon, and I think they felt that it was pulling them in a direction they didn't want to go."

The Raincoats wasted no time in utilising the magic that was happening between them all, and busily started work on their first album for Rough Trade. Which was just as well, as Palmolive was not to stick around for long.

Ana: "We did a very clever thing and did a record with her. The Slits did a Peel Session with Palmolive, but I think they should have done those songs with her as an album and then moved on in a different way. I think they were into making it, on their own terms of course, but I think the spiritual side was maybe a bit embarrassing."

The Raincoats celebrated in Palmolive what so many people criticised – her timekeeping. What they wanted and needed was different to The Slits at that time, and they loved her playing all the more for its ragged edges and mutability.

Gina adds, "With classical music what you've got is feeling and emotion and the way people play is to do with the gentle nuances of a crescendo or a speed change – OK we're not talking about classical music, but what we're talking about is emoting. I saw a programme on BBC4 about the guitar, with all these men talking about how they found it easier to emote through their guitar than through talking. For us, our emotions might have had more to do with our timing or our nuances. For Palmolive, she had incredible energy and emotion."

It worked between The Raincoats and Palmolive, she was happy in a way, but again, it didn't take long until she felt this was not the change she needed. She explains: "In my mind it was the problem with the group (The Slits) and the direction of the group, so then I joined The Raincoats, and then I realised, 'No, it's not the group!'"

While she related to The Raincoats, Palmolive finally made not just any change, but the right change for her. She says: "When you're a teenager you protest this and protest that, I felt my life was what I had made it, I couldn't blame someone else.

"It was like something in me was saying, 'You need to take responsibility for where you are at! If you want something else, you have to make it.' I was strong-headed and when I see something I go for it, but I was able to look at my life and say honestly, 'I don't like it, but I have done it.' So I had started to look into spirituality, Hinduism, yoga and meditation, and decided I'm not just going to sleep around, you go to a party and you go with someone and you don't even know why, I felt there was no dignity in that, there was something not right. The dope, the cigarettes, it was almost like a survival thing.

"I felt like I was drowning, something was going on, something I didn't like, I just felt like I was hurting me. So that was the beginning of me taking my life in another direction. Someone spoke to me and said, 'This is God, Jesus is God', which sounded crazy. I heard it from my brother-in-law one time and I thought, 'That's nuts, it's so narrow-minded'.

"But at one point in my life when I was really running out of answers, something in me thought, 'Well ...'"

Palmolive – now Paloma McLardy – lives in Cape Cod, Massachusetts, and remains a committed Christian to this day.

After her departure from The Slits, the group kept a positive, affectionate slant on the story when they were interviewed by *ZigZag*'s Kris Needs, admitting how tough it must have been after everything Palmolive had worked towards – but while they missed her, they made it clear that plans for their debut album and Palmolive's vision were poles apart.

"Tessa: 'She didn't feel at all bitter or anything.'

"Ari: 'At least, she didn't show it, whatever she felt, just having two years cut off.'

"Tessa: 'She's against big companies, even Island.'

"Viv: 'It's just gone right, you know. It's just fate, it turned out right. She's found something closer to her heart.'

The Slits now had to find a drummer who could take them to new heights. It was an opportunity to sharpen up their act and find someone who would have just the right balance of stability, versatility and lightness that would give their songs a livelier backdrop. And it didn't necessarily have to be a girl.

Chapter 9

"As far as I'm concerned, being any gender is a drag." – Patti Smith

When Island signed The Slits, the group were confident they had found the right label. Island's roster at that time was right up their street and with independence and rebel music in its bones, not to mention an honourable history, the label seemed perfect for The Slits. They were a niche group, after all, and had no intention of being swallowed up and forgotten by a major label concerned solely with commercial success.

Ari Up recalls other offers from record companies that were loaded with clear intentions to exploit the "novelty" aspect of a girl band. Island, on the other hand, made it clear it took The Slits and their music seriously – and could put its money where its mouth was. "Island offered good money," she says, "and offered us a real type of deal that wasn't based on cashing in on gimmicks. It was a proper record deal taking a group seriously as recording artists.

"Most of the typical media was against us, and the typical audience was against us. But Chris Blackwell had vision. He gathered up all these different acts, reggae groups, Jamaican and local groups, and there was room for us on the so-called 'punky reggae' side too. We found a home with Chris Blackwell."

"It was always going to be Island, because of their roster," adds Viv, "apart from Eddie & The Hot Rods! Of course, there was all that happening at the same time, pub bands, that sort of thing, but there was also all the soul and reggae [and] that appealed. We thought it suited us – but we were probably wrong again!"

With hindsight, Viv wonders whether the band shot themselves in the foot by being so bolshie, so inflammatory and determinedly experimental. They would frighten people off by digging their heels in and, at times, refusing to act on well-meant, sound advice. For certain outsiders, a band unwilling to compromise was something to be celebrated but it probably did The Slits no favours in the long term.

The question of whether Island had any underhand intentions with regard to The Slits, of making them do their bidding, telling them what to do, or what was what, has never really been answered. According to Don, this was not the case. "Other than saying, 'A record's round with a hole in it,' no!" he says. "That's why they didn't get any further than they did because The Slits were bloody-minded, they knew exactly what they wanted, and they weren't malleable, they couldn't sit within that corporate structure, no way. And more power to them for that. It wasn't a business plan."

A key reason why The Slits were in a position to go their own way was their insistence on having complete artistic control written into their contract. This enabled them to record the songs they wanted in the way they wanted, select the album cover they wanted, and generally assume an attitude towards their career and output that brooked no dissent from anyone at the label. Such a contract was generally bestowed by labels only upon those with proven track records, such as former Beatles, or pre-packaged certainties like Led Zeppelin. In the case of The Slits it was not only unusual but hindsight suggests it may have been a double-edged sword. At the time, though, they were delighted with it.

Ari recalls: "We made sure we signed with a lawyer and – and this is very important – we were not only the first girl band to do this, but one of the first bands period, to have artistic control written into our contract. We had a lawyer who dealt with all the groups at the time. At the time I was a kid, it was a bit over my head. I didn't understand it, and I didn't know what was going on, I just thought it was all too much to have such a big lawyer, but I realise we needed it.

"It's a huge thing, huge. We're girls and, when the time came, we were able to do the cover we wanted. We must have found that lawyer through The Clash. It was a must. Jimi Hendrix, because he didn't have artistic control, couldn't have the album cover he wanted on *Electric Ladyland*."*

In regards to album artwork, it was just as well that The Slits had insisted on this clause in their contract since Island's art department had plans for their pending album cover that were far from appropriate for The Slits. Somewhat inevitably, they were veering towards glamorising the group, which didn't sit well with the girls at all.

Ari explains, "They wanted us to be like glamorous Charlie's Angels with fog on our faces, special light effects and special back-combed hair, all glamorous. Then they wanted to have a trashy, fluorescent album cover with zippers all over it. Like insinuating that when you open the zipper, there's The Slits, going to the pussy image, and we were just like, 'Hmm... that's corny'. So there was quite a bit of argument about the cover when we were signed."

The group had strong ideas about what they wanted, and they certainly weren't interested in charming their way around A&R men, or anyone else for that matter. The press in particular got it in the neck. Island was already holding "pre-recording parties" in Ari's words, and get-togethers to raise awareness of The Slits. But if journalists had failed to do their research, or tried to force the band to endure a cliché-riddled interview, there'd be trouble.

"We were a strong gang, in your face," says Viv. "The thing about punk was that you said what you thought. It was all about honesty, and honesty is pretty brutal – so some journalists would ask a boring question

* Ari is referring to a well-known industry story. Hendrix had asked Track Records to use a Linda Eastman photo of his band sitting with a group of children at an Alice In Wonderland sculpture in New York's Central Park, but his request was ignored in favour of the label's own art department's idea – a bunch of winsome, nude dolly birds posing against a black background. Hendrix hated it. Experience Hendrix, which nowadays controls the musician's estate, has since ensured that the image is no longer used.

like 'What are your musical influences?' [and] you'd get so sick of it. With punk, you turned things on its head. We were turning things on its head so why weren't the journalists? They were just going down the same old route so we were winding them up like mad. Most music-industry men were like dinosaurs."

They were fortunate that Chris Blackwell at least was cut from the same cloth as they were. It was thanks largely to the Island boss's open-minded attitude that The Slits found a place where they could set down (albeit temporary) roots and have their wild, creative ideas nurtured and encouraged.

Their first meeting with Island's head honcho at the label's headquarters in Notting Hill's Basing Street remains etched on Viv's memory: "The first time we met Chris was in a dark room in Island with lots of cushions everywhere. He'd been betting on the horses, and I'd just had a pair of shoes stolen and he said that if he won he'd give me the money for the shoes! I was so broke and I'd spent a fortune on these shoes – he didn't win! But that stands out to me. He was fun, charming, perhaps not absolutely moved by us though.

"He also had Marianne Faithfull with her new album, and frankly he was more into her. She was more his generation and that was more exciting, whereas we were just this bunch of wild girls."

Ari: "Chris Blackwell didn't really get us musically, he always admitted that. He saw a whole image thing, but not in a gimmicky way. He let us be who we were and he kind of liked the idea that it was radical. So he gave us full support, gave us a good advance."

Island Records was a hub of excitement that suddenly connected The Slits to their reggae heroes on another level. No longer were they just listening to them or dancing to their records, now they were watching them pass in and out of the same rehearsal rooms, and Tessa was sufficiently motivated by it all to remain around that potent area for years to come.

"I had a lot of respect for Chris Blackwell," she says. "He was with us when we recorded '(I Heard It Through The) Grapevine' and 'Typical Girls', and there's a great picture in one of the music papers where he's like James Bond and we're like the three Bond girls around him!"

Sounds a bit un-Slit? You'd better believe they were taking the piss. Ari explains, "Chris was very shy and very much a 'behind the scenes' guy, he'd never made a press interview with pictures before – but he did one with us with a picture of him doing the James Bond pose with us like Octopussy girls.

"I thought that was great. We were really anti Bond girls at the time, we thought they were so corny and sexist, so we took the piss and totally mocked it. We didn't look like James Bond girls!" The image certainly made an impression, showed The Slits' sense of humour, and in future manager Dick O'Dell's eyes, was "obviously the greatest signing picture of all time".

Tessa continues, "It was a great time to be signed to [Island]. There was a cook, Lucky Gordon, who was part of the Profumo scandal*. He's still around. It was a great atmosphere in Island Records, you had really interesting reggae acts, you could get some great records for free. I've got some very good memories of that studio, Sarm."

Ari adds, "The studio was on the famous road with all the Jamaican food, we had ginnip juice, rice and peas, salt-fish and ackee and all the Jamaican stuff that they'd cook. You'd hear all the sounds in the street, they were great times, you always heard a bass somewhere."

The Slits would spend many happy hours at 10 Basing Street. It was here that they rehearsed the songs for their first album, reworking many of their older songs and working out arrangements for the newer ones. They would record their first track there too, a unique version of the Marvin Gaye Motown classic '(I Heard It Through) The Grapevine'.

The studio was state-of-the-art, Island offered just the right amount of support, and the band were on their home turf of Ladbroke Grove, which made it all feel right. "When we were at the studio rehearsing, Chris used to drop in on us now and again and see how we were doing," says Ari. "We were a pet project. He was looking out for us to be the next big thing, I think."

There was just one problem – they still didn't have a drummer, and time was of the essence. They had to find someone just right, if only to cut the first track before they moved on to the residential recording

* Gordon was one of Christine Keeler's lovers.

studio Ridge Farm near Dorking to start recording in earnest. It was easier said than done – The Slits needed a particular kind of drummer: versatile, open-minded and aware of all kinds of music.

"We went through tons of auditions, lots of guys," says Ari. "There were no women drummers, it's even hard to find one now who can play more than one style. They usually play very average rock 'n' roll, one-dimensional. All the guys who auditioned were accidents. Not just their attitudes, but they weren't educated in their musical backgrounds, not like today where people are exposed to all kinds of world music, reggae, drum and bass."

The Slits finally settled for a talented local reggae session drummer called Maxie, who backed Jamaican reggae artists when they toured England. He didn't know the song very well – which was a good thing, because The Slits were determined not to ape the original anyway. He also didn't know The Slits, and he thought they were completely bonkers. But they were used to that.

"We didn't do many cover versions at that stage," says Ari. "And we thought, if we're going to do a cover it's not just got to be a song that we love, but a song we can make our own. We always knew that. Don't try to copy it the way it was, make it your own vibe. We wanted ours dancey, dubby and funky.

"Maxie was perfect for 'Grapevine'. He hardly knew the song, he just came in and clicked into it, he didn't play it all soppy, it was hardcore with reggae drum fills. Reggae drummers have to tune the skins a certain way, you have to spend time on that, maybe dampen the snare with a T-shirt, and he knew that and did that. That's why you have that crisp snare and those heavy toms. The guitar sounded funky, the bass and drums sounded reggae. And instead of concentrating on guitar, we focused on the bass line instead."

'Grapevine' remains a popular Slits track, and is often the first track of theirs that people come across thanks to its ubiquitous inclusion on punk compilations, and its enduring status as one of the top cover versions of all time. In *The Observer*'s own list, it sits proudly at number seven, with the write-up: "The Gaye classic is a study in self-lacerating paranoia. The Notting Hill femme-punks delivered it as an eccentric, dub-disco jump for joy…"

As with so many artistic flourishes, like bolts of lightning cast without pretension or self-consciousness, this track was a one-take wonder, recorded as live, and mixed by a lady who, apparently, was up to that point in charge of making the tea.

"We just played it live," says Ari. "We ran into the studio and we had all the time in the world, but they used the first take of us, it was as if it was a live gig.

"I came in the next day to do the proper vocals, because I'd only done guide vocals the day before, just singing along with them, fucking around. And we ended up using the vocal that I was just fucking around on! We tried to get that vibe and that vocal when I came in the next day but it didn't work. It needed to be live."

"Ari did a fabulous vocal," Viv adds. "But they wanted to have another one to choose. She did try it in different ways but nothing came up to that first take. She does it beautifully."

Ari: "I was making funny sounds, monkeying around, and that's the one we ended up using." So every yodel, yelp, gasp, giggle and tremulous vocal quiver that are now Ari's trademarks are there. You can even hear her counting quietly in the middle eight and Maxie mumbling at the end. Knowing the history of the recording session, listening to it now is like eavesdropping on a magical moment in time, where the group, Ari anyway, are just playing around.

The Slits were without a producer at this stage but things were happening fast, so an interim figure would have to be brought in to mix 'Grapevine', which Island hoped would be released as The Slits' debut single. Who better to have at the mixing desk than a legendary reggae artist from Jamaica? Island suggested the singer Dennis Brown – known as the 'Crown Prince of Reggae' – who was Bob Marley's favourite artist, and who fitted in perfectly with the Island image, as well as The Slits' image. The Slits agreed and Dennis was more than happy to oblige. It all seemed perfect. Apart from the fact he had never mixed a track in his life.

Ari recalls, "He came in with a friend, all hyped up, all excited, 'We're in the big studio for a big hot-shot group' sort of attitude, showing off.

"Then he got to the desk and he couldn't do anything! Couldn't touch a button, they didn't know what they were doing. They were fucking around, and we were just watching and looking at each other. Dennis Brown is not a mixer, he's a singer. The guy he brought with him was a bit of a Mafia guy. So Dennis came in with this no-talent crook and they just didn't know what they were doing.

"There was this girl called Rima from Jamaica who came as an extra helping hand, she wasn't doing music, I think Island wanted her to make the tea. She'd met us at the studio and got the whole Slits fever! She'd been oblivious to us before, she'd just been used to these chauvinistic hot-shot reggae guys coming over, women were nothing really.

"But she had started getting familiar with our sound and us, and she just took me aside and said, 'Listen, I've got a bit of experience I've picked up from hanging around in studios, I know a little bit of what's going on,' so I said, 'OK,' and we threw Dennis out, we dismissed him. It was a peaceful parting but he'd come to con us anyway."

By this time, other than Rima and The Slits, there was no one else in the studio. Island had no idea Dennis Brown had even been given the boot. They were on their own, and between themselves, they mixed the track – the first time they had ever mixed anything – just by muddling through.

Ari continues, "We had the place to ourselves, we could have done a whole album in that time if we'd wanted to! If we had that time now, I'd have done at least four songs, but it took us forever to get mixing because Dennis Brown had fucked it up.

"Rima just came and took it over. She was able to manipulate the big desk in this huge studio. She was experimenting and looking around, what does this do, what does that do? We were all joining in, 'Where's the reverb button?' etc. Maxie thought we were crazy, by the way.

"We played around a lot, I recorded a soft backing vocal – 'Heard it through the grapevine' – and a screaming one too, and we put the screaming one in the background with an echo and the soft one up front with a drier sound. This was our ears, our thing; that's what I mean, The Slits make their sound, we have that sound on that track because of *our* ears. The Slits were always part of our own sound. Again, that was in the contract, artistic control."

Island were thrilled with the results, and knew straight away that 'Grapevine' would be the perfect debut single for The Slits, that a

Ari, Tessa and Viv get back to nature before shooting their infamous *Cut* cover shoot at Ridge Farm Studios, Surrey. 1979. (PENNIE SMITH)

Live at the Music Machine, October 1977. (JILL FURMANOWSKY)

Palmolive, Tessa and Ari bedding down in Nora's (Ari's mum) van during a stint in Germany, 1978. (VIV ALBERTINE)

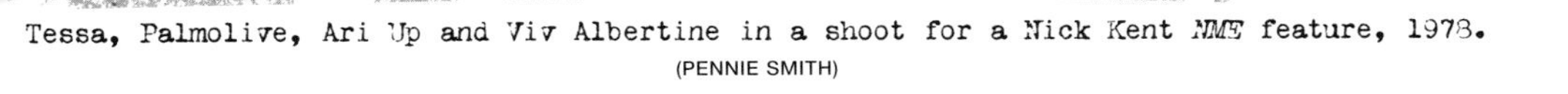

Tessa, Palmolive, Ari Up and Viv Albertine in a shoot for a Nick Kent *NME* feature, 1978.
(PENNIE SMITH)

The Slits backstage, not long before Palmolive's departure, 1978. (PENNIE SMITH)

Tessa takes the mic for 'Adventures Close To Home', live at the Sid Vicious legal fund benefit gig, Music Machine, December 1978. (MICK MERCER)

Jazz trumpeter Don Cherry, who toured with The Slits in 1979. Don brought his teenage step-daughter Neneh on the tour, and she quickly became an honorary Slit herself. (DAVID CORIO/REDFERNS)

Shooting the promo for 'Typical Girls' in Regents Park, London, summer 1979. (DESMOND LETTS)

Viv and Slits comrade Iv-I take a break during filming, Regents Park, summer 1979. (DESMOND LETTS)

The cover of *Cut*, released in September 1979. (COVER PHOTOGRAPH BY PENNIE SMITH)

The dubmaster Dennis 'Blackbeard' Bovell, The Slits' 'lollipop man' and producer of *Cut*. (GAB ARCHIVES/REDFERNS)

Tessa and Ari befriend a horse in a neighbouring field to Ridge Farm, 1979. (PENNIE SMITH)

Three Slits in the bath, at Ari's west London flat, 1979. (URBANIMAGE.TV/ADRIAN BOOT)

Bruce Smith of the Pop Group, drumming for The Slits, March 7, 1980. (PHILIPPE CARLY)

Viv onstage at the Alexandra Palace, 1980. (DAVID CORIO/REDFERNS)

Ari backstage at the Alexandra Palace, 1980. (DAVID CORIO/REDFERNS)

Viv and Ari onstage with Neneh Cherry, American tour 1981. (COURTESY OF VIV ALBERTINE)

unique, danceable version of a much-loved hit would be a great introduction for the record-buying public.

Everybody was convinced except the group themselves.

The Slits were proud of the track but they were also determined to release one of their own songs as their debut single. To Island's increasing concern, they weren't particularly focusing on what was going to sell. "Chris wanted it as the first single quite rightly, but we said, 'No, we want our own track'," says Viv. "We should have gone with 'Grapevine'. It would have been such a good in, like Chrissie Hynde when she did 'Stop Your Sobbin'".

"When you hear a band cover a song it helps you reference them a bit more, but we were so stubborn. I think every choice we made we steered ourselves further and further away from any sort of commercial success without knowing it. So that happened, we insisted that it had to be our own song – 'Typical Girls'."

'Typical Girls' was released as The Slits' debut single in October 1979, with 'Grapevine' duly consigned to the B-side. Whatever doubts may now exist about the wisdom of the choice, Tessa is still convinced they did the right thing. "Island really wanted 'Grapevine' as the A-side but we thought that would be too easy," she says. "It was our first major single so it was important that it was one of our songs, not a cover version, we didn't want to be a cover version group.

"Who knows, maybe it would have sold better if we had used 'Grapevine' as an A-side but I'm still happy that we chose 'Typical Girls'."

Maxie the drummer was only ever going to be a stand-in, and even before 'Typical Girls' was recorded or a producer selected, the overriding issue for The Slits was, of course, finding the right permanent drummer. Their 'fifth Slit' of choice was their beloved pal Paul Rutherford, if only he could play the drums. However, it was through their friendship with Paul that they met the next link in The Slits chain – Budgie, aka Pete Clarke.

"We first met Budgie in Liverpool," remembers Tessa. "We met him when we were staying at Paul's. We all got on really well. And he could handle working with three crazy Slits!"

Budgie had played in The Spitfire Boys with Paul, and was at this stage drumming for Big In Japan, another Liverpool band, which starred Paul's future Frankie Goes To Hollywood cohort Holly Johnson and the then skin-headed Jayne Casey, famous for performing with a lampshade on her head.*

Big in Japan were all about "ideas rather than proficiency" according to their guitarist (and future Lightning Seeds frontman) Ian Broudie, a theme familiar to The Slits in their earlier days. Budgie meanwhile had been keen to move forward. It was hard to get gigs in Liverpool, and the group he originally wanted to join, Deaf School, had disbanded. But The Slits had been on and off Budgie's radar for some time.

Paul: "They came up to Liverpool in their big tour bus and were staying at a hotel in Sefton Park, and they all hated the hotel so much, so I said, 'Why don't you come and stay at ours?'

"It was just me and my dad as my mum had died a while ago and my sister was off somewhere. So they came out to Cantril Farm – if you know Liverpool, well, ask anyone what Cantril Farm was like! So The Slits came to stay with the roadies and everything, and they had the bedrooms, I took the front room, and my dad got up and made them breakfast in the morning!

"It was just such a funny thing having The Slits and this tour bus on this housing estate, which was a bit like *Shameless.* It was like something out of a film, my favourite band, coming to sleep over! How fantastic is that? It really was so much fun, Ari Up with my dad in the morning, it was so funny. My dad loved it, he knew Pete Wylie and Pete Burns and Holly Johnson. He got quite used to all the punks hanging out."

The Slits were very fond of Paul. They'd kept in touch throughout the punk years – sending him postcards and letters from around the world on sanitary bags and tampon packets – and they ideally wanted him to join the group when the opportunity arose. "They were interested in me as the fifth Slit!" laughs Paul. "They said, 'If you could play drums, we'd have you...' They asked me if I minded if they had Budgie, and I said,

* Jayne Casey would later mastermind Liverpool club phenomenon Cream, and subsequently the smaller club BabyCream and Creamfields festival.

'No.' I was mad jealous of course, but you know, Budgie and The Slits, how fantastic is that?"

Managerially, at this point The Slits were working with former Deaf School manager Frank Silver, who was very aware of Budgie and how appropriate he would be. At the time Budgie was working with Clive Langer, also managed by Frank. To get by, the future Banshees (and Slits) drummer would sleep on Clive's floor in Camden when he was down from Liverpool, and take on jobs as a decorator.

"I'd pretend to do tiling jobs, decorating people's flats and things," he recalls. "One time I was decorating Steve Jones' pad. He had a Trimphone, and I thought that was really cool. I thought, 'I could phone Liverpool on that,' but I didn't. And he had a stage in the corner of his room, he was quite a rock god. There was no door on the bathroom, I don't know why."

Budgie was a hard-working, imaginative drummer, creative and adaptable but controlled and disciplined, which was perfect for a band that needed a light but unwavering heartbeat at its core, and for Tessa to mesh her bass lines with.

Frank invited Budgie to spend some time with Ari and talk about the possibility of joining the group, and within a couple of days he was in, although The Slits later teased in an interview that it would take him a year to become a 'full-time Slit'. "I came down to meet up with Ari at her mum's flat, with under-floor heating, it was a cold night," says Budgie. "Ari came to the door in a T-shirt and a pair of knickers, little socks on, masses of hair, scarves. It was like being entertained by this wild child, and I was pretty green, pretty quiet, but I was really enjoying it.

"She took me through her record collection, which was all reggae and Tamla Motown stuff, things I loved as well, and she rocked back and forth – and I rocked too! I'd never seen anybody else doing that. I used to destroy chairs as a kid. I'd sit there on Saturday nights with the lights off, rocking, had to be in time. I had to figure out double time and half time – it was impossible to do double time – but I was my own metronome, my early drumming was destroying furniture. And Ari did the same thing, I thought, 'I like her, she's a bit crazy but I like her and I like the band.'"

The Slits started rehearsing 'Typical Girls' with Budgie, working out ways to keep the rhythm constant, moving on from Palmolive's erratic style without losing any of the colour. "It was getting the time signature to stay the same," says Budgie. "Going from the straight four to the swing, keeping the snare constant, this was new, this was learning. Everything that Palmolive played started off in one tempo and quickly demolished it, stopped and started, nothing really continued, it was just the way things went. They were written as they sounded, there was generally never any kind of flow, but usually it just got faster and faster and faster. So the idea was to do something approaching consistency."

Close pal Don Letts noticed a major change right away, not only in the sound, but in the vibe of the group. "There was 25 per cent less fighting for a start," he says. "Budgie is an amazing drummer, and because he delivered, there was no confrontation, not that I ever saw. I guess he was the most technically proficient, and he was experimental too."

Certainly, the chaos seemed to lessen after the departure of Palmolive. One of Budgie's early memories is seeing The Slits supporting Siouxsie & The Banshees at the Greyhound in Croydon, and he recalls the Banshees being somewhat upstaged as they started their set because there was a pile of Slits wrestling on the floor behind them. But once Budgie had joined the group the ambience seemed to become more balanced. Chaos had been a huge part of what made The Slits who they were, but they couldn't behave explosively much longer and still make the music they wanted to make.

"Budgie was a very feminine guy," says Viv. "Fantastic drummer - very important to us, the drumming. He was so sensitive and tight and creative, and had a massively wide taste in music and didn't have to be told not to ride a cymbal or bish bash bosh all over the place. The skippy rhythms from reggae, and the jungle rhythms and all that mixed with a bit of glitter rock, you almost didn't have to say it. He was disciplined, and you've got to have a disciplined drummer. You don't want them all over the place like these big Yes bands. To punks, Yes was like the anti-Christ really."

Keith Levene must have kept his admiration of Steve Howe quiet at the time, then, although we now know that Buzzcock Steve Diggle also loved Yes, while Steve Jones was a closet Queen fan. This was considered to be highly classified information during the punk era, incidentally.

Budgie rehearsed much of what he would play in place of Palmolive's arrangements by playing the songs live, as he was thrown straight into touring with The Slits in support of The Clash on the long, UK-wide Sort It Out tour from October to December, promoting the album *Give 'Em Enough Rope*. The tour kicked off in Belfast and culminated just before the New Year of 1979 at London's Lyceum Theatre, off the Strand.

Budgie got to know his new bandmates very well very quickly, and there was no shortage of drama. "Every night Viv would have a big argument with Mick," says Budgie. "I just remember this one night, it was terrible, they were having this big barney behind the stage, and then the stage wings came out this way and that way. Everybody was in the theatre, people weren't quite sure whether it was a set-up for a film or something.

"The Clash were on a bus, stayed in nice hotels. We were in a smaller van, staying in B&Bs. Sometimes it felt like we were all sleeping in one big bed! I always remember Tessa put more clothes on to come to bed, she didn't even take her boots off, it was so cold! People would ask me, 'So are you sleeping with all of them, then?' And I was like, 'What?' I was a little shocked. Certainly more clothing went on when we went to bed.

"I got to know Clash drummer Topper Headon, [and] he showed me a lot about tuning drums. His set-up was really good, he had a great technician, and he was just an amazing drummer to watch, he held the band together completely, and I thought, 'OK, I see how that works.' I modelled my sticks on his. I had my little gold Beverley drum kit – my first kit – and part of my thing for doing The Slits tour and album was that they refurbished my drum kit. It would have fallen to pieces otherwise."

In the outside world, where punk culture was still a festering sore on a smooth complexion, the musical *Grease* had hypnotised the nation, with slick-haired John Travolta and cutesy Olivia Newton-John wiggling around in all their faux-Fifties glory. Ari liked to be sufficiently tuned in to pick up on mainstream references like this, feeding them into Slits songs on stage, throwing in 'Tell me more, tell me more!' here and there, or shrieking out her own Slit version of Seventies ballads like 'A Man And A Woman'. One example of this can be found on the recording of The Slits live at the Gibus Club in Paris, considerately translated as 'Une Homme et Un Slit', the genders deliberately swapped round for extra humour.

One night, as The Clash's entourage checked into their hotel, The Slits were hanging out in the foyer with The Clash's road crew when they spotted Bruce Forsyth in the reception, and bellowed the inevitable, "Nice to see you!"

Budgie: "He did a little shimmy, soft shoe shuffle thing, and charmed everyone. Then, in Bournemouth, I remember Topper skidding into reception naked. He'd gone skinny-dipping on the beach with his girlfriend, and someone had nicked all his clothes. It was a funny tour, and it got us well integrated. I learnt how to get the kit sounding better, and just enjoyed playing really, it was quite an event, you were never quite sure what was going to happen next with Ari."

Once the tour had finished, The Slits started rehearsing in the Fall-Out Shelter, Island's basement studio in Chiswick. Jamaican artists would flock straight to Island after getting off the plane at Heathrow, and they were none too impressed when they arrived to find Budgie's original take on reggae drumming for The Slits' material. The Slits didn't want to completely copy anything, and weren't trying to be a reggae band per se, but these were rigid times, especially as far as your authentic reggae artists were concerned.

"These guys would be coming in, looking at my kit and looking at me and trying to figure out what this music was," says Budgie. "They'd be like, 'No, you can't play the beat, mon!', you know, 'White honky, you don't know how to do it,' but I thought, 'I'll show you!' When I was a kid, the skinhead era had started first time round, they were all listening to The Upsetters and The Cimarons. The Upsetters' *Return Of Django* was the first record I bought. It heavily influenced us all … we didn't want to become reggae bands but we wanted to somehow adapt.

"After we recorded the album though, the nicest compliment I ever had was at the Music Machine. I was introduced to the drummer of The Police, Stewart Copeland, and he said to me, 'But I thought you were black?'"

Nobody within the scene was bothered by the fact that The Slits were no longer an all-girl band. That was never the point. This came as an extra, albeit unintentional, snub to those militant feminists who wanted to adopt the band as their mascot. However, it was assumed by outsiders that Budgie was merely an interim drummer who'd stick around until they found the right girl. *NME* archly wrote in their '*T-zers*' news column: "Budgie is filling in with The Slits while they look for a drummer with the correct chromosomes..."

The feminist question would still be trotted out occasionally by right-on journalists, but to The Slits, it was much more empowering to simply play with the people you liked and respected, regardless of gender. The Slits were just getting on with being musicians.

Tessa: "It was no longer an all-female group, which is not a bad thing. I didn't even think about the new 'male' dynamic; we didn't think we had to go and find a female drummer as Palmolive had gone, it just had to be someone who was right. I like a bit of balance in the group, so I think it's not a good or bad thing Palmolive going or Budgie coming in, it was just a new phase."

And it was a phase that would eventually include some of the leading figures associated with the avant-garde London Musician's Collective. This was – and continues to be – a fertile, exciting scene. In the late Seventies, you could find Vivien Goldman and Viv Albertine mixing with artists such as guitarist Derek Bailey, drummer John Stevens, Evan Parker, David Toop and, of course, The Flying Lizards and Steve Beresford. This was no time to be small-minded about gender.

Tessa continues, "We would soon have lots of different male musicians playing with us, Flash on sax, Steve Beresford on all his crazy instruments and percussion and keyboards, and they all added more flavour to the music. Too much female energy can be difficult for me personally."

Chapter 10

"I prefer to accept only one type of power: the power of art over trash, the triumph of magic over the brute." – Vladimir Nabokov

The Slits now had a drummer on whom they could rely and a label with which they felt confident. They were soon to have another new manager in Dick O'Dell, who also managed their Bristolian contemporaries, the post-punk jazz-heads The Pop Group, and they had an important album in the pipeline. Whether they knew quite how important it would be to those outside of the group is uncertain, but it was always going to be a study in going against the grain, against all odds. They just needed to make sure that, while they continued to befuddle the outside world, the circle of people who would be working with them would need to be, if not completely of a like mind, at least flexible enough to trust The Slits' decisions.

Budgie would be a vital part of the alchemy that would make their debut a success, and he also came up with the name for the album – *Cut* – during a meeting with Island Records. "We were all racking our brains," remembers Viv, "and Budgie said, 'You just want something simple, just one word, you know, 'Slits, cut'.' Like he was saying you've got to cut through the crap, you want something sharp, and it was the cut of a record, we were The Slits, cut. We knew it was *Cut* the minute he said it."

Ari can list a million reasons why the title *Cut* was absolutely ideal. It was immediate, it had impact – and it had a touch of violence, a hint of what they had to go through every day, and the insinuation of fighting back. More importantly, the words 'cut' and 'slit' had a far greater significance to the group themselves than their obvious sexual connotations.

"People would just cut us out. Maybe that's why the album was called *Cut*," muses Ari. "We wanted to make it clear, it's not so much about our vaginas, but it's a cut of songs, get this cut, we're being cut out of so many things in life – and we're cutting because we symbolically have our knives out. We weren't violent people ourselves, but there was a symbol in the aggression of *'Cut'*, cut it out, you know?

"We also wanted to make it clear that The Slits' name was more to do with *that* meaning – slit, slice, cut – rather than the vagina part. But we didn't mind if people wanted to take it as that. I personally am very proud of my pum-pum."

Things were coming together, and the group were looking forward to heading down to the luxurious Ridge Farm Studios in the Surrey Hills. Despite The Slits' aura of craziness, they were to take the making of *Cut* very seriously, and they needed a particular kind of producer to help them turn their ideas into an entrancing reality of which they could be proud. It couldn't just be anyone from the world of punk because punk in its purest, original form had already become boring and brutal, and some groups just hadn't progressed; no, The Slits were never going to be one of those groups but they couldn't move forward in the way they wanted to on their own.

Keith Levene was in the running to produce the album, but in the end, after discussions with Island, there could only be one man for the job – dub maestro Dennis 'Blackbeard' Bovell. *Melody Maker*'s Vivien Goldman described him at the time: '(He) almost always wears a peaked cap over his dreadlocks, other times he'll tie them back and appear daredevil-style, piratical. Always in motion, at times he seems a rhythm machine, even when he's talking to you, percussion person, clacking heels, and slapping hands, he'll take a piece of paper and make it whistle round a comb, he'll take a lighter, bang it and you'll be skanking to the sound."

Ari: "When we were at the rehearsal, we were always thinking, 'Who's going to produce this?' More than thinking about the album cover, we were thinking, 'Who's going to mix this?' And that's where we all decided with the A&R guys on Dennis Bovell. Dennis had mixed all kinds of stuff aside from his roots, there was Matumbi – and he was the dub master."

Asked by Goldman about his work with The Pop Group, whose debut album *Y*, a work of dissonant, jagged beauty, was also released in 1979, Bovell explained: "It's an experiment with sound as opposed to pretty chords and lovely hoo-ha singing. How do we know that singing is pleasant? We do because it is tuneful, and for years it's been ingrained in us to say that this is the right thing. But how do we know A is A or B is B or C is C – how do we know anything? Every man does his thing a little bit different." It was that kind of attitude that attracted The Slits.

Don Letts remembers, "Dennis they had admired from afar for a long time. He had Matumbi, the fact he was into dub and he lived in London, it was an obvious choice really, obvious for The Slits anyway. Might not have been so obvious for Dennis. But the path had been kind of set and the idea had been implanted that some kind of punky reggae mix could be attained. And they went for it."

Even though they had artistic control, The Slits were still not entirely relaxed. With so many mixed experiences behind them, they were never quite sure if the decisions they were making would backfire, especially when it came to involving West Indian men. They were very keen to get Dennis Bovell on board, but equally concerned that he wouldn't 'get' them. They needn't have worried.

"It's that edgy thing, like always on the cliff, hanging there before you might drop off," says Ari. "By the time we got to Island it was still like that: 'Are we going to get Dennis Bovell without there being a huge problem?' He's a guy from the West Indies, and they have their standard mindset about how girls should be and look [but] Dennis wasn't like that.

"Luckily Dennis really enjoyed that we were completely different and free, he would take the piss all the time and laugh because he'd think we were crazy – a good thing at the time. The people who thought we were crazy in a good way and weren't offended, they became our friends. We couldn't get people thinking we're just normal girls, expressing ourselves musically or in our clothes or our art. We couldn't be seen as 'normal'.

"I didn't understand that, but that was the good side. The people who didn't understand us at all didn't just think we were crazy – they thought we were threatening."

Dennis Bovell didn't find them threatening, but he was initially in two minds as to what they were about. He was hugely respected and serious about getting things right, and Island realised that, in the case of the raw talent of The Slits, they would have to get the producer in situ in order to proceed with their plans for the group. And they'd have to be persuasive too, because Dennis had already announced in an interview with Vivien Goldman that he was stepping back from producing in order to pour his energies into Matumbi. Famous last words.

Bovell recalls: "Chris had asked his art editor, Dennis Morris, to ask me if I would get involved with The Slits. And the first thing I thought was, 'Girl band? I've got to see them to see if they can actually play these instruments, as opposed to it being some kind of concoction that you lot are trying to get me involved with and it's all going to go belly-up and then I'm going to be famous in the press for aiding and abetting talentless people, and my production name will be in shreds.'

"They said, 'It won't be possible to see them except for in the studio.' So I said, 'Well, I'll have to see them in the studio then.' They said, 'Yeah, well, we've booked Ridge Farm Studios, and they're going to do this album.' So I went along and heard their stuff, and I really liked Ari – the voice and her ability, all the different voices she did, and she played the piano as well, so I thought, 'Well, this is a musical person.'

"Then I met the others – Viv is a very tactful guitar player, quite girly, but actually plays some good guitar. And Tess – wicked bass player, amazing bass player. Tessa was always quiet, never spoke a lot, but could play her instrument and for me that was the most important thing.

"Budgie's an outrageously talented drummer. Just to work with Budgie alone would have been a plus, you know? He's such a vibrant player. And so they had him as the engine room, and it was an amazing combination.

"I knew I could pour in the different bits of this and cook a really good meal out of the song ideas, from hearing all the music, but I thought, 'It's going to take some time to put it together properly', because I was very fussy about things that were out of time or not intentionally out of tune."

The Slits loved Dennis for his reggae expertise but also for the magic he had worked the year before on The Pop Group's *Y*, which had also been recorded at Ridge Farm. On *Y*, Dennis was able to display his open, versatile and resourceful production skills and assist the group in merging their love of free jazz, reggae and funk. He would play things backwards, make sound effects out of the most unlikely sources, always aware and intelligent. The Slits wanted to experiment, merging dub and reggae with their own quirky brand of punk, they wanted to be free and able to express their ideas and try things out without being trampled on, manipulated or judged. Dennis was perfect.

However, in many ways so was Keith Levene, the inventive guitarist who had walked them, Viv in particular, through difficult times, supported them, and was now making serious waves himself with Public Image Limited.

Viv: "I think because of Island and pressures to be... well, we just didn't have the confidence, you know? [Keith was] a young mate, basically he has the same mentality as Dennis, the creative open mind, loved all different kinds of music and was this beautiful guitarist. [But with Keith as producer] It would have gone a different way."

At the time, Keith wasn't best pleased when he realised he wasn't going to be asked to produce their album. He felt protective and proud of The Slits and felt rather hurt to be passed over. "I wouldn't have minded producing them, and I was a bit miffed I didn't get to," he says. "It's not that I was so busy with PiL, I was fucking there, and they didn't treat me right. It doesn't matter, I don't care, but it did happen.

"I get why Ari got Dennis Bovell in, and it made sense to me in the context of The Slits, so fine, it wasn't a career move for me to produce for them, but I thought it was a natural move. I was with them and doing stuff and suddenly I wasn't and they were with Dick [O'Dell]. He kind of did me a big favour taking them off my hands, it wasn't like we had any deal with each other, and I did have to move on. But when it came to the recording they could have said, 'We're recording, you should come in,' but they didn't.

"But what happened happened, and it was great working with The Slits, I really had a lot of fun doing it. It was right in between The Clash and PiL for me. I don't think I had anything better to do at night anyway..."

When Viv heard after The Slits broke up in 1982 that Keith had expressed in an interview how he felt that she had never talked about him, she was shocked. "There was about a page of this interview about me, saying I never mention him even though he'd been so good to me, and of course he has, I always thought that in my head, I never thought for a minute that he hadn't been," she says.

"We were all mad about him as a person, absolutely adored him. He was the best friend you could possibly have as a boy. Obviously I hadn't said in a way that had been public to him, or in interviews, if they don't want to go down that route...so I didn't want him feeling that I didn't know, because I really do know and appreciate what he did for me. Keith is fantastic and I want him to know I think that."

Viv's song 'Instant Hit' was written for Keith and planned for inclusion on the album. At the time, though, Keith had no idea he was to have his own dedication on the album he felt so excluded from.

"He says I didn't take any notice of him and that song's for him," Viv continues. "You hear him at the end talking. He doesn't know that. That little bit at the end had been recorded (a conversation with Keith that would feature at the end of the track) at Ari's house with a little tape recorder, he didn't know..."

Dennis Bovell was immediately charmed when The Slits played 'New Town' to him, particularly because the words were unlike anything he'd ever heard. His imagination was already whirring... "I like the lyric of 'sniffing televisena'. I was like, 'What?!' 'Taking footballina'? Like a drug. Brilliant lyric. Positively Hendrix!"

Although the themes often dealt with what affected The Slits personally, what they observed (things that would often pass others by), loved or hated, they were determined their music should not be seen as exclusively for girls, just because they were female. They could identify with music made by men, and they wanted their own music to be just as open.

Viv: "That was all very carefully thought about, we very much wanted boys to respond to our music, not on the level of, 'Oh, that's a nice girly song,' but something they could feel was as cool to listen to as a girl would."

And they were to succeed. After proving themselves to the discerning Bovell in the leafy seclusion of Ridge Farm, they were ready to hole up, reinvent the tracks they had chosen and take on the world – if the world was prepared to open its mind and give them a chance.

"And it wasn't all just about rage and madness," muses Don Letts. "When they actually came to cut a record – pun intended – they actually were delivering something really fresh and new, they had original ideas and that wasn't just following the same punk formula of loud fast guitars. Punk was never about that – punk was about freedom, and The Slits were one of the first groups, along with The Clash, PiL and a few others, that kind of stepped out of that box that punk had created, and went where nobody had gone before."

1979 was to be an important year musically, with several high-calibre albums released by different, very important, artists. The Fall would release their second album, *Dragnet*, PiL unleashed the icy but poetic *Metal Box* to knock everyone sideways (and it's still doing so), The Clash's *London Calling* was on its way and, of course, The Slits would smash expectations, charm, disgust and thrill with *Cut*. It would take time and patience on everyone's part, but it was going to happen, and it was going to be special.

Ari: "I think making *Cut* was the result of years and years, or what felt like years to teenagers, of just absorbing what was around us. I think the vision for *Cut* had been growing for all those years – every year that passed up to that point really had felt like ten years to us.

"1977 was the big explosion, revolution, 1978 was the in-between stage, 1979 was already the beginning of bands like The Pop Group, and new styles and experimental groups, PiL for example. Every time all these bands started a totally new music and new culture, a new revolution. These bands, including ourselves, were growing with the new sound, new culture, new clothes. We were all just inspired by each other and a mixture of everything we'd seen all our lives, integrated into our personalities and our social mind-set."

The Slits were taking the raw punky tribal sound from their earlier days and were keeping the bass heavy and powerful. They were also determined to retain the way they sang, their trademark upfront backing vocals, like playground chants and rounds, sometimes playful and boisterous, sometimes haunting or menacing. "The chanting was almost Celtic-sounding," says Ari. "We kept that from our roots, we wanted to continue that onto *Cut*.

"We were like untamed, wild horses, and that's what we wanted to put into the *Cut* album, musically and culturally. It was like, whatever you've heard about women before that, or what they're supposed to be, wipe it off your memory because it's not going to be like that any more."

Chapter 11

"1979 is the year of after-punk and there's a battle of ideas going on that is much more interesting than the original punk argument about commerce and cop-out. The debate is no longer about music as a commodity, but as art." – Simon Frith, *Melody Maker*

The Slits headed down to Ridge Farm to record *Cut* in March 1979, and while they had to work long and hard on the album, their time at the sprawling residential studio in idyllic Capel, near Dorking, was an intensely creative, enjoyable and challenging period they would never forget. It did them good not just from the point of view of their musicianship, but for their general well-being too.

Ridge Farm – one of the UK's first residential studios – was situated at the end of a long private drive flanked by woodland, which led to a group of beautiful black-and-white 17th-century buildings set in 13 acres of perfectly tended land.

The main building had originally been a medieval farmhouse and the studio itself was in a converted barn. The farm, operating as a recording facility since 1974, was very much admired as a world-class studio and had already seen Queen, Magazine and Roxy Music record within its warm, comfortable confines.

For once, rather than living on their wits, defending themselves and staying in damp squats or on people's floors, The Slits would be well looked after. They'd sleep in proper, warm beds in the peaceful ambience of the countryside for a start, with bedroom windows that looked out on fields and woodland. It was the first time they'd eaten quite so heartily in a while too, as there was always an abundance of healthy fresh food available for them and they'd all eat together in a big, cosy communal area. Ridge Farm owner Frank Andrews recalls marvelling at the amount of food The Slits could put away, and watched them go from wiry punks to wholesome, well-upholstered country girls in an alarmingly short space of time. They were surrounded by warm, friendly people who ensured they were taken care of. It seemed a million miles from angry, dirty Seventies London, despite being just over an hour away.

"It was so exciting going down to Ridge Farm," remembers Tessa. "I love being in the country. And there were just huge amounts of food every evening on the table, home-cooked food, and that's why we all look a bit plump on the album cover!"

Viv adds, "I was a city girl, I didn't have any contact with the country so it was quite strange, in a nice way. We had this fabulous food, vegetarian, organic, which in those days was amazing. There were these girls cooking, Denise and Vonnie, Denise was Ian Dury's girlfriend at the time.

"Denise gave off a very beautiful vibe, very chilled, she had that lovely, gentle angelic vibe that was very rare at that time in London. It was great to have someone like that making the food, and we'd all eat together for dinner. It was a lovely experience and you felt like you were a real rock band. Being trapped together, that was all right, I don't remember it being particularly argumentative."

The only downside to being out in the sticks was the wildlife, which seemed almost inevitably attracted to Ari's ever-developing nest of dreadlocks.

"Ari got nits, and I think Tessa might have done too," Viv remembers. "You know my drawing on the inside cover (of *Cut)*, with them all flying out of her hair? She was ridden with bugs! It was very funny. It all got a bit country-ish with bugs and beetles, and Ari had all these things living in her hair..."

Dennis Bovell and The Slits lived together for weeks at a time, and from the word go Dennis had to become a kind of father figure to ensure everything went to plan. The excitement of being at the magical Ridge Farm could be too much for Ari in particular and she didn't want to waste a moment. If it wasn't for Dennis laying down the law about bedtimes, albeit with a twinkle in his eye, sleep would have been off the agenda entirely.

Dennis: "We spent a lot of time together, we ate together, we messed around together, we worked together, and I was the one in charge, having to say: 'Right, that's it, girls, go to bed.' And they'd go, 'NO! Who do you think you are? You're producing the record, not our lives!'

"I'd have to say, 'Go to bed, because you're going to have to be fresh tomorrow morning. I don't want you to be all pissed off because you haven't had enough sleep. And no one's breaking camp either.'

"Ari used to yell, 'Look at him! Don't speak to me like that! Who do you think you are?' She was the rebel. The other girls would see sense but she'd be the one to say, 'Who do you think you're talking to? You're not my dad!' All that attitude. But she would give it her all when it came to it."

The intensity of living and working together at Ridge Farm would make The Slits themselves even more like a family – and it was an all-embracing one that included Budgie and Dennis. Dennis, meanwhile, had been seriously looking forward to working with Budgie, and often tried to steal a bit of time with the drummer when The Slits were asleep. Ari didn't miss a trick, of course.

"Sometimes I used to try to send the girls to bed so that me and Budgie could have a bit of a jam!" Dennis laughs. "And then Ari would discover us and say, 'You think you're going to have a jam without me?!' And then the three of us would have a kick around for an hour or whatever while the others had gone off to bed.

"And then I'd have to say, 'Right, go to bed, even me, I'm going to bed now! Seven o'clock in the morning you've got to be up!' We could have hung out all night. I mean, Ari was little more than 16 – she *never* wanted to go to bed!"

Budgie remembers, "Dennis would show me how to get all these different sounds out of the hi-hat and the drums, hitting them in different ways, which, again in rock, there's no room for that kind of subtlety. I came from that 'play as loud as you can as fast as you can' mentality, because you didn't have much time to be on stage. To get three notes out of the hi-hat and all this was an education to me.

"When everyone had turned in for the night, or when we were sitting around the dinner table, Dennis would say, 'Can we go and play some stuff?' and I'd think, 'He's going to teach me about some reggae,' but he wasn't – he'd put a six-string electric guitar on and wanted to play rock 'n' roll! 'After Tonight' was the song we played. It was lovely."

Viv recalls the studio as being "like a palatial church", and Budgie admits that, after going back in recent years, he was struck by how much smaller it is than he remembers – but the intense experience of making *Cut*, and the knowledge of who had recorded there before them, made Ridge Farm seem huge and imposing at the time. "It had been host to Bad Company and Roxy Music, Simon Kirk and Paul Thompson, both heroes of mine," says Budgie. "When I got there they were like, 'Well, Simon set his drums up over there, and Paul set his up over here, which sound do you want?' And I go, 'Roxy Music, Bad Company…I'm with The Slits - neither! I have to find my own spot.' We put my drums under the control room."

The recording of *Cut* would be the first time The Slits had had anything recorded and mixed properly, and they would be using the very best equipment – Yes's equipment, in fact. Yes weren't allowed to know that either.

Again, it is more than a touch ironic that in the face of the punk/prog gulf this seminal post-punk album would be recorded on equipment belonging to Jon Anderson. Ari redressed the balance by cheekily carving her name into one of his top-of-the-range consoles.

Dennis admits that this was the moment the game was up, but he'd managed to get good use out of Jon's expensive gear: "He'd bought this recording equipment, MCI, I think. It was left there while Yes had gone off on tour. Roxy Music were the guinea pig at Ridge Farm (with *Manifesto*), then I did the album with The Pop Group, and then on the back of that I did The Slits album. And on the back of that I did an album with a singer called Marie Pierre for Trojan, and then I did the Matumbi album for EMI – so I was in Ridge Farm for about two years while Yes were out on tour!

"When Ari found out it was Jon's equipment, she etched something on it, 'Ari woz here', rude-girl style. So of course then Jon would know that we were using the equipment when I don't think we should have been, because I think Jon was intending that for his own personal use. Naughty girl.

"Mike [Dunne] the engineer was most upset, he was in charge of the thing and then suddenly of all things Jon's going to know about it. It was fantastic recording equipment, as I say I recorded about six or seven albums on it and it was a fantastic sound."

Jon Anderson's link with Ridge Farm was Frank Andrews, who still owns the studio today. Frank was initially a lighting technician for Yes and Deep Purple – and he also met Dick O'Dell during this time.

Dick's first meeting with The Slits left a lasting impression on him: "They were wild girls!" he laughs. "Wild, wild, wild. I'd seen them a few times at the Roxy with The Clash, but I didn't know them at all.

"It was when Dennis Bovell came on the scene. The Slits had already been through about 12 managers, and Dennis had said to them, 'What about Dick O'Dell?' So, they were recording at Ridge Farm, where The Pop Group had made their album, and he'd obviously liked it. I'd put him in there with The Pop Group because I knew the guy who ran the studio – he was a tripping buddy of mine from the old days.

"So I drove down there. They weren't in the studio, they were in the main house, in this huge lounge with loads of couches, chaise longues. I walked in this room and they were all draped around in an incredibly nonchalant fashion, obviously thinking, 'Yeah right, mate, we'll test you!' and it started from there, basically."

They did test him, not least because their experiences with managers had left much to be desired. But Dick, who now manages the cult group Bat For Lashes, was simpatico to The Slits' direction, and he admits that it was his time spent with the group that equipped him for working with an all-female outfit – and much more besides.

"They did a lot for me," he says. "Not just as a manager and a group, but as a man with three women, because you learn a lot about women when you're virtually living with them. Guys are rubbish, they think they're clever, but a woman just knows stuff immediately. 'You're trying to take the piss? I'm a woman. You're an idiot.' I learnt that one quick enough.

"I stayed (at the studio) more than I would now. In fact, I meddle way less now than I did then. I'm sure they probably hated me for it at the time! I was young and foolish and you kind of want to be part of everything.

"No one had really taken them seriously before, [and] most of their managers had treated them like a joke band. It's harsh but true. They had [been told] that they're the bastard offspring of what The Clash were doing or the Pistols, and because Ari was so wild onstage, some people turned their noses up. But I didn't. I fell in love with it and I thought it was wonderful and they were wonderful."

The Slits were getting serious in the studio. It was nerve-racking and while they had fun, their confidence, Viv's and Tessa's in particular, was shaky. Dennis Bovell was an incredible perfectionist but at the same time he was understanding, and was prepared to take them by the hand and help them realise their ideas. However, he wasn't going to let them get away with being out of time, or out of tune.

Viv: "I remember my confidence was very low because I felt I really couldn't play. I think it highlights it, when you come to record and you've got to be in time and in tune and everything. I felt incredibly inadequate, I don't know if Tessa felt the same.

"Dennis was a great musician, Ari had a fabulous ear. There's a spotlight on you, you're down in this pit and they're up there in the booth and you're on your own, and everyone's listening to that part in isolation, it was really scary but Dennis made it great. He wasn't that judgmental, but he just had to get it right, and Ari was also a perfectionist, as I am too, but I despaired sometimes, of myself. I don't know if every album is like that, but that's what it was like for me.

"It was different to the Peel Sessions as that wasn't isolated instruments, that was playing as a band, everyone speeding along together and careering to a stop. This was isolating each instrument and then everyone listening to the playback of just your instrument. Dennis was such a perfectionist, you had to get it right. He wasn't cruel about it, but you know, get it right!

"I used to say, 'I thought that was perfect, that take!' 'No, it's still out of time, you're still just not hitting it right on the beat.' I don't know. It tightened us up though – after recording that album we could play 100 times better."

Tessa adds, "It took us forever, but we wanted it to be excellent, however long it took. Ari has a whole orchestra going on in her head, she's a real musical director, she can hear everything, she has a really sensitive ear like a dog. I'm a bit tone-deaf, sometimes I can be a semi-tone out and I can't hear it unless someone tells me! I'll be thinking it's all right…"

Admittedly, the point was not to polish The Slits to the point of taking away their raw magic, or ruin some of the deliberately clashing notes and sounds they had written into their songs. Part of their unique sound came from their bravery in breaking some rules and creating beauty from something dissonant and wild – and Dennis was wise enough not to trample on that.

He explains, "We did intentionally put some things out of tune to go with the lyrics so that it would grate well. You know, attempting to do that when everyone's attempting to sing perfectly in tune, then something else has to be out of tune [affects an Ari scream] and then it's perfect!

"It was like I was in a chemistry lab and I had all these different potions, I was like, concocting something – and it was great fun. Ari wouldn't give up until she'd achieved what she'd intended, you know? So nowadays people are still buying the record."

Chapter 12

"The artist's first responsibility is to himself." – Miles Davis

Dennis Bovell has often referred to himself as 'the lollipop man' who helped The Slits across the road, but over the years a rumour has persisted that *he* actually played all of the instruments on *Cut*, rather than The Slits.

Anyone who knows anything about this group and their attitudes to their work would find it highly unlikely that they would blithely step aside and let that happen. This was long before the era of routine auto-tuning or Pro-Tools, and even if it had been, The Slits would have had no part in it, and would have gone for the flawed but honest approach. They hadn't waited all this time for the right moment to make an album only to let a more experienced musician push them out of the way and do it all for them. But this enduring suggestion was later perpetuated by reports that Dennis had done exactly that with former Slit guitarist Kate Corris and The Mo-Dettes.

Kate: "I don't know how much Dennis Bovell had to do with the playing on *Cut*. I saw the way he worked on a couple of Mo-Dettes tracks, and afterwards I remember Bob Black (the manager) saying, 'Viv didn't play any of the guitar on *Cut* either!'

"Dennis would just take over, he took my guitar off me because he had his ideas about how it should sound and didn't want to bother explaining it! He let me play keyboards, but he was very much a control freak, although he got good results."

Nevertheless, The Slits have had to endure the repeated telling of this frustrating and unfair myth since the release of the album in 1979, and Dennis insists it really is just that – a myth. In fact, The Slits deliberately barred him from attempting to shoehorn his own contributions in for the very reason that they knew people would be suspicious when the album was released.

He remembers: "I tried to get in there occasionally and play things but they all said, 'People will know!' There was one time, I forget what song it was, but I played something on guitar that I thought was very close to brilliant. Everyone's going 'Yeah!', and then I looked over my shoulder and Viv's in tears. She said, 'Rub that off.' I said, 'But it's great!' and she said, 'Yeah – no one's ever going to believe that I played that. So rub it off.' I didn't even take a cassette of it – it was an acoustic thing, like Segovia. Off it went.

"The thing is, I had to make the album *them* – because they would then have to go out and play the album live, so I didn't want to stick too much crap on there and then defeat the object of what they were trying to do in the first place.

"I'd hear that live they weren't always that together. So rather than see them at their worst, I wanted to have them at their best, and then see how they could make their best better. Give them some motivation and something to aspire to, so they can say, 'Right, we've done this in the studio and we know it can be done, all we need to do is rehearse a bit more.' I couldn't go, 'Out the way, I'll do this' – and then on *Top Of The Pops* they'd have been like, 'Er, we can't actually play it because the producer did it all…'

"I was just there to help them get it on that tape and have the patience to sit there and go, 'No, one more time again, yes, you're getting it,' using the old drop-in technique. Even if it was a patchwork quilt at the beginning, by the end it was a silk sheet."

Some of the newer songs, which featured Viv's lyrics, were still in the process of being arranged and worked out at Ridge Farm. Budgie remembers watching Ari working out the piano part to 'Typical Girls', and Viv going through the words to 'Spend, Spend, Spend', the darkly witty ode to retail therapy, marrying up her lyrics to Ari's complex melody.

"Ari had this Teutonic pronunciation," says Budgie. "In 'Spend, Spend, Spend', the words were so good, 'I am trapped in a flat but at least it's raining... it's not pills and gin stopping me from committing a crime.'

"I always remember Ari going, 'Imogen myself moving in the kitchen...' and Viv going, 'Ari, it's not Imogen, it's 'imagine'!' I love things like that, Ari's delivery was very Nico."

While working with Dennis saw The Slits turn their songs on their heads in many ways, they retained some of the elements that had always been so compelling about the way they performed up to now, and one of those is their gang-like backing vocals, harmonising in rounds.

Viv: "We very much tried not to sing all girly like Cerys Matthews does now, we were like a gang, we didn't pitch our voices all high. We were very careful because they were rigorous times and you did look at everything under a microscope, so we made sure our voices came out at the pitch they are, not heightening them into girly voices like Girls Aloud."

They weren't trying to sound like boys, nor were they trying to sound overtly feminine, and as a result their backing vocals on the recordings sound unusual, because we are actually hearing what girls sound like when they sing naturally and without affectation. And this is still very rare. But they were feminine in the most honest way, and the way they played reflected this. The intense depth and velvety warmth of Tessa's bass lines, the light sparkle of Ari's piano-playing and shivering, quivering vocal idiosyncracies (very much the Björk of her time), and Viv's bright, tactful but pointed guitar work and diary-entry-style lyrics were all uniquely female.

Dennis agrees: "Viv is a very female guitar player, very accomplished too. Even the way she held the plectrum was very feminine. Very talented, great lyricist. Tessa came up with some wicked bass lines. And Budgie was a good foundation for Tessa to rest her bass lines against, a solid, confident drummer."

However, both Dennis and Dick O'Dell were coming to the realisation that Budgie was getting itchy feet with The Slits, and Dennis knew there was another punk group that Budgie was very keen to work with. "In my mind he always wanted to be in the Banshees," he says. "In The Slits he obviously gave his all, but he'd always seen himself as Siouxsie's drummer, and when, later, he got the call he was in there like a shot."

Despite this potential clash of loyalties, Budgie's musical contribution to *Cut* is substantial and a key element in what makes it so impressive. Dennis managed to utilise Budgie's sensitivity and imagination, as well as his skill, to make their album exactly as the group wanted it to be, beyond what they'd hoped for even. And Dennis had the laid-back humour to ease the way.

The dub super-producer drew on his inexhaustible imagination and encyclopaedic reference points to turn the songs of The Slits around, and the results were inspired. And all of this, by the way, was happening while he was also producing Linton Kwesi Johnson's album *Forces Of Victory* for Island: "I'd leave The Slits in the evening and go to London to work with Linton and be back with The Slits in the morning. I'd sleep on the train – Dorking to London. I think there were about three or four days where that happened. Being expected to be in two places at once. So Linton was the nocturnal one and The Slits were in the day. I had to be there at 10am to work with them, work until 7, then be in London by 9, start working with Linton at 10 and work through until about 5 or 6am. And then get the train back to Dorking. For that time I slept like four hours a day. But I was young then!"

Miraculously, his energy didn't seem to be diminished, and he still managed to work his magic for both parties; in the case of The Slits, cutting out anything messy or unnecessary, and paring back the sound so that it reflected them at their best. In this respect, *Cut* was an appropriate name for the album.

"The songs were transformed by Dennis," says Viv. "He just took things out, made space in them. And we were ready for that as well, we'd been listening to a lot of dub and reggae and really appreciating the fact that you take things out, and the spaces you leave are vital."

The space in the album – what wasn't there – was every bit as important as what was there. Keith Levene, for one, can point to the musical decisions made between Ari and Dennis in particular that dictated *Cut*'s sound. "The producer stepped in, cut all the shit out," he says. "The producer definitely bonded with Ari, no bad thing.

"You know Ari, she's like a big fucking St Bernard, she's got the strength to do anything, so she's dealing with Dennis Bovell, and he's saying, 'I think this, I think that, don't do this any more, do this, I want to get this many mics on the drums because we're going to do that with it,' and so on, and Ari bounced off that."

But as the alternative choice of producer, how different would *Cut* have been had Keith been at the controls? "I think they were better off coming out with a focused album like they did with Dennis, than doing some kind of possibly experimental thing with me that might have got mixed up with PiL," admits Keith. "People would be thinking it was some kind of extension to *Metal Box* even though it wouldn't have been. So they were much better off with the single identity. It doesn't matter what I was miffed about when I was a kid."

The Slits were keen to incorporate their love of sound-system music into their album – and while the dub aspect is never overplayed, it is there and it lends a spatial ambience and a hypnotic echoing element to tracks such as 'Spend, Spend, Spend' and 'Ping Pong Affair'.

"We were up for that," continues Viv. "And I think it made things beautiful. He's got a massively eclectic musical taste. You could say to him, 'Oh, that song in *Mary Poppins*', or Jimi Hendrix, you could say anything, and he'd like it and know it and appreciate it. He was the most eclectic guy in that way, and so naturally musical. He heightened things; if we wanted a tinny sound he'd make it tinnier, there was still a beauty, there was a real finesse, a delicate touch – and he made me love our music, he made it magical. A guy!"

One of The Slits' fondest memories of Dennis was his imaginative treatment of 'New Town', and while Viv admits she went through considerable anguish getting her guitar parts just right, the track ended up being the group's favourite – it was worth the blood, sweat and tears. She explains, "We totally rearranged the structure of the song, we made certain changes and tightened it up and made more sense of it.

"It took bloody ages to get my guitar part right on 'New Town'. They would be all up in the booth and all you'd hear would be these disembodied voices going, '(Click) No, that was out of time again, Viviane. Do it again.'

"So I'd play it again as tight as I possibly could. 'No, you're coming in just before the beat. Try it again.' In the end I just thrashed at the guitar and they went, 'That was fantastic!' That's how the guitar part evolved, and it sounds great now, but it came out of absolute hell, I was at my wits' end."

'New Town' became infused with a sharp delicacy it didn't have before. Tessa's ominous bass line, such a potent part of the original version of 'New Town', remained and was pushed to the fore, but the rhythm stayed constant, no longer suddenly accelerating in the middle. It was sprinkled with sawing stabs of guitar and – the *pièce de résistance* – Dennis' inspired percussion track, which paid homage to the druggy theme of the track.

"There was something missing going through the track," explains Viv. "Then Dennis said, 'I'm going to put some rhythms on it. I'm just going to wing it.'

"On the table he laid out a box of matches, a glass, a pen, a spoon; it was like one of those games where you have to memorise the things on a tray and they take it away! The engineer pressed play and we were all upstairs thinking, 'What the hell is he going to do?'

"The song starts and he starts to do these little things like a shake of the matchbox, and then striking one, that's how he underplays things. Just with four things in front of him, he did a rhythm all the way through, and he was totally in the zone. That was it, one take and it was absolutely brilliant. We were all just goose-pimply, there was absolute silence in the booth, just couldn't believe it, he brought the track to life."

Tessa adds, "'New Town' was my favourite. Dennis adds his own flavour by dropping the spoon and shaking this big box of matches, like the tools you would use to cook up your fix. I've just never heard a song like 'New Town'."

"They were all going, 'He's mad!' says Dennis of his percussion track for 'New Town', "but it was so right at the time."

'Shoplifting' was another old song made new. The tumbling bass line at the heart of the song would be brought into prominence in the mix, with the peripheral sound heard on earlier live recordings now cut out entirely in the verse, while the chorus remained as chaotic and adrenaline-led as ever, all spiralling screams, escalating, jangling guitar and, of course, those lairy shouts of "Do a runner". Indeed, Ari's screams provide the most memorable moments of this short, sweet, cheeky gem of a track, and she certainly put her all into it...

"She screamed so loud that she wet herself!" laughs Dennis. "And at the end of the scream, she shouts, 'I pissed in my knickers!' She put so much into it, she wet herself. I kept what she said in the mix, it's audible. If you know what you're listening for you can hear it. Like satanic messages!"

Speaking of hidden messages, Keith Levene is convinced he's picked up on something in the album version of 'Instant Hit' that no one else will admit to. Keith heard *Cut* for the first time in 2008 after regaining contact with Viv. He listened to Budgie's drumming on 'Instant Hit' and, throughout the track, laced with snapping, cracking rim-shots, he heard the unmistakable sound of a ticking time-bomb – a musical metaphor for himself at the time.

He says, "With Budgie, it sounds like a time-bomb waiting to self-destruct, it's like 'tic-tic-tic-tic' on the hi-hat all the way through. I checked it with Viv, and said, 'Was it your idea, the ticking bomb?' And she said, 'What ticking bomb?' Checked with Ari, 'Bomb? I know no bomb?' So I thought, OK, I'll drop the question, but I know what's going on here."

The song refers directly to Keith's then problem with heroin. But Keith is relaxed about it. "I really liked it, I'm fine with it. Good song. Viv said, 'Well, you proved me wrong with this one. The song is saying, 'Shame he won't be around for much longer, but nice guy'. Well, here I am. And I knew I'd be around because I knew what I was doing."

Palmolive, now ensconced with The Raincoats, had, as we know, insisted that Tessa sang her song 'Adventures Close To Home' on the album. It has a special quality and is a rare treat for Slits fans to catch the bass player stepping forward to sing as Ari takes over the bass-playing duties. "I've always felt really insecure about that song," confesses Tessa. "I'm not really a singer. It was one of the last songs Palmolive wrote before she parted company with the band, and then The Raincoats did a version, because it was a Palmolive song. Latterly I had people coming up to me and saying, 'Oh, I much prefer The Raincoats version!'

"Ari just gave me a tape of us doing that song live and I sound like someone from *X Factor*. Not one of the people who gets through either! I like the song, but I think I could have done a lot better."

Much of the song's charm lies in the sincerity of the vocal, while the overall track creates a welcome shift in energy on the album. "It's really quirky," says Viv. "It changed the vibe. And it worked beautifully with Tessa – plus she had the nerve to do it. I wouldn't have."

Budgie also remembers being struck by how brave Tessa was, not only by singing on the track but also handing her bass over to Ari, who, impressively, picked up how to play it straight away. And as with most Slits songs, the bass would be playing a complex little melody of its own, not just a simple walking bass line, but Ari nailed it.

Budgie says, "Thinking from my point of view, I'd be put out a bit if someone picked up my instrument and played it very well. It's taken me a long time to be comfortable with my limitations, and if I see someone who I think is technically good, I can very quickly think that I'm not any good. It can take a long time to feel confident, it took me until about five years after the band [the Banshees] stopped. I knew I felt inventive and creative, but to think of myself as someone who should be a musician? It's recent.

"Looking back on 'Adventures Close To Home', that was really tough to have the singer, who has, like, a three-octave vocal range and who's pretty gifted musically, to pick up the bass like that, *and* you've got to sing in front of her as well. It was on the spot in the studio, and Ari was helpful and unhelpful at the same time. She'd be saying, 'It's good, it's good!' one minute and, 'You can't sing at all!' the next. I'm full of admiration for Tessa because she did it."

Another Palmolive song, the eerie 'FM', seems to pay the closest homage to Palmolive's urgent drumming, opening and closing with a crescendo and a diminuendo of toms like a heartbeat, and featuring The Slits' trademark harmonies, hauntingly distant and low in the mix in comparison with Ari's expressive lead vocals.

It wasn't just The Slits themselves who struggled at times to get their parts right. 'FM' was a particularly challenging track for Budgie. "That was a really difficult one for me, it was hard to keep playing this beat over and over. Reggae is very critical when it comes to time-keeping, it's got to lock in and stay there, and my way was to push and pull and push, especially on choruses, or I'd just get totally excited like Palmolive did and go faster and faster and faster, and these guys were like, 'No, you've got to sit there in the dance groove.'"

Having made the decision to use so many of Palmolive's songs on the album, The Slits were determined to do things properly and ensure their former drummer was credited. After all, she was the founder and main songwriter for The Slits, and there was no question that they would deal with things fairly. Viv: "We put her name on the other songs so she'd get a quarter. She'd totally been The Slits up to that point because all her work had gone into it, so we felt we were fair."

But it would be a Viv track that would make it as their first single. They turned 'Typical Girls' into a reggae-fied merry-go-round, swerving between rhythms and, of course, performed with as much wit as ever. Ari's vocals bounced off Tessa and Viv's and the result was full of surprises, oddball changes spontaneously conjured up in the studio and plenty of that irresistible Slits humour.

"A lot of the stuff they used on *Cut* was pre-prepared but the final touches they put on were in the studio," remembers Dennis, "like on 'Typical Girls', Ari was determined to go, 'Typical girls buy ma-a-a-agazines!'"

They were rightly proud of 'Typical Girls'. But not only did they want it as the single – they wanted it *their* way. Mick Jones, by now known as a force to be reckoned with when it came to arranging songs for the 'biggest band in the world', The Clash, was convinced the song would zoom up the charts if they changed the rhythm and made it more accessible.

"I remember Mick saying to me, 'If you make that into a 4/4 song, you could have a hit with that,' but we refused yet again!" says Viv. "'No, no this is how we hear it!' skipping and bumping along in this mad way. Some jazz guy once said to me, 'Are you using some sort of mad time like 9/13 or something?' We didn't know...

"If we turned it into a proper catchy pop song we could have had some success with it, but we said no."

To be fair, it would have taken away part of what makes the song so much fun to listen to and dance to. The Slits wouldn't have been true to themselves if they'd changed it solely in the hope of achieving some commercial success. From the outside – certainly from the point of view of their contemporaries – The Slits appeared to be keener than before to be commercially successful, but the reality was that they simply wanted the opportunity and the means to make the album they wanted to make.

Chapter 13

"In my music, I'm trying to play the truth of what I am. The reason it's difficult is because I'm changing all the time." – Charles Mingus

Because it took longer than expected to make, The Slits recorded *Cut* during two separate visits to Ridge Farm. Initially they hoped that the record would be released in June of 1979, but it wasn't to be, and Dennis didn't want to rush them.

"I think all in all we did about 10 weeks of recording," he explains. "I envisaged it taking a fortnight, maybe a month. But we were there over two months. At one time I had to tell the record company, 'Look, I know we've taken this long, but we really are not finished, we need more time.' But I'm glad we did it that way, because it's stood the test of time. Put it on now and it still sounds great. I don't ever remember feeling that we weren't going to do it or it was a mistake to start it. It just needed time and patience.

"They had all the ideas, they just needed to be afforded the time to exercise their ability. They were well ahead in their heads in what they wanted to do, but whether or not they let frustration get the better of them . . . I'd be there to take them through it, hold their hand. I didn't have to do it that much."

Island Records was understanding and supportive – up to a point. The label certainly made an effort to promote the album and get The Slits out there and talking to the music papers. Lest we forget, to the naked eye at least, The Slits had seemed to have gone underground for a while – to the extent that *Melody Maker* had started to describe them as a 'mythical band'.

Despite their general antipathy towards the press, there was at least one journalist who didn't come in for The Slits' wrath – and that was *ZigZag*'s Kris Needs, who interviewed them on several occasions. In the spring of 1979, *ZigZag* put The Slits on its birthday issue's front cover, with an image of them digging their hands messily into a giant cake that had been baked courtesy of Island Records. The cake inevitably ends up getting hurled at Kris Needs himself of course, but not before he found out a bit about their hotly anticipated release.

"Viv (to Kris Needs): We'd like it to be sunny when it comes out. It's got a good atmosphere and suits the sun more!

"Ari: The songs are so you can see a whole film in front of your eyes. Visual pictures - you won't recognise them!

"ZZ: Why did you choose Dennis Bovell as producer?

"Ari: He's a good producer. He gets good sounds, he doesn't just get reggae sounds, he can do anything. You can't really label reggae sounds anyway. He's inventive. You've got to be an artist to be a mixer. Imaginative."

In June 1979, Dennis' own song, 'Silly Games', sung by Janet Kay, would rocket to number one in the British singles charts, making Janet the queen of Lover's Rock, Dennis even more of a star producer than before, and, perhaps more surprisingly, ensuring Ari Up was immortalised on *Top Of The Pops*. Yes, Ari. And, less surprisingly, not in the conventional way.

Dennis: "The funny thing is that while I was producing The Slits, I'd done that song with Janet and the record company had released it and I thought nothing of it. I didn't expect anything much to happen with it… and Ari burst into my room one morning with a huge ghetto blaster on her shoulder and 'Silly Games' was being played. I thought she'd helped herself to my cassettes – I used to play it to them, 'Listen to that, you lot'." Once I'd played that song to Ari, she loved it to bits. She'd heard it before Janet had sung on it, she'd heard it at the writing stage."

Ari remembers falling in love with the song, and how excited she was when Janet Kay herself visited Ridge Farm to go through it with Dennis. "She'd come over and sit at the piano. We were hanging out because I was always sitting at the piano too, and she would play me that song and sing it. I saw the birth of it."

So when Ari heard the song in its final incarnation in the Top 40, she could barely contain herself. Dennis remembers, "She came into my room going, 'Dennis! Your song's on the radio!', and I thought she was winding me up! So I was like, 'Get out!' Then the DJ goes '...just in at number 20...' And I was like, 'You're joking! I've got to go to London, you lot!' I had to speak to someone.

"Three weeks later it was at the top of the charts. The one *Top Of The Pops* that we did live, I took Ari to see how it was done, 'This is where you lot are going,' kind of thing. And Ari, just as Janet's about to come on, shouts, 'Dread at the controls!' Audible – gone out.

"I got a bollocking from the directors. 'Who's that?' 'Her.' 'Who's she here with?' 'Dennis Bovell.' 'Right...' Ah, well – she wouldn't be a punk otherwise!"

But Ari remembers it not as a punk trying to grab attention on *Top Of The Pops*, but as someone standing up for Janet Kay, who, Ari felt, wasn't being treated properly. So the reason she yelled out was not simply to pay tribute to Clash cohort Mikey Dread, whose first reggae album – entitled *Dread At The Controls* – was released that year, but to make a point.

"I remember that, and I was thrown out too," recalls Ari. "I bet (Dennis) doesn't remember what brought it on. I was backstage seeing Janet Kay crying before the show because they forced her to wear lipstick. Not only did she not wear lipstick in everyday life but this one was extra horrible and shiny. Women [could have] a hit but no say – the price of fame! So it was 'dread at the control' in context to this story."

Other than this occasion, The Slits never appeared on *Top Of The Pops* – the make-up artists alone must have breathed a sigh of relief about that.

Between recording sessions, The Slits would spend their time listening to music – by now they were absorbing a lot of jazz – and they would go to gigs. Viv Albertine started attending free improviser Derek Bailey's

Company events at London's ICA, which comprised of ever-changing line-ups of artists. These happenings had a huge effect on her own playing, prompting her to state later that it was only once she started going to these gigs that she really started to enjoy playing the guitar. Viv got to know the experimental group The Flying Lizards on these occasions, and Steve Beresford in particular, whom The Slits had bumped into over the years. Steve would soon be, in Ari's words, very much a 'boy Slit' when he later joined the group.

In July, The Slits were reported to have gone to see the avant-garde group Throbbing Gristle at the London Film Co-operative – and it was also reported that they started a bloody riot, "a pitched battle between the band and members of The Slits and The Raincoats – a clash of ideologies between arties and social realists", Jon Savage wrote in his book, *England's Dreaming*. But this wasn't true; in fact The Slits weren't even at the gig.

The reality of the situation was that The Raincoats – with Palmolive (making up the 'Slits' quotient of the story) – were at the Throbbing Gristle gig with their manager, Shirley O'Loughlin, and some friends. One of their friends was drunk, and as they were standing close to the stage, she started reaching up and playing with some of the wires at the musicians' feet.

According to O'Loughlin, a member of the group suddenly brought a guitar down on top of the drunken girl and she crashed to the floor. The Raincoats rushed to her aid and managed to get her to hospital quickly. Another man who rushed to the scene, who happened to be a journalist, asked if there was anything he could do to help. He saw what had happened first-hand, but in the next issue of *Sounds,* it was reported that "The Slits and The Raincoats" had kicked off at the gig, causing a violent affray. The Raincoats were so staggered that they wrote an open letter, which was printed in the following issue of *Sounds,* giving details of the true story. But unfortunately, it seems, the more sensational version of events continues to be perpetuated. Never let the truth stand in the way of a good story…

Life was taking different turns for The Slits during the period in which they recorded *Cut*. On a personal level, Tessa suffered the loss of her father the day after her 20th birthday in May. Understandably she felt completely numb after first hearing the news, but the ill-timed arrival of some guests at the studio didn't make it any easier.

Tessa: "John Lydon's brother and some of his mates came in. I was just waiting for the rest of The Slits, and they just cornered me and started taunting me – 'You don't look very sad, your dad's just died...' – I've never forgotten that, I just felt cornered like an animal.

"When someone close to you dies you don't always show it in your face, at first you go numb. I was dazed until I just went into the field and started crying. I think that's a typical reaction to when someone close to you dies. I had a similar thing when my daughter's father, Sean (Oliver), died. I went completely numb, and then it came out later in waves of grief."

In a very different way, Viv was experiencing changes personally too. Her relationship with Mick Jones had finally dissolved and she had started dating The Pop Group's Gareth Sager, whom Dick O'Dell introduced her to when the Bristol art-funkers visited Ridge Farm. But despite what many might like to think, there was rarely a time when anything came between The Slits during this period, nor indeed The Slits and the rest of the Ridge Farm collective. They wouldn't stand for any nonsense; they were taking their work seriously. "They were strong characters, especially Viv," recalls Dick. "Occasionally we had sparks, but I have nothing but respect for her. Even when she was going out with Gareth, when it was Slits time, that was it, Slits time. Fair enough."

Ridge Farm owner Frank Andrews remembers The Slits with affection: "We all got on well, it was a very happy time. They liked to think they were a bit outrageous but they weren't really."

Tessa adds, "We all got on fantastically. I can't remember any arguments. It was like being with a family and having fun and working together. Plus we couldn't have done the album with a better person (Dennis), not only because he got the right sound but because he was just hilarious, he was such a laugh."

Pop Group drummer Bruce Smith was also around at Ridge Farm, even making an appearance as 'the boyfriend' character on 'Love And [now Und] Romance'. The Slits loved Bruce and were keen to work with him, which was just as well, because Budgie was ready to move on.

Budgie explains, "I remember sitting outside the cottage on the grass saying to Viv, 'I've got to go now,' I'd just had enough, it was a bit crazy, everyone was a bit frayed, we were all tired. I might be flattering myself but I think they were upset. But it had been very good to be around them. There was nothing pretentious or girly about them, it was smells and all, no 'stinky fake smells' as they say in 'Typical Girls'. It was an eye-opener really, very different, and I felt very akin."

Dennis: "I said to The Slits, 'You'd better work with Bruce Smith.' Those groups would not only have the same producer but the same drummer, it was like a big family. The vibe changed because Bruce was more of a jazz-rock drummer, but they were both fantastic in their own individual ways. And they both knew what to do, to adapt to this girl band."

Bruce continued to work with The Pop Group, and also played with Linton Kwesi Johnson's group and in Dennis' own Dub Band, even squeezing in a stint with PiL as well. He was on the threshold of his busiest years yet. "I've no idea how he kept it all going but he's retired now!" laughs Dennis.

Budgie, meanwhile, found himself to be a much sought-after musician, and before long his impressive, creative foray with The Slits actually secured him the gig he really wanted. "I eventually got playing with a few other people," he says. "Glen Matlock, Danny Kustow, who was the guitarist with the Tom Robinson Band, and Steve New, who was the other guitarist in Glen's band. We did about six gigs as the Jimmy Norton's Explosion. It would be billed as 'Glen Matlock, Danny Kustow, Steve New and featuring Budgie'. And all these heavy metal fans turned up because they thought it was this band plus the three-piece Welsh heavy metal band Budgie." The group folded after a six-date run, but still managed to squeeze in a Peel Session at the end of July.

Just after the release of *Cut* in September, Siouxsie & The Banshees released *Join Hands*. The group were already touring the album, and doing the usual round of in-store signings. Budgie continues, "John McKay, Kenny Morris, Siouxsie and [Steve] Severin were signing copies in this record store in Aberdeen while the album was playing over the speakers.

"John and Kenny, the drummer, thought it was very uncool to be signing your albums with your own music playing, so they said, 'Let's not play this, let's play *this*' – and it was The Slits' album, which was brand new at the time.

"It caused a big argument and John and Kenny left that day, that's the story anyway. For me it's an amazing link, the album I'd just done was a catalyst in these two guys deciding they didn't want to be in a pop group – because the Banshees were a pop group." Sex Pistols drummer Paul Cook, who lived with the Banshees' manager Nils Stevenson at the time, had, meanwhile, recommended Budgie to Nils on the strength of his drumming on *Cut*. The rest is history.

Once The Slits had recorded the tracks for *Cut*, they stuck around to help with the mixing. This was their album, and they weren't going to go swanning off just yet. Apart from their collaborative effort on 'Grapevine', The Slits had never had anything mixed properly before, and as a result, their experiences of recording up to this point had largely left them frustrated and feeling more than a little exposed: "You can put it down but your flies are open," Viv had told *ZigZag* editor Kris Needs in an interview that April. "If you do demos, your knickers are on show," added Ari.

This was their opportunity to craft their sound as it was in their own imaginations, something that could only be done with all three of them actively working with Dennis at the desk. Which makes it all the more galling for The Slits that the general opinion all round was, and has remained, that they had everything done for them.

Ari complains, "We never get credit. Yes, it did take a lot of work to get it right, yes, it was challenging and hard, yes, Dennis Bovell did help us a lot, and helped us put things together and create, but we're the songwriters and arrangers, we arranged our own rhythms and songs. Dennis was brilliant, by then he knows our sound, knows his studio. But, but, BUT, having said that, remember he still needed to get into our heads and understand how we wanted it to sound. We had to sit there every day with him, creating it.

"I'd say, 'Hey, that guitar needs to go up more, the bass needs more reverb,' balancing the instruments. We were there. We didn't just sit back like most of these big star girls, hand over the product, finish singing, go home and let the producer do everything. Blokes [do that] too, most guys get their big record deal with their big producer, finish recording and leave it up to the producer.

"That's not me and it will never be us. I will always want to be in the mixing room to make the end product. We were like that even in the Peel Sessions, from day one."

Tessa adds, "In the mix there were sometimes three people or more pushing up or pulling down buttons, it was the old style of mixing, 24-track analogue. No computers back then."

The assumption that female artists have little or no input in their own projects beyond singing or the basic playing of instruments is still prevalent today. This was brought home in the summer of 2008 when Icelandic artist Björk published an open letter on her website addressed to a Reykjavik music paper, called, coincidentally, *Grapevine*. The journal had conducted an interview with a local DJ who was expressing admiration for her 2001 concept album, *Vespertine,* particularly Valgeir Sigurðsson's instrumentals and production. The local DJ was evidently unaware that the instrumentals and production were all Björk's work, and that Sigurðsson was a programmer and engineer on the album. After seven years of hearing credit go to other people, always men, for her music, Björk decided it was time to right some wrongs.

Björk wrote: "It feels like still today after all these years people cannot imagine that a woman can write, arrange or produce electronic music. I have had this experience many, many times that the work I do on the computer gets credited to whatever male was in a 10 meter [sic] radius during the job.

"It could be that this is some degree of sexism. MIA had to deal with this with the respected website pitchfork.com where they assumed that (DJ) Diplo had produced all of her *Kala* album without reading any credit list or nothing. It just had to be, it couldn't have been MIA herself!

"People seem to accept that women can sing and play whatever instrument they are seen playing, but they cannot program, arrange, produce, edit or write."

According to The Slits, it was during their time at Ridge Farm that the concept for their infamous semi-naked album cover was born. Island's art director, Dennis Morris, who, to be fair, thought he was going to be the one to create the cover, wanted to shoot an image of slashed up pink nylon, so the cover looked 'slit'. No chance. Too obvious, maybe. And it was The Slits' first album, so it had to be The Slits' concept. Island accepted this – although they were in for a shock when they saw the cover image the girls came up with.

The Slits wanted to appear on the cover like defiant, fearsome savages in the not very wild surroundings of rural Dorking; tribal, earthy and dangerous but also quite funny, given the context. Photographer Pennie Smith, who took the shot, remembers that their real inner Amazons took a bit of coaxing.

"I got to know them through The Clash, and I enjoyed working with them because I didn't find them girly," she recalls. "But I expected them to be more ferocious. They wanted to look savage, but at first it was much more polite than I'd imagined. They'd just put lippie on their cheeks."

It was when Pennie noticed that the flower beds had just been watered that someone suggested they could do a bit better than lipstick war-paint. One thing led to another and what resulted was a very brave, controversial album cover – and some extreme reactions.

"Oh my God, outrageous," laughs Dennis Bovell. "Listen, when they said they were going to do that, I thought, 'Bloody funny.' But I thought they were just going to do it on their faces!"

As we know, the album cover was originally to be shot by Dennis Morris and, at the time, he was not best pleased to be pushed out of the picture, so to speak.

Tessa: "To do a cover like that you have to feel relaxed but there was the guy lurching around from Island Records. We just shooed him out of the way! He was just hanging around gawping at us. But it was quite a childlike thing to fill a bucket with mud and cover each other with it, it was liberating."

Viv adds, "We thought it was funny to be covered in English mud, and it was an English cottage with English roses behind us, and there we are like three savages in England.

"We only thought of getting our clothes off on the day we shot it, I don't know what happened there! We were saying we wanted to be covered in mud or something, and a friend of Dick's who'd just come back from Africa was saying, 'This is how they do the loincloths,' and showed us how to tie them. We were thinking, 'Well, that's OK, it covers us more or less'..."

The classic shot that was used for the cover was of course of the three Slits – Tessa, Ari and Viv – topless, covered in mud, wild-haired and standing defiantly straight to camera. No posy positioning, no sucking in of stomachs, no come-hither expressions. Just three strong tribeswomen giving off the ultimate: 'Here it is, so what?' vibe. True, the reaction of the public would range between shock, lust and disgust, but that was their lookout. The Slits' message was clear. This was no pin-up, although that wouldn't stop it from being treated as such once it hit the outside world.

Pennie: "I didn't give a thought about impact, I don't think about the outside world. To a degree I wish it was even less posed."

Luckily Chris Blackwell was amused by the cover, not that he really had much choice thanks to that artistic-control clause that The Slits had inserted into their contract. Ari reiterates, "If we didn't have that written into our contract, we would have ended up like Jimi Hendrix with *Electric Ladyland*. Everyone's worshipping Jimi Hendrix, where's our worshipping? We need to be worshipped just because we were one of the first bands to do that, we were teenagers, girls!"

The only real concern over the cover for The Slits was, in hindsight, the fact that, thanks to the new healthy lifestyle they were living, their spindly figures had rounded out, and when they saw the resulting photos, they were convinced they looked fat. Not that that stopped them from using the image. It would have been very un-Slit to do that.

Viv laughs, "You can see on the cover we'd eaten quite a lot. You couldn't do that now with those bodies, could you?! We just look like three quirky different bodies, I suppose."

"We ate so much," adds Ari. "There was a great chef there. They were cooking traditional English recipes, really hearty food. We were just playing music and eating, that was it! Nothing but countryside – we'd have done horse-riding if we could, we love riding horses, but there weren't any there. We just had food." And mud.

The Slits and Pennie were having a great time. It was the men – Dick, Dennis Bovell and Dennis Morris – who were, for different reasons, getting antsy; Dick because he knew he'd get into trouble for letting this happen, Dennis Morris because his services were apparently surplus to requirements, and Dennis Bovell because he feared for his reputation if he was photographed supposedly cavorting with three muddy, naked Slits.

Bovell: "They're loinclothed up and they've got mud all over themselves. I thought, 'You lot are mad...' So while they're doing that, of course, no work in the studio. So I went for a swim in the swimming pool.

"When they'd finished, they were de-mudding themselves, and someone said, 'Oh, it will be a lot easier if you just jump in the pool, I'm going to clear it out later anyway.' And I was like, 'No, no!!' So they decide to get in the pool. And someone grabs a camera and goes, 'Photo!' (click) and then I'm being asked by *Melody Maker* or *NME* to sanction a photo of me in the pool with three naked Slits with mud everywhere – it's all over me as well now – and I'm demanding the negative! The minute the photo was taken, I thought, 'God, my reputation! It cannot be published.' Now looking back I remember it being quite a laugh. But at the time – not!"

Dick refers to the whole episode as "the great and very controversial photographic incident which I got royally bloody caned for.

"Most people assumed it was my idea. It was not, I could never take credit for it as it wasn't. I was basically just standing there thinking, 'Well, this is fucking brilliant fun, but am I going to get a problem with this or what?'

"Ridge Farm had a manicured lawn and a really nice pool, a proper English country home, and there was that lot, all covered in mud from the actual garden, and then after the shoot they jumped into the pool, drove them all mad! 'The fucking pool! Get out of the fucking pool!' Rolling around with just the loincloths on, hilarious."

Viv confirms that Dennis Bovell, at the time, didn't find it hilarious – and not just because he was worried about his reputation. "It was very hot in those days and there was Dennis sort of trapped here for all these months with all these girls. He got a bit hot under the collar, to be honest, although he won't admit it," she says.

"We didn't see it at the time, but then suddenly one day it clicked with me he was being all grumpy and irritable all the time; all the female hormones, all the oestrogen, us with all our clothes off and he was the only guy there!

"It really didn't strike me until late in the day that this was going on for him a bit. I had a flash of, 'Oh shit!' But he was very respectful, a perfect gentleman. And we didn't think of ourselves as sexy at all. I mean, my little girl's eight and she's aware of sexuality, and how to flounce and flick. We weren't aware, either you sort of fancied a boy in a very clean way, or you liked how he made you laugh, but it wasn't all about bodies or money… so we didn't think we were in any way attractive to Dennis or that he might find it difficult with us flouncing about with no clothes on in front of him. Quite funny."

According to Viv, there was another man getting hot under the collar too – although he handled it in a different way. "One of Island's A&R men was trying to get me chucked out of The Slits. But that's what it was like, it was back-stabby; maybe he kind of fancied you but you weren't interested, or you said the wrong thing or you didn't kowtow or flutter your eyelids.

"So he tried to have a meeting with Island to get me chucked out of the band, and everyone just said, 'You're joking, she's the songwriter in the band, you can't chuck her out.' Dennis Bovell had to stand up for me.

"I got my own back many years later. I was a director on TV working on an arts show called *01 For London*, and this guy had an exhibition, and now of course he was sucking up to me because I was directing this show. In the end there were too many pieces for the show that week so I said, 'I think we should drop that one…'"

The Slits were an odd combination of worldly and innocent, so it is unsurprising they were slow to see the potentially sexual side of what they were doing. They certainly didn't anticipate the cover being used as a masturbatory focus as soon as it was released. Sex was not part of the picture, so to speak. Ari, for one, was still an unsullied maiden at the age of 17, of which she is proud; it was a personal issue that was about respecting her body until the time was right for her, or in her words: "pum-pum power".

"I'm a big pum-pum power girl," says Ari. "I was a virgin and remained a virgin for a very long time. I was still a virgin when the *Cut* album was made, and let me tell you, it was pum-pum and punk power and everything mixed. But people freaked out at that."

By the end of the summer of 1979, *Cut* had been mixed and was ready to greet the world. The Slits returned to London, Island prepared to unleash *Cut* on the press and the public, while Dennis Bovell took a well-earned two months off in his homeland of Barbados for the first time since he was 12. "Being at that farm in Surrey reminded me of my upbringing on a farm in Barbados, suddenly I was longing to go there, it brought it all back," he said later.

One listen to *Cut* and it was obvious that The Slits had come a very long way from punk. They had imprinted something of themselves as individuals onto those tracks, the wit, the cheekiness, the intelligence and the ingenuity. But were the public ready for it? Some still aren't, even now. Once the opportunity to shout, pogo and smash things at their punk gigs of yore had transmuted into something more cerebral, challenging and interesting, more people than ever simply didn't know what to do with them. But many were grabbed and inspired by their evolution – and would support The Slits in their ongoing journey.

Chapter 14

"Caroline Coon wanted to write about Cut, and her editor said: 'No! They're fat, ugly, disgusting!' This is a reflection of how men viewed that cover, they didn't get it, they didn't get the humour, it went right over their heads." – Tessa Pollitt

As review copies of *Cut* hit the desks of music journalists across the land, and giant posters of our muddy heroines were pasted all over town, Island Records braced themselves for the response. They didn't have to wait for long. Just days into the poster campaign, a motorist would try to sue the record company because he was so stunned by the spectacle that he crashed his car.

While The Slits' friends and contemporaries and other like-minded people could appreciate what they were trying to put across, the cover almost inevitably succeeded in exposing the unpleasant side in the sort of people to whom bold originality was anathema. It also created a misunderstanding among feminists, with some convinced they were trying to use their bodies to sell their album. But at least, as Tessa observes, it was making people think and talk: "It was quite menacing, like warrior women, a powerful cover whether you like it or not – it made you think."

Friends of The Slits wondered why some people were so shocked –

what did they expect? Why were people so upset at seeing girls covered in mud when such sights were seen on a far wider scale at festivals like Woodstock during the Flower Power era? The difference was that there was an edge of threat and danger in The Slits' cover – it wasn't about peace and love. Don Letts: "The reaction to the cover of *Cut* was as expected – outrage, scandal. To the rest of us, The Slits were so out there that when they did it we were all like, 'Oh, well it's The Slits.' You expected no less from them, pushing parameters, being provocative and polarising public opinion. Which is what it did – and still does."

While up to this point it was dangerous to be a Slit, it now became dangerous for a Slits fan to carry a copy of *Cut* visibly in public. Christine Robertson remembers, "I had a copy of *Cut* on me as I got on the train to see my brother, and I got attacked by two Pakistani guys who obviously took offence, they started on me. I was on my own in this empty carriage and it was late at night. I just got really aggressive and they backed off. So it was shocking."

"We made history with that cover," adds Ari. "We had big posters made, and they were everywhere, all over London. Even if people didn't know The Slits, they'd see these posters and say, 'What the fuck is this?' People were outraged of course, or some of the rebels of society, who would be like regular everyday people in the street now, would be curious.

"The black community, those who were not so into the punky reggae connection, more into calypso and soca, they were intrigued. We would get reactions from some of them asking what it meant, questioning. They weren't all, 'Ooh, disgusting, it's filthy…' although a lot of people reacted like that."

Journalist Vivien Goldman had supported The Slits from the very beginning, and had been waiting with great anticipation for their first album. The moment she received her copy she was like a child on Christmas morning, but the sight of the cover was too much for some editors. Whether it was burgeoning political correctness or basic misogyny and confusion with the mixed messages they were taking from The Slits' defiant stares and nakedness, it was enough to cause real upset.

Vivien remembers, "I was on *Melody Maker* and I was very excited about the *Cut* album finally coming out. So I rushed into the editor's office brandishing *Cut,* shouting, 'It's here! It's fantastic!'

"He looked at it and he said, 'Oh my God, this is disgusting! Why aren't they wearing any clothes? Look at them, they look terrible. They're fat, they look disgusting.' I was just so appalled because apart from anything else – they're not even fat! That response was something that freaked *me* out and turned my stomach as much as his, so that cover was truly provocative. But in fairness to him as a journalist, he did give me the space to say it was a very significant record."

Keith Levene is equally upset that people were offended: "What's disgusting about it? What is possibly disgusting? They've got no clothes on and they're covered in mud, is that fucking disgusting? Is that more disgusting than the shitty news that comes out every day that is a lie anyway?

"Listen to the record mate, it's not about that! And women are bigger anyway. They've got big arses and they've got big tits. Doesn't matter. I'm glad it creates something, it's supposed to. I think it's great, it's tribal and earthy."

When *Cut* hit the shelves some took the cover for what The Slits had intended it to be, but countless others persisted in damning the band as "fat and disgusting" or simply viewed the cover in a carnal light, sneaking a copy home for their own private use. Vivien Goldman spoke to the group in the light of these reactions to the cover and found them slightly stunned at the response but nevertheless defiant. Asked by Vivien how they felt about becoming a masturbatory focus of many a teenage boy, she found that The Slits genuinely hadn't thought about it that way at all – and had no intention of giving it any thought either.

While she could see that the intention was never to create a punk pin-up scenario, not everyone else was prepared to see their cover so positively, as she wrote in *Melody Maker*: "You have only to see Viv standing so defiant that she looks like the statue of Dame Edith Cavell to know that *Playboy* pinup thrills are not foremost in their minds ... They're (theoretically) reclaiming their bodies: 'Here we are, that's it, what's the big deal?'

"In fact there is a big deal. The Slits are crucial role models for a new generation of British women musicians who are finally beginning to step forward, and their sleeve has already created quite a furore. One feminist who works at Rough Trade reckoned that the shop should slot

The Slits in with The Stranglers and refuse to stock it, as intentions apart, it's merely another record sleeve using naked women's bodies to sell records ..."

Despite her concerns, Vivien had herself picked up on the tribal aspect of the image straight away, and being aware of their growing closeness with The Pop Group, whose singer, Mark Stewart, was Vivien's boyfriend at the time, she saw possibly subliminal but no less present parallels with The Pop Group's cover for *Y*, which pictured the Mud Men of Papua New Guinea.

Vivien: "That cover was very influenced by The Pop Group. They did the whole mud men thing, and they were very into this Pagan 'get naked' sort of idea! The whole idea of the integrity of the primitive was very important, so there was some bond at the time between the two albums. I just loved it."

Other journalists hooked on *Cut* included Vivien's *Melody Maker* cohort John Orme, who emphatically advised readers to screw up and throw away whatever preconceptions they might have harboured about The Slits ("They are not a female Pop Group and they are not a forgotten hangover from another era") and celebrated their creation of a "concentrated and startling package of skipping ideas, unfettered enthusiasm and groundbreaking originality". Lester Bangs was positively evangelical about them in his review for *Rolling Stone* magazine. The Slits had achieved one of their ambitions – boys were enjoying their music as much as girls.

Bangs wrote: "... the news from such magazines as England's *New Musical Express* was that they hadn't quite, ah, *gelled* yet, though they certainly were trying. I don't know what those limey critics' ears are made of! Because both live and on their debut LP, The Slits prove that they're not only charming but can hold their own as a band..."

Their contemporaries were just as fulsome with their praise of the record. Keith Levene, who heard it in latter years, was impressed – and found it poignant that he could hear himself in Viv's playing. "It reflected that she listened to me, and she went into some very good areas. Put it this way, she didn't come on like any other rock guitarist, she was like an artist who started to play guitar. I gave her a palette of guitar, and she picked it up good. As the guy that taught her, I'm proud of what she did on *Cut*. I can hear me in it, but I think she's got her own style and I think The Slits were really lucky to have her."

Former Slits guitarist Kate Corris was also a fan of the album, and could see the move upwards from straightforward punk. "I loved *Cut* when I heard it. It was a watershed for them, after *Cut* they were a separate entity to punk, and their whole presence changed radically. I thought they really grew up around that album."

Members of the more hardcore punk faction, however, found it difficult to adjust to the new sound of The Slits, and didn't like the way their heroines had progressed. But punk was never about staying the same, it was about striving for new and more exciting ideals, musically and as people. In any case, rifts were already starting to appear in 'punk' with artists like John Lydon and PiL, not to mention The Slits themselves, moving on into more expressionistic territory, and it was around this time that 'street-punk' or Oi! came into play to cater to the tastes of those keen to retain the angrier, less cerebral side of punk. There were still good reasons to be angry – Thatcher's iron grip had taken a hold of the country, the outlook was bleak and, for some, the sight of their formerly nihilistic idols fulfilling themselves creatively and trying new things felt like a betrayal. The Slits were between a rock and a hard place – after working hard to improve and thus throw off slights about their musical ability, they were now being snubbed by a section of punk fans who didn't want to see them move on or, basically, enjoy wider success.

Bruce Smith: "The reaction to the album was confusing for those who knew them as the original all-girl punk band, I can tell you. It was pretty riotous. I heard them before *Cut* a couple of times, and it was abrasive to say the least. It was very original and compelling but a bit all over the place. So some people were like, 'Oh, The Slits have sold out, trying to do a pop record.'

"But I think they made the record they wanted to make. By and large it was really a ground-breaking, original record and it still is. There was nothing really that sounded like it; the synthesis of the rhythms and Dennis' production, and of course Ari's very musical. So largely it was extremely well-received, it was such an innovation."

Vivien, from the point of view of being a reggae expert, appreciated the dub aspect and oddball sound effects, especially those used in 'New

Town': "The glass, the matchbox, spoon, that's very reggae. On Bob Marley's *Exodus* there is one track that rides completely on this scraped bottle."

'Typical Girls' was also popular, and while, as Island predicted, many journalists preferred the B-side of 'I Heard It Through The Grapevine', they could see that, given the attention it deserved, The Slits' chosen A-side could be a big hit. In the event, it only got as far as number 60 in the singles chart, although *Cut* peaked at a respectable number 24 in the album listings.

Dennis Bovell: "I thought 'Typical Girls' was going to be a huge hit, I really did. I thought 'Typical Girls' was going to be a smash. I don't know what happened. I didn't hear it on the radio. Radio 1 bloody well turned their noses up at it – or the plugger didn't do his job, I don't know."

The Slits were working hard themselves to raise awareness of *Cut* and, during the break in the recording of the album that summer, they had teamed up with Don Letts to create a visual side to their work, a collection of short films within a film called *Slits Pictures*.

Don, ever busy with his Super 8 camera, was fast becoming the go-to man within the punk scene for music videos. He had already made the video for PiL's debut single, 'Public Image', in 1978, and by the end of 1979 he would have created The Clash's atmospheric promo for 'London Calling' for its release in December. So it seemed only right that he should try to do something similar for The Slits.

Don hooked up with Mick Calvert, who had been making a promo film for The Pop Group, and, taking The Slits' choice of *Cut* tracks, made a selection of music videos that Island Records could use as a promotional tool. "The video age was just starting to bubble up," says Don. "Me and Mick Calvert decided to say to the record company, 'Give us £10,000 and we'll make a half-hour film, and within that half-hour film, you'll get two or three videos.' We went out and that's exactly what we did – an abstract promo-type half-hour film.

"It was interesting because it sort of pre-empted the advent of these things you get today where you get a CD with a DVD – and this was a long time ago, we're talking about 30 years ago. But if it wasn't for us being such big fans of The Slits, there wouldn't be that kind of documentation around."

Tessa: "It was like having a scrapbook done on Super 8 film. A Slits scrapbook! It's good that it's documented, in those days there wasn't so much filming going on. It's quite hard to get footage of The Slits, and Don was always there with his Super 8 camera just documenting the whole thing, not just our gigs but everywhere. It's brilliant."

This wasn't the first time The Slits had been captured on celluloid. Apart from Don's *Punk Rock Movie* (in which you can see just how continually and carefully The Slits had to tease their hair to keep it looking unkempt), they had also appeared briefly, with Palmolive, in Derek Jarman's dark punk film *Jubilee* as a street gang who tear an abandoned car apart. Getting the best out of The Slits on camera was no problem, especially for a close friend like Don. And the familiar madcap quality of the group reminded him that they were as funny – and feared – as they ever were, even though Ari had told *NME* that at this stage they "couldn't afford to be naughty". It's all relative.

Don remembers, "When we were shooting the film in West London somewhere, there was one point when Ari wanted to change and she saw a bureau de change and said, 'Well, I'll change in there.' We started to film it, and then the police were called and it all ends up being in the film. It was the bits we filmed that were outside of the plan that are the most interesting.

"We were filming in Notting Hill Gate and Ari wanted a drink, so we went to Sainsbury's and we gave her a shopping cart and she ended up getting chased by the store staff around the store, and that ended up in the film. And then of course there are the set pieces, 'Spend, Spend, Spend', 'Typical Girls', which is filmed on the bandstand at Regent's Park."

A promo for 'Instant Hit' was filmed around some mansion apartments, with The Slits running up and down the different levels. It's a slice of late Seventies London from the beginning, where you see individual Slits in their respective homes getting ready to go out, strutting down the street, jumping on buses and swarming all over that elegantly wasted Thirties block.

Viv: "I loved the one for 'Instant Hit', at those mansion flats in Shepherd's Bush. I always used to walk past them because that's where me and Mick were at art school. Penhurst Mansions I think they were called. The design reminded me of rhythms because they were so repetitive, the balconies.

"The one for 'New Town' I adore, it's so great. We didn't know what they were going to do as it's such a moody piece but Don said, 'Don't worry, Mick and I are going to take the camera, we'll do something in the spirit of the song, and you don't even have to be in it.' Anyway they went off to this very seedy hotel, with blue light, and Mick, who's a very extraordinary-looking guy, sort of wired-looking, gaunt bloke, just looks like he's having a nervous breakdown through the film, the light swinging, and him, angst-ridden.

"'Typical Girls' was a lovely one on the bandstand, we just got loads of mates down and it was a beautiful day, and there were all these ordinary English people just in deckchairs dotted around. There was a lovely boy there called Iv-I, with dreadlocks and a very beautiful face, he got murdered in LA. He'd come from Jamaica and had only been here for about a week and we immediately clicked with him." The Slits later dedicated their second album, *Return Of The Giant Slits*, to his memory.

Slits Pictures was screened a month after the release of *Cut* at The Scala in London's Kings Cross alongside Mick Calvert's Pop Group film, and was well-received by a curious press. One particular favourite was the vignette for 'Spend, Spend, Spend'. The song may be a study of the obsession with consumerism, but The Slits and Don avoided the obvious and shot it in a reggae club featuring dancing Slits among a skanking crowd and Ari as DJ with the Moa Anbessa Sound System.

Don experimented with split screens, solarisation and expressionist lighting in *Slits Pictures*, while Mick used a more stripped-back approach for his Pop Group film, which critics compared to the work of Kenneth Anger. The Pop Group film featured tribal concepts and African imagery, while *Slits Pictures* hinted at The Slits as elemental 'demon dryads' (albeit ones that attended St Trinian's) hurtling through woodland and charging around Notting Hill frightening the locals, as *Melody Maker*'s Debra Daley observed.

She wrote: "The Slits are let loose in London like St Trinian's runaways, and in their rage for disorder, claim a supermarket and a bureau de change as helpless victims. Their antics are varying degrees of funny, and they produce some terrific music ..."

By the time *Slits Pictures* made it to the outside world, the group themselves were already on their promotional tour for *Cut* – the Simply What's Happening tour.

Bruce Smith had now joined The Slits on drums while also remaining in The Pop Group. Both groups were at the peak of their powers, but exhausting as it could often be, Bruce engaged himself completely with The Slits.

Pop Group and Slits manager, Dick O'Dell, remembers, "Bruce was more involved, definitely. He is very good at responding and he played brilliantly with that band, both of them, The Pop Group and The Slits. And luckily Bruce didn't mind being bossed about."

Bruce also played a part in deciding who they invited on the tour. As the memory of the initial punk explosion faded The Slits were listening to more and more jazz, and when they started to get hooked on something it quickly spread. Paul Rutherford remembers, "The whole '77 thing was coming to a grinding halt, and The Slits were still into reggae but they were getting more into the free stuff, Ornette Coleman. They made me listen to lots of things like that and I ended up buying tons of mad jazz records! I think The Pop Group were a big influence there."

Bruce had introduced them to the music of trumpeter and Coleman cohort Don Cherry. They fell in love with his sound, and in true Slits-style, weren't just content to listen to the records. They invited him on tour. "They went that step further," says Bruce. "It was extraordinary."

They wanted three artists on the tour, and in order to put across the message that they were all as important as each other they would swap the order of the bill round every night so The Slits were not always in the traditional headline slot. It made sense that the third artist should be a reggae star, so the quirky Jamaican toaster Prince Hammer – a performer known for his penchant for bounding on stage with vampire teeth and a cloak – was invited on the tour too, backed by the respected British dub band Creation Rebel.

The Slits met Creation Rebel when they became friends with white reggae producer Adrian Sherwood that year. Adrian was young, talented and ambitious, and everyone on the scene who was into dub and reggae respected him. Dennis Bovell admits Adrian was more of a hardcore reggae producer than even he was, and credits him for bringing a lot of those influences into the punk scene. As well as The Slits and The Clash, PiL – John Lydon, Keith Levene and Jah Wobble – were all admirers of Sherwood. Apart from anything else, the fact that Adrian had tried to help Keith kick heroin stood out to the guitarist as a brave and appreciated, if unsuccessful, move.

Keith: "I really like Adrian and out of all the people I knew when I was in PiL, Adrian was a friend, he fucking cared. Now I think he sees me like I'm still the guy I was when I was 25, like I'm a naughty boy who fucked up.

"It can be awkward, but you try being in fucking PiL and not being totally mental, mate. I can still play guitar. But he's a fucking great producer. And I know the real Adrian, he's a caring, nice guy – and he was just getting on with it. I thought it was amazing what he was doing. And I used to think, 'Wow, he's so grown-up and responsible, owning a house and stuff.'"

In contrast to many of those on the 'punk merging into dub' scene, Adrian was particularly together. He might have just turned 20 but he had already started up his own small reggae label and was recording his own albums, putting together groups, working with reggae artists from Jamaica, and had managed to save enough to buy property too. He was one sorted individual.

"I had a record label called HitRun," explains Adrian, "and on the label I had Creation Rebel, who were our own band, and one of the best reggae bands at the time in England, certainly one of the first to do a live dub show.

"The band were organised to initially back Prince Far I, Prince Hammer and Bim Sherman and we did a tour in '79 called the Roots Encounter tour. Ari in particular came to our gigs, and she invited us to go on their 1979 tour, The Slits with Don Cherry and Happy House, who were Lou Reed's backing band, and they had us on the bill with Creation Rebel backing Prince Hammer."

Dick O'Dell: "We initiated that kind of line-up in The Pop Group days, we had The Pop Group, Cabaret Voltaire and Linton Kwesi Johnson for their tour, and now people say, 'Ooh wow, what an amazing concept, this fusion idea,' but at the time, we'd just look around and think, 'Right, what's going to make a really cool bill?' That was it. As a group of people, the kind of music we listened to was not just contemporary pop music, it was reggae, jazz, Ornette Coleman, Charlie Mingus, Don Cherry. We listened to those guys."

While it wasn't a problem convincing Don, Prince Hammer or Creation Rebel to join the tour, organising the run of dates hadn't been plain sailing. The Slits still had a reputation for being wild and unmanageable, and some of the more powerful promoters didn't want to go near them. John Curd, a London-based promoter who worked with many new wave and punk bands at the time, was unwilling to get involved with them. "He refused to have us because of our 'reputation', so we called him John Turd," says Ari.

The Slits wanted to treat their fellow artists well on the tour, and decided to pay for everything themselves with their advance from Island, which amounted to £45,000. They flew Prince Hammer (and his entourage) out from Jamaica at great expense, Don Cherry over from the States, and they ensured they had the best hotels they could afford, while The Slits themselves survived on a wage. Dick took care of sound, Gareth Sager joined them to play keyboards, Steve Beresford would turn up for the US leg with his bag of sonic tricks and effects, and The Slits met a girl who would quickly become an honorary Slit, a teenager with fluorescent hair called Neneh, who'd asked her stepdad if she could hang out on the road.

Viv remembers, "She was very punky, and very New Yorky, not at all the ethnic princess sort of person she is now! She was very wonderful and had a very warm matriarchal quality, and she was only about 14, 15. She was telling us she'd been a complete dropout in New York, having quite a difficult time, but she did have this amazing grown-up warmth, which I didn't have, and she was much younger than me."

"I was stunned when I saw her," remembers Tessa, "this cheeky 14-year-old with bright orange hair and a real style of her own. She was a bit younger than us, and we all just took a real shine to her."

Chapter 15

"I improvised, crazed by the music. Even my teeth and eyes burned with fever. Each time I leaped I seemed to touch the sky and when I regained earth it seemed to be mine alone." – Josephine Baker

The Simply What's Happening tour ripped through the UK during September 1979, enthralling and bemusing as it went. Most audience-members would come out of those gigs exhilarated, but many old-school punk fans didn't know what to make of an avant-garde jazz artist like Don Cherry, mesmerically strumming an African stringed instrument, or Prince Hammer, who would hurtle on, beaming manically, waving a Sten gun and bellowing in "a voice that attacks the back of your knees", as one reviewer put it.

At best, these fans were confused, at worst, racism would rear up. Despite the fact that punk was supposed to break down prejudices and give people the confidence to be themselves, enough people had jumped on the initial bandwagon simply to shock or be aggressive. Being open-minded was all very well when it came to doing what *they* wanted to do, but when it came to accepting new sounds and different people, other rules seemed to apply.

"We got into a couple of fights in Newcastle," remembers Adrian Sherwood. "It was rough in those days, a lot of racism. There'd be pitched battles between football fans outside the chip shop with glass everywhere, it was mental.

"In Newcastle and places like that at the time, we were racially abused, not me personally, being white, but my mates were racially abused, assaulted, and Prince Hammer went in there and sorted out about four people on his own.

"He was a very strong warrior type. He didn't beat anyone up, but he terrorised everybody, he didn't want any trouble, but he fronted out when he heard that Don had been insulted. So he went down to the bar on his own. There were about 30 people and no one would have a go at him. That's how menacing he was. Very powerful Jamaican man, still is. He was the leader of a huge gang in Jamaica and he's a very serious character. And he fronted out all these racist wankers in a bar in Newcastle. That's one of my memories."

The spitting was still a problem. While it was a sign of quasi-acceptance from the punk fans' perspective, it never got any less repulsive from The Slits' point of view. And Prince Hammer and Don Cherry literally didn't know what had hit them. "They would just shower Don Cherry in spit," says Adrian. "On one occasion, after about 30 seconds he just left the stage, it was completely inappropriate."

Viv adds, "The further north you went the more you got spat at, and the more gloopy and phlegmy it was. It was colder as you went up north and they all had consumption or whatever! But generally the people were warm, intense and alive, you had lots of Hell's Angels who seemed very scary but were actually very protective. There's a hardness that can be seen as scary but actually isn't; it was good for me. I won't judge a person by how hard they look particularly. And touring … [takes you] straight in to certain sections of society you don't get to see if you just visit a city. You get taken to the underbelly and it's a bit more interesting."

The Slits certainly saw it all thanks to their travels to some of the odder areas of Britain. One night spent in a hotel in Portsmouth was particularly disturbing. "This little boy was exposing himself in the hallway," says Viv. "We'd pass him every time we had to leave our room to go to the loo. He was only about nine or 10. He'd just stand there all night with his big thing out. It was freakier than any of those heavy guys in Scotland. I wonder now whether it was because it was a port, and sailors may have stayed there, you know, he might have been abused.

"Paul Rutherford was with us at the time, and he was more freaked out than we were! When I passed this little kid, I said, 'Oh, very nice,' sarcastically, and then a while later a note came under the door: 'I think you're very nice too.' Spooky."

The Slits were trying hard to bring together the music they loved and demonstrate how the styles linked together, and how it was possible to be open to all kinds of music. Fortunately, because they had chosen such potent characters in Don and Prince Hammer, the audiences could often be won over, or at least be provoked into thinking about what they were seeing and hearing. Don wasn't just a jazz artist, he was experimenting with 'world' elements, introducing ethnic influences directly into his music, and Bruce Smith insists the trumpeter should be credited for creating the term 'world music'.

Bruce remembers, "This cultural challenge was so adventurous for The Slits to put together. They were kind of frictional gigs! There were members of the audiences who were like, 'Fuck this, we're just here to scream and see The Slits.' [It was] extremely brave on their part to put that on. Those audiences were out for blood.

"Don was knocked out by The Slits. He probably wasn't expecting some of those audiences, but I'm sure he saw it as an amazing opportunity to play his music in a very different context. He was really a magical person, and absolutely one of the greatest musicians ever. From our point of view, every night something extraordinary happened, because this combination of these three different bands and what was going on was highly unusual, I can't really think of anyone doing that before. So it was frictional and magical!"

Tessa got on with Don particularly well. "I had so much respect for Don Cherry," she says. "I really romanticised about the Fifties, I love the jazz period; I think you often romanticise about the decade before you. That's why a lot of people of my daughter's age love punk."

Dick O'Dell may have jocularly described that month on the road as a "magical mystery coach trip to Blackpool" sort of affair, but with so many bright, strong people brought together in such a confined space, there was bound to be some tension. Tessa and Don Cherry clicked immediately, Neneh and Ari almost became like one person, but Viv got off to a bad start with Don, and ended up feeling isolated for the rest of the tour.

"It was so exciting when we were cooking up the idea for this tour with Christine and Dick in the office in Victoria," says Viv. "We couldn't wait. Then on the first day, we all got together and we were sitting on this great big coach that we'd hired. For some reason the subject of junkies or heroin addicts came up, and I said, 'Oh, I hate junkies.' Don Cherry looked at me very coolly and said, 'I hate hate.' I was crushed, as I was meant to be, I think. It was such a cutting thing to say.

"I had my reasons for saying what I said, I'd had unpleasant dealings with junkies from being very young, but he must have thought I was a silly girl just saying the first thing that came into my head. Of course I had no idea that *he* was a junkie.

"So all I knew was that this guy, who I had massive respect for, had taken something that I hadn't said lightly, looked me in the eye and cut me down, basically. I couldn't really talk to him again after that, I was really hurt, I felt foolish. That was a bad start for me, and it made me self-conscious, foolishly probably, but it knocked my confidence. I didn't feel confident to talk to him much, and I don't remember talking to Prince Hammer much either! Touring is difficult, there are all these things going on with people, you have to almost set up your own little camp."

Dick was busy trying to keep everything under control once the groups got into the hotels. Unlike the White Riot tour, this time around it wasn't The Slits who were attracting attention from the staff. "Prince Hammer would get absolutely blasted," remembers Dick. "I'd sometimes get a call from the hotel people, and they'd go, 'Mr O'Dell, I think you need to open the windows in room x', and I'd go down there and he'd be all over the place!

"Prince Hammer couldn't believe he was doing a tour with this mad white Rastafarian girl, which is a fucking trip in itself. There's a whole other subtext there if you want to get into that. There was a lot of that. Rastafarians were really arsey about that, I thought their attitude to women was bullshit really, but then again you have to take into account

Chrissie Hynde, Debbie Harry, Viv Albertine, Siouxsie and, in front, Poly Styrene and Pauline Black, in a shot taken for the launch of the short-lived music magazine *NEW MUSICAL NEWS*, in 1981. This picture was taken for an article called 'Pop's Punk Princesses', although, according to Pauline, "We had very little in common other than all being women and musicians." (MICHAEL PUTLAND/RETNA LTD)

The Slits in Finland, sampling some questionably named sweets, 1980. (CHRISTINE ROBERTSON)

Ari on stage at Alexandra Palace with the Pop Group, 1981. (CHRISTINE ROBERTSON)

The Slits emerging from the sea at Malibu, California, during their American tour, 1981. This picture was intended to be the cover of their third album. (CHRISTINE ROBERTSON)

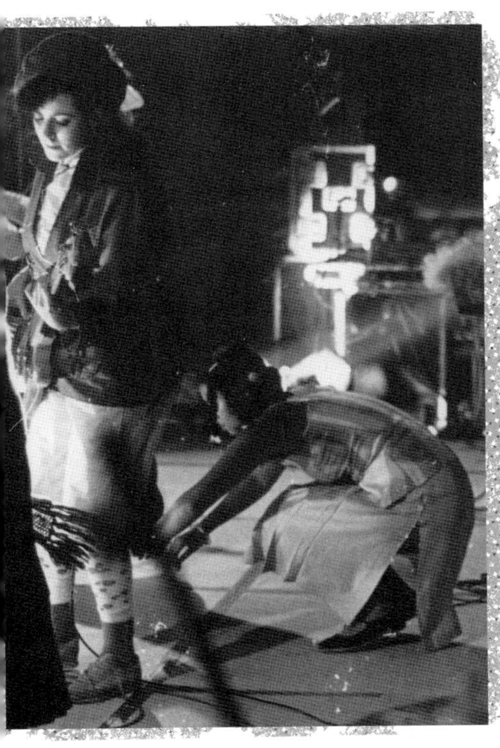

Tessa and Neneh on stage, 1981
(COURTESY OF VIV ALBERTINE)

Viv and Ari make friends with a Mexican kitchen assistant, Los Angeles, 1981.
(CHRISTINE ROBERTSON)

Neneh's wedding to Bruce Smith, 1983, with The Slits and journalist Vivien Goldman.

The Slits, Bruce and Neneh, 1981. (PENNIE SMITH)

Tessa, at '30 Years of Punk' at Selfridges, London, March 14, 2006.
(TARA BIRCH/RETNA CELEBS)

Tessa, author Zoë Street Howe and Viv at Mick Jones' Carbon Casino, Inn On The Green, Ladbroke Grove, January 2008.
(COURTESY OF ZOË STREET HOWE)

Viv, Don Letts and Tessa at the Carbon Casino, January 2008. (COURTESY OF ZOË STREET HOWE)

Dub producer and DJ Adrian Sherwood at his North London home, 2008.
(COURTESY OF ZOË STREET HOWE)

Former Slits and Banshees drummer Budgie, at the author's home, December 2008.
(COURTESY OF ZOË STREET HOWE)

Ari and Zoë, Denmark St, London, November 2008. (COURTESY OF ZOË STREET HOWE)

The main house at Ridge Farm, 2008. (COURTESY OF ZOË STREET HOWE)

The studio at Ridge Farm, 2008. (COURTESY OF ZOË STREET HOWE)

The Slits' 2008 reincarnation, in New York: Ari Up, keyboard player Hollie Cook (daughter of Sex Pistol Paul Cook), drummer Anna Schulte, Tessa, and guitarist No. (JANETTE BECKMAN/REDFERNS)

people's backgrounds, you can't just go, 'Oh, well you're a fuck.' But it was good fun. And Don Cherry, top fucking man."

To cheer things up a bit for Viv, her then boyfriend, Gareth Sager, joined them on tour. Gareth, like his Pop Group bandmate Bruce, was a huge Don Cherry fan, and he would eventually end up on stage with The Slits when their session keyboard player, Penny Tobin, let them down. The Slits had thrown everything they had at this tour, but it was starting to become complicated.

"Penny was quite a downer actually, not very interested," says Viv. "She was quite slick and a bit jazzy, not really right for us, but we just needed someone to fill out the sound. She agreed, rather offhandedly, to do it.

"Then she started having a thing with one of the guys in Don Cherry's band, and one night she just didn't turn up for the show. She was very cavalier about the whole thing anyway. She got bollocked obviously. It was quite fraught. So after that Gareth stepped in that night, and he was better, frankly, he's a multi-instrumentalist, so he could play a bit of trumpet, keyboards, bit of guitar.

"I also remember our roadie Dave, who looked totally like a roadie, coming onstage and playing extra guitar to the point that we got quite reliant on him adding to the sound; he played quite nicely, but he looked dreadful. Then he started feeling like he wanted to be paid more, which I suppose he should have been, then all the dynamics went funny. One minute he's on stage with us, the next he's humping our gear around, honestly it was such a mess. Why didn't we just get another person?"

The Slits would bound onstage in mismatched bits of school uniform, basketball shoes, rags in their hair and "blowing whistles and toy trumpets", one reviewer reported, "skipping, hopping, fooling around".

The Selecter's Fred Perry-clad singer Pauline Black made sure she saw The Slits when they made it to the Coventry Theatre. The group first caught her eye not during the first wave of punk, but just after the release of *Cut* itself during 1979, the year The Selecter and 2-Tone exploded, suited, booted and trilby-hatted, out of the Midlands. Pauline: "I've always thought hybrids of music, like The Slits' punky-reggae hybrid or The Selecter's punky-ska hybrid, was the way to go. Crossovers always breed something vital and interesting and free up public perceptions about gender and race.

"I only discovered The Slits on September 8, 1979 in an article in *NME* entitled 'Up Slit Creek'. I would've probably ignored it, except The Selecter's first interview appeared on the next page. A photo of three semi-naked women smearing themselves with mud caught my attention. The photo looked so joyous, innocent and natural that it just seemed like a celebration of womanhood rather than any cheap titillation that might garner a few more sales."

Watching The Slits on the concert stage proved every bit as wild and joyous. They transcended punk and personified its true spirit at the same time. "From the moment they came onstage it was like being invited to a Greek Bacchanal," continues Pauline. "Conventional formulas had been thrown out of the window, both musically and performance-wise. They sounded like they were doing exactly what they wanted to do, writing songs about what they wanted to sing about, and having a lot of fun in the process, and in the end, that's what punk was all about. They were the real deal, no punk posturing, like so many of the all-male bands. From then on I was a fan of the phenomenon that was 'The Slits'."

The group played songs from *Cut* and also new tracks, including 'In The Beginning There Was Rhythm' and 'Walk About', both of which ended up being extended jazz-tinged explorations, laced with African percussion. Bruce's drum part on 'Walk About' was just hi-hat and a wooden block, while Dick O'Dell mixed the sound.

Dick: "It was all just really great fun. I got to do the sound, and like any West London boy I was into my dub, which suited them. 'Grapevine' was very sexy, dubby, and live we worked out a whole section between them onstage and me dubbing it up. It really took off." Dick also recorded them live from the sound-desk, and, once he had taken some recordings from their forthcoming tour of America and added a handful of vintage Slits studio recordings, would release the result as an 'official' bootleg album called *Bootleg Retrospective* at Rough Trade through his own Y Records label the following year. Viv recalls, "Dick did a fabulous bootleg. We bootlegged ourselves and sold it on Portobello!"

Adrian Sherwood remembers becoming a true Slits convert while watching from the wings. "When you're on tour, you stay on the side of the stage and you're listening to the band. And I got more and more engrossed in their music.

"I never was a fan of the remake of 'Grapevine', I'll be honest with you, it didn't do a lot for me, I was stuck in my ways with the reggae. I'd been completely immersed from the age of about 20, and I'd done about 20-odd reggae albums. I was completely reggae, reggae, reggae, but 'New Town', from that day to this, that melody comes to me in my dreams! It's a fucking mighty, mighty track.

"And a lot of their other songs, I loved them because were just so charming. A lot of it was because of Ari's absolutely unique personality, combined with Viv's vicious guitar and Tessa's dubby b-lines and everything. Those are my memories, it was serious, serious."

The Slits were fortunate to have a new ally in their midst, Christine Robertson. Formerly an art student and promoter, Christine had begun working for Dick O'Dell in his office, and she would eventually take over the management of The Slits herself. "Dick was the official manager, but he was actually more into The Pop Group, and he was more interested in getting involved in production," says Christine. "I liked being involved with The Slits and I loved the music.

"After *Cut*, I really knew they were very important. I just thought they were doing something that hadn't been done and I identified with it as a woman in this new world of possibilities that was emerging. I became really involved. But they did this tour, which was not artistically disastrous but it was financially disastrous..."

Christine had been brought up to be sensible with money, creative but pragmatic. She had always made sure she was on top of her finances, and quickly realised that her grasp of economics would be an asset in her new employment.

"*Cut* came out in September, the summer had been spent planning the campaign and the tour, and in typical Slits style, well, their grasp on reality, like a lot of artists', was a little bit slippery. Island had thrown quite a lot of money at them, I understand. Not that it all reached The Slits but there was tour support, Prince Hammer had to be brought over from Jamaica with his entourage – which was huge – and it was really Prince Hammer that broke that tour; he swallowed up the essential tour support.

"There were hotel bills of nearly £2,000 per night, just when we were touring, and air travel was not cheap in the Seventies – to fly from Jamaica was a lot of money, not even comparable to today. Air travel was still for the rich in those days.

"They played venues that were too big, so they were playing in the main to half-empty halls. London was OK, the Rainbow, that was full, there were about 2,000 in there. But generally the halls were so big we weren't making [a profit] on the door. They did go bankrupt but luckily it didn't mean too much to them at the time, it just meant they were barred from being company directors for five years. It didn't really have any impact later on."

The London show, at Finsbury Park's Rainbow Theatre – since converted into a church – was stressful for Creation Rebel for different reasons. Their drummer, Style Scott, went down with acute appendicitis in the night and was rushed to hospital. "We ended up doing the gig with the guitarist playing the drums," remembers Adrian. "So no guitarist, on the one show that would have given us a bit of exposure; the real benefit in those days was the key London show that everybody came to."

Nevertheless, The Slits achieved creatively what they had set out to do, and by sharing the tour with such inspiring acts, their imaginations had been stoked and they were already writing prolifically for the next album, with new ideas taking shape and extra dimensions being added. Other groups might have been more immediately accessible, but The Slits were still not about to start compromising.

Adrian adds, "At the time they were competing with Siouxsie Sioux. We'd play Manchester and the Banshees would have four times as many people at their gigs across town. But I tell you what, you play a Banshees record from that period, it doesn't stand up. Not slagging Siouxsie Sioux, respect to Budgie and all that, but The Slits' stuff shines out like a beacon."

While The Slits' UK tour was coming to a close, The Clash had been taking on America, the country The Slits would be expected to tour in the not-too-far distant future. It would be their first trip to the States as a group – and in Christine's case the first time she had ever been on a plane – but this was several months away, and after the concentrated excitement of September, The Slits fell down to earth with a bump when they returned to London at the end of the Simply What's Happening tour. They wouldn't be the first musicians to feel that way at the end of an exhilarating tour, as if life had suddenly stopped and nothing was happening. But they couldn't have been more wrong.

Ari settled in to a squat in Battersea with Adrian Sherwood and Neneh Cherry while Viv and Tessa moved to a flat in Victoria near Dick's office. Gareth Sager, still Viv's boyfriend at this stage, was a near-constant presence.

Tessa was a "slow-moving, graceful personality", in Dick's words. She kept her own counsel and as a result it was difficult for those around her to tell if something was amiss. Her experimentation with heroin was also something that passed others by, as it fitted with her personality – dreamy, calm and introspective. The fact that Tessa could fall asleep outside airports while jumbo jets roared overhead just struck Dick as a handy skill to have on tour. It never occurred to him that it might have its roots in something darker.

"Tessa was like a narcoleptic," says Dick. "She could go to sleep anywhere. There was this one fucking amazing time when we were on tour in America and we flew into LAX, and they went off to get the flight cards and Tess fell asleep on a bench with planes taking off over her head and those tannoys bellowing 'You cannot park here' really fucking loud. She could fall asleep anywhere at any time. But it's quite a useful thing when you're on the road.

"However, I've never been that great at spotting when people are out of it, and I was never quite sure with Tessa... I remember I took heroin once and it made me sick. So I was like, 'Well, this is crap!' But I get it, it's a dreamlike state, I was just never about that."

After the tour with Don Cherry and Prince Hammer, Tessa began to feel disconnected and disappointed, and a "dreamlike state" was at least something she could privately retreat into. But she had been taking the barbiturate Tuinal daily, and it was having a soporific, lowering effect. "I was feeling a disappointment in life," remembers Tessa. "I was at a tender age and was trying to fathom things out, but I think when you're in your twenties you're still a child really."

While living together, Viv became used to seeing Tessa snoozing the afternoon away on the sofa while she and Gareth got on with the day, but one occasion was different. "I didn't think anything was particularly wrong," says Viv. "She's kind of a low-energy person anyway, Tess. She'd mooch about, a bit Eeyore-ish. Not a pessimist though.

"Me and Gareth came in and Tessa was asleep on the sofa. It got to half eight, nine, and she still wasn't awake. I put some music on really loud to try to wake her up, then I started dancing around the room and she still didn't wake up. I was like, 'Bloody hell, Tess!'

"Then I cranked it up to top volume and she still didn't wake up. I went over to look at her, and then of course I knew she was unconscious. I thought, 'My God, I've been farting about, eating, turning on the music, dissing her, and she's lying on the sofa unconscious. I knew it was drugs."

"I had basically taken about 22 Tuinal," explains Tessa. "It wasn't like, 'I really want to die,' it was more like, 'Whatever happens, happens.' Because I had been taking these Tuinal once a day, it was affecting me, it was making me a bit down. I can't say it was one specific thing that made me want to do it. I think it's connected with the whole heroin thing, that's like a slow suicide, but it's not so dramatic or violent."

Viv immediately rang the drugs helpline Release, whose advisor told her to get Tessa on her feet, walk her around the room, try to get her to drink some coffee. But when Viv and Gareth attempted to get Tessa up they realised it was impossible. She was out cold, and had been for several hours.

"We went to the hospital in South London," continues Viv. "They strapped her all up and everything, and I remember after that going there every single day to sit by the bed, Dick would go every day as well. She was just out. She looked very, very beautiful. Her skin was always great but it went a sort of translucent white, she looked like Snow White."

The outlook became so bleak that Tessa's mother even brought a priest in to read the last rites over her body. "They didn't know if she'd ever come back," says Viv. "It went on for what seemed like forever.

"They told us to talk to her as it would help bring her back, and she did eventually come round. She seemed very changed, very smiley and soft. She's sort of been like that ever since, almost a happier person really.

She was glad when she came round; I asked her, because some people don't want to be brought round of course."

Tessa: "I obviously felt bad afterwards, to do that to your mother ... my father had died of course, so I don't know if that had an effect. But I put it down as a life experience and I was lucky to pull through. Obviously my work wasn't finished on Earth, I was kicked back down! I did feel ashamed afterwards. I think that's natural, but I was really thankful to the doctors and everyone that I got through.

"It definitely changes you for the better. I always felt like a misfit or an outsider and I felt I couldn't connect to the world. I still feel like that now, but I've accepted that's the way I am, and I'm happy with it."

After this traumatic experience, Dick was understandably reluctant to involve The Slits too heavily in another big issue that was hanging over them. All was not well as far as Island Records was concerned. There are various versions of what happened between the label and the group, but the official line at the time was that there was a dispute over money.

While Dick thrashed things out with Island, and ultimately prepared to take them to court, Ari and Adrian were cooking up some ideas for another cover version for The Slits to get their teeth into. Their cover of 'I Heard It Through The Grapevine' had attracted a positive response, and while they had been writing plenty of their own material since *Cut*, they knew they wanted to work their magic on another classic song.

All of The Slits loved the John Holt song 'Man Next Door', which was a particular favourite of Tessa's. Adrian recalls, "Ari was getting more and more into reggae so I played her loads of my favourite tracks, Bob Andy, Junior Byles, Bim Sherman. We were in the flat and did 'Man Next Door' in one evening. Ari was playing bass – she's great with b-lines – because Tessa was in hospital at the time. We got this great drummer called Cecil, because Bruce wasn't around, and we cut it in about three hours."

There has been some confusion over who played bass on the Adrian Sherwood-produced 12-inch of 'Man Next Door', but while it has been a mystery to Tessa herself for some time, the reality is that she played on The Slits' second release of the track, through Rough Trade. She also designed the artwork for the original single, an eerie monochrome etching of a stooping man with wild hair, a tail and a hat, looking over his shoulder with a compelling leer. It was the kind of illustration that would give The League of Gentlemen something to think about.

The first recording of 'Man Next Door' took place during the period while Tessa was recovering, and it was some time before she was ready to record again because, despite her return to consciousness, her thumb and two fingers were still asleep, and showed no signs of moving.

"I didn't know if I'd be able to play again," remembers Tessa. "My thumb and two fingers were all pins and needles and I thought, 'Oh my God, have I lost the use of my bass-playing hand?'

"It's been said on the internet, 'Tessa's not playing on that track,' and I thought, 'What are you talking about?' But when I heard it I thought, 'That's not my playing.' It's definitely me on the second release, with Bruce Smith. Ari has always told me it is my playing on the first release, but maybe people were just covering so I didn't get upset!

"But that's why I wasn't on it, because I'd lost the feeling in my bass-playing fingers! And thank God I got full feeling back."

The Adrian Sherwood-produced version was mastered by the acclaimed engineer George 'Porky' Peckham and released eight months later. But it had already become a classic Slits tune thanks to their live interpretation of the song – the thick, padding bass line thudding moodily against rolling, echoing, fill-heavy drumming, twisted spaghetti-western inspired guitar, backing vocals straight out of *The Good, The Bad And The Ugly* and Ari's emotive wails and Apache-style hollers and whoops. But this single would not be released on Island, because by the end of the year the band were no longer on its roster.

Melody Maker announced in November: "The Slits and their manager Dick O'Dell were preparing to take Island to court over alleged breach of contract but both sides feel the dispute will be settled this week... Island business manager Tim Clark said the argument was about two amounts of money – one for the album, which has sold 20,000 copies in the UK, and the second as a contractual advance.

"He said that Island had been very generous when the band had 'wildly exceeded' their recording budget, but The Slits and O'Dell were claiming that about £7,000 was owed to the band in the last four months. Island's option on The Slits is up for reconsideration shortly and O'Dell said it was inevitable that Island and The Slits will part company."

There were other reasons the group felt their time with Island was up: "I think they were more interested in putting their energy into other bands and we felt a bit let down," says Tessa. "We didn't have their full support, which we thought we would have when we first joined."

Dick adds, "I think they thought The Slits were a bit too much of a handful anyway. Now I don't think that would be the case. There are plenty of women now who are strong and intent on doing things their way, but The Slits really played a key role in making that happen for other women, big time."

Adrian Sherwood has his own theory on why they had to part ways, and it's simple, sad but very likely – The Slits were no longer marketable in Island's eyes, and this goes back to the thorny issue of artistic control, because what Island saw as marketable for them was not in sync with the way they wanted to be perceived. The phrase 'to thine own self be true' was more appropriate to The Slits than 'integrity never paid the bills'. Adrian: "If you sell lots of records, the record company will always put up with you. No matter how awkward you are, or however much of a shithead you are. But The Slits didn't play the game how Island wanted it.

"*Cut* is revolutionary in the area it's going, they had a reggae engineer who understood their sensibilities, which was a genius move. But the record company would probably have loved it more if they'd gone in and made a record that sounded like everything else.

"Going back to Siouxsie Sioux, bless her or whatever, no disrespect. She was five, six times more massive than The Slits. She wanted to be a success, [and she] played the game. The Slits refused to play the game. I respect Siouxsie a lot, but The Slits were the real deal, end of story."

Christine Robertson agrees. While importance and integrity didn't necessarily equate to mainstream acceptance, no one could deny the difference between The Slits and more immediately accessible groups like their old pals The Clash. "The media ban on The Slits didn't help things," explains Christine. "It was too dangerous. Because of their reputation on stage, they never got invited on things live. Ari would have done something mad.

"But put The Clash and The Slits side by side and say which was the more important band – it would have to be The Slits. But The Clash were a rock band – they can buy huge houses on what they earned, The Slits can't buy a pair of shoes. It isn't down to the quality of the music, it's down to the acceptability of the music.

"It became very obvious very soon after *Cut* was released. I mean, I thought it was great, Dick thought it was great, The Slits thought it was great, everybody in the business thought it was great, and people bought it but not in huge amounts like they would The Clash. And they never conquered America. You can imagine what the Americans thought of The Slits..."

The Slits were about to find out what America thought of them, and while they might never have become a mainstream hit like The Clash, their journey across the pond would alter their musical direction, exposing them to influences that would yet again spark their imaginations and ultimately add to their sound, with hip-hop and funk the most obvious injections into their enduringly dub-infused output.

Going to America for The Slits meant experiencing the differences and similarities of New York culture, winding up DJs at university-town radio stations, absorbing the music of the streets and the silence of the desert, and making a pilgrimage to Philadelphia to see Sun Ra, the jazz musician and composer who believed he was from Saturn. People might have treated The Slits like they were from outer space, but here was one musician who could say that he, in his own mind at least, actually was.

Chapter 16

"It was brilliant. I'd never seen a stuffed pizza before. I was very naïve." – Steve Beresford joins The Slits for their tour of America.

By the time The Slits were heading to the US, Dick had stepped down from his managerial role and had handed over to Christine. Of all the managers who'd chanced their arm taking on The Slits, Christine would turn out to be the most successful in forming an advantageous band-manager relationship. Dick continued to tour with them and mix the sound but, as Christine observed, it took a woman to manage The Slits.

Christine: "I took care of the business side, and I also did set design and lighting, but the management was my priority, and that was quite creative too. I wasn't afraid of it at all."

It was a time for looking ahead, and not least because a new decade was around the corner. Like many musicians, the members of The Slits remained largely unperturbed and unaffected by what was happening in the outside world, and simply continued to get on with what they were doing. Everyone hated Thatcher but their music was more important than worrying about what they *didn't* like. Their contemporaries, however, were feeling dubious about the Eighties. Siouxsie Sioux shared her predictions with *Melody Maker*: "There'll be mass hysteria. The news has been getting so heavy of late. People are starting to panic, getting more suspicious of what Thatcher is doing.

"There'll be more gadgets to save time, silicon is coming into the home. I heard someone say there'll be no such thing as burnt toast. That says a lot for everything."

John Peel's producer, John Walters, shared the sense of dread, but more from a musical point of view: "One just hopes it won't be a hippy revival. What I really want is for all the young people of good intent to make the supreme effort to try to free rock once and for all from the clutches of people who can play. The more musos came in the door, the more jazz, for one, went out the door, and all that lot are writing suites on commission now."

The Slits might well have been more in tune with John Walters' concerns for the new decade, but they weren't taking sides at this stage as they were far too busy getting ready to tour the States for the first time during the closing weeks of 1979. The Slits were particularly looking forward to their New Year's Eve slot at the New York club Hurrah's, with the surreal Canadian multi-instrumentalist Nash the Slash in support. Nash the Slash would appear onstage wearing a tuxedo, top hat, sunglasses and Invisible Man-style bandages covering his face.

The Slits were also set to play opposite the 'Africa Must Be Free By 1983' singer Hugh Mundell, avant-garde saxophonist John Zorn and experimental singer Shelley Hirsch. But more exciting than any of this, as far as The Slits were concerned, was simply discovering America for the first time, its landscapes, people and atmospheres. Not to mention the fact you could buy a book and a coffee at 3am in New York, if you were so inclined. It made Seventies London feel very colourless in comparison.

"That tour in America was amazing," says Dick. "We went round San Francisco, we did Berkeley, Santa Cruz, New York, Chicago. It was a really great tour. And they were absolutely on top of their game."

Viv agrees. "Touring America was fantastic. I loved the country so much, I was knocked out by the landscape of America, the towns, the cities, I just loved everything about it, and don't forget in those days you hadn't seen it on TV in the same way, so it was completely new. We did a radio interview in every town we did, and we got wilder and wilder as we went round."

The American audiences were curious about The Slits, and while the New York crowd reflected that of London to a certain extent, in other towns people would turn up just to see what would happen. They quickly realised they didn't have another Runaways on their hands.

"I enjoyed every night, it was great," says Bruce, a native New Yorker. "A lot of people were interested to see them. You never really knew quite what was going to happen, it wasn't rock 'n' roll. And yet the association was still that The Slits were the original all-girl punk band, that was the history. What that meant in the US was a reinterpretation of three-chord rock 'n' roll, it wasn't anything more progressive than that. But the more interesting music came after."

Part of what made The Slits' tours of America so magical would be the musical input of Steve Beresford. Steve was the first choice to replace Gareth Sager's contributions to the live Slits sound, extending the injection of keyboards, hand percussion and sound effects that had featured on *Cut*.

Dennis Bovell: "The main keyboard parts on *Cut* were either done by me or Ari, but she was too busy leaping around, as Ari does, to play them live on stage. So Steve was brought in for the live stuff, then following that he became part of the band."

"Steve is a great musician," adds Bruce. "He had all these noise-making things around on a table. We, The Pop Group and The Slits, were listening a lot to music from people like Don Cherry and Sun Ra that had those improvisational qualities, and I think we collectively found that pretty exciting, certainly more exciting than trite pop songs. Steve brought this whole other element."

In addition to the times they had bumped into each other over the years, The Slits and Beresford's paths had also crossed indirectly via dub hero Prince Far I when he recorded with Adrian Sherwood. Prince Far I (originally known fondly as King Cry Cry, as a result of his tendency to burst into tears if something made him cross) ran the UK branch of his Jamaican label, Cry Tuff, through HitRun. In 1979, the Prince came to London to create *Cry Tuff Dub Encounter Volume III*, which would include Beresford and the experimental musician (and fellow Flying Lizard) David Toop on effects, whistles and noises, with Ari Up, Viv Goldman and the reggae singer Elizabeth Archer on backing vocals.

Steve Beresford: "We got asked by Adrian to play on this Prince Far I session, and we loved dub music, and listened to Jamaican music a lot. We went to a studio in Berry Street in Clerkenwell, and we ran dub tracks, just had a pile of things and played them over the top. It was brilliant.

"The only problem was that no one could understand a word Prince Far I was saying because he spoke in incredibly thick patois with a very, very deep voice. He really did talk like that all the time."

Beresford would throw things at the piano strings, shake and hit little objects he'd picked up, tinkle away on toy pianos and play a range of brass instruments. This made him just right for The Slits, and he was inspired by how they, and The Pop Group, broke through a lot of punk conventions, because by now, punk had itself become a convention in many ways, lacking in imagination and creativity.

Steve: "I had always thought the rhythms were very weak in punk music. It always did the same thing. I grew up with Motown, Stax, James Brown, that music was rhythmically very interesting and creative. I just couldn't understand why in punk the drummer would always play the same beat in every tune. But Bruce Smith is a very different drummer, very spontaneous, very light. I always thought of Bruce as having more of a jazz touch.

"I was replacing Gareth on keyboards and things, and he played lots of racket all the way through. But when I did it, I felt that when we played 'Grapevine', I'd quite like to play the chord sequence on the piano. I liked having different roles throughout the tunes. Sometimes I would make horrible noises and sometimes I'd make quite conventional noises. We'd do dub versions with elements of free improvisation, and really I could do anything with them.

"It was great playing live with them, although at the time, I sometimes thought it was not so great. Ari would keep coming up to me, shouting, 'Improvise! Improvise!' and I kept saying, 'Well, I *am* improvising!' There was a lot of running around and being a bit bossy on stage. But it was a nice group feel, and we could take tunes where we wanted them to go at that particular point.

"Sometimes Tessa would drop a beat, but we loved that, we'd just lock in with Tessa. She's got fantastic time, but some of the best people do that – the drummer Terry Day used to turn the beat around all the time.

People hear rhythm in different ways, I liked that, it was just another form of deconstructing the music."

Touring in America would expose The Slits to sights and experiences they would never forget, but it was more intense than before, and the group had to toughen up more than ever in order to protect themselves from undesirables who would sometimes home in on them.

On one occasion, The Slits spent a night in Death Valley. The now distinguished Dutch photographer Anton Corbijn had hooked up with them in California for a photo shoot and, after The Slits offered to pay for him to travel with them, took some truly haunting pictures of the group amid the lunar desert surroundings. However, it was also less than comfortable because a rather strange promoter was hovering about making Viv, in particular, feel uncomfortable.

"He was this Vietnam vet who was very weird," begins Viv. "He'd become a promoter in San Francisco, and I always remember that when he laughed, the pain in his face ... you don't often see that, but there was agony in his face, it doesn't go together, it was terrible to see. He'd been obviously so disturbed by what he'd done and seen.

"So he was promoting us in California. We went out to Death Valley, where those Anton Corbijn pictures were taken. We camped out overnight, and this Vietnam vet showed us how to survive in the desert, but he kept watching me all the time, even when I went to have a pee behind a bush, it was awful. I just got really pissed off with him in the end and we fell out over that!

"We're just young girls on tour, and it's not only nice people who come into your orbit, you get real weirdos, people who want to use you, have sex with you, you're constantly vetting people and putting barriers up all the time, and you don't always get it right."

This might explain the slightly guarded vulnerability in one of the now legendary black-and-white images Corbijn took of the group – four Slits huddled together despite the enormity of the space around them; Ari looking like a watchful Navajo, locks bound up and a headband tied across her forehead; Viv looking similarly serious, clutching a small parasol and wearing one of her trademark little girl dresses with socks tied in her hair; Bruce standing close to the others, facing resolutely inwards; and Tessa, by contrast, showing a hint of a smile, arms folded, eyes gazing confidently down the lens. Corbijn would pay homage to that set of moody shots with the iconic pictures he took of U2 for *The Joshua Tree* album in 1986, also in Death Valley.

The Slits' night in the desert was a magical affair, sleeping under the stars, coming to terms with the sheer space, silence and emptiness. Tessa fell in love with it straight away, and Anton's images of the group remain her all-time favourites. "I love the desert in America, and it's such a perfect background for pictures. Anton had this genius eye. He had such humour too, which is such a big thing for The Slits. He was really fun, a very easy person to be around."

Christine was similarly inspired by the alien beauty of the desert, and, armed with a borrowed camera, she started taking movie footage of The Slits at this point of the journey. She had wanted to film more of the group onstage too, but her managerial duties took over. However, her snatched moments of Ari, Tessa and Viv playing around amid the cacti – a riot of colour against the sun-bleached backdrop – or on Malibu beach, jumping over waves, wading in silhouette hand in hand in the sea, are funny, poignant and beautiful. "The desert was where I started filming them," says Christine. "Anton was taking stills and I was taking Super 8 – badly!

"I was always busy when they were playing. It was very rare for me to pick up a camera. But when it all ended I wanted to do an MA, so I thought I'd try to get funding on the back of a piece of work. I took what I'd got, film of them basically, and made a soundtrack, sampling off the radio, snatches of their music, and a really fast edit montage of them.

"The problem with the film was that it had nudity in it. If you're on a beautiful private beach, well, you're going to get your kit off, aren't you? It was never publicly shown until it was included in the punk season at the NFT in 2004 (titled 'Typical Girls'). It captures something of that time, it was emotional."

Back in San Francisco, the group made sure they had plenty of time to explore and meet people. Among their fondest memories is the time they hung out with some reggae musicians who were rehearsing, not least because this occasion felt like a quiet triumph for Steve Beresford, who felt he had to stifle the more technical side of his musical knowledge lest he be teased for being terribly fusty and academic. Even admitting to recognising a note was enough to attract unwanted attention.

Steve: "Ari did have classical piano lessons, although they always tried to pretend they didn't know what a C sharp was. They did really. There was this actual ban about mentioning chords. Oh yes, I was constantly derided as an incredibly academic person because I knew what a C sharp was. But I think Ari always knew what a C sharp was.

"But then we went to see this very old-school reggae band rehearse and they were talking about C sharps. I think everybody just assumed that reggae musicians just knew how the tune went without talking about it. So they suddenly went, 'Oh, they say things like you say, Steve!' Then it was all right to say E major etc, and nobody would say, 'Oh, you're being hideously academic!'"

The Slits felt there was one person on board the tour bus who definitely did need an education, but not necessarily in the musical sense – and that was Dick. They reckoned that if he was going to stick around he'd better get clued up in the mysterious ways and workings of women. Dick was in his late twenties, older than them, but The Slits still wanted to make sure he was going about things in the right way. If they could only change one man's approach then it was still going some way to benefiting womankind. A biology lesson was called for.

"They bought me this book in San Francisco called *Our Bodies, Ourselves,* which is, like, a woman's book," chuckles Dick. "Everything. Every single thing – it was an education. 'We think you need this book,' they said. It was really sweet, I didn't take offence at all.

"The other thing was periods. They all used to have their periods at the same time, you'd become trained to watch out for it. When you're on the road, that was that, and I'd fucking know about it big-style. Narky, seriously narky. But it's magical, proper sort of paganish, the moon and all that, I love it."

Another issue with touring was finding the right kind of food. Every day it was Viv and Steve's mission to find a good vegetarian restaurant in the town they were in. It got them out of bed at a reasonable time, apart from anything else, and provided a healthy focus. "They were all into that," says Christine. "There was never booze on tour, might have been a bit of weed around. There was other stuff that involved certain members but I wasn't aware of it. Basically they were clean-living. When I started with them I possibly had a bit of a drink problem but I stopped when I was with them, and I still don't drink to this day. They were always sober on stage with the exception of one member, and Bruce liked his beer..."

The fact that The Slits looked after themselves was quite unusual at the time, especially for touring musicians who traditionally let their hair down, particularly after shows. Viv and Ari were drug-free, and Viv also shunned cigarettes as a result of her asthma. It made sense to eat healthily and steel themselves to the often exhausting life on the road. "That was quite a progressive thing to do in that time," says Keith Levene. "It was almost rebellious in the arena we were in. It was a mistake that it was rebellious, but that's what it was like.

"A lot of people were getting fucked up. I'm speaking for myself too – and I can speak for a lot of other people because half of them ain't here, and half of the other half might as well not be here, and I don't know what happened to the other half of the other half of that half ..."

Philadelphia – home of the 'cheesesteak', no doubt left unsampled by The Slits – was a city the group were excited to visit. Steve wanted to go to the Museum of Modern Art to see the Marcel Duchamp exhibition, and The Slits were determined to meet one of the region's most unusual residents, Sun Ra, known to his mother as Herman Poole Blount. Sun Ra was a musician who presented himself as a sun god from the 'Angel Race'. He wasn't actually from Philadelphia. He apparently wasn't even from Alabama, where he was born. He was, in his opinion, from Saturn.

The Slits adored Sun Ra's jazz compositions and the power of his Arkestra ensemble. His style would range from big band to electronica, afro-jazz to ambient 'space' music. He had apparently had a vision as a student in the Thirties that changed his life forever. It was akin to a religious experience – he claimed to have been surrounded by white light, and, as far as Blount was concerned, he was being teleported to Saturn where he was about to receive some career advice from aliens. He said of the experience: "They had one little antenna on each ear. A little antenna over each eye. They talked to me. They told me to stop [attending college] because there was going to be great trouble in schools. The world was going into complete chaos... I would speak [through music], and the world would listen."

After living in Chicago and New York, Sun Ra and the Arkestra settled in Morton Street in the Germantown district of Philadelphia in the late Sixties, and while they were sometimes reprimanded by their Philly neighbours for making too much noise, their apparently drug-free lifestyle and general warmth meant they were popular, if unusual, residents. Saxophonist Danny Thompson even started up a convenience store in the neighbourhood – the Pharaoah's Den.

From 1979, Sun Ra and the Arkestra had become the house band at New York's Squat Theatre, trundling up together on the train from Germantown, rehearsing all day, and playing at night. Which meant they unfortunately weren't in when The Slits came to call (although Tessa wonders whether they weren't just hiding).

Steve remembers, "We looked him up in the phone book, and there he was – Ra, Sun. So we said, 'Let's ring him up,' but they said, 'No! We're going to drive to Sun Ra's house, and we know he's going to be there because... well, we just know.' So we didn't ring him up and we drove to his house and of course he wasn't there.

"The lady next door was very nice and said, 'Yeah, I'm sorry they're all out, they've got a gig.' And we drove through some really interesting areas of Philadelphia, saw all the wooden houses, I remember that. And then I got a cab especially to see the Marcel Duchamps in the Museum of Modern Art, but when I got there they were all away in Paris. So we didn't meet Sun Ra or see the Marcel Duchamps."

Bruce Smith recalls New York being his favourite date on the tour. On top of everything else, it was where new music was springing up, scenes were merging and spawning new sounds and The Slits would be exposed to hip-hop for the first time. "We were the headlining act at Hurrah's and then we'd go to parties downtown. There was an amazing synthesis between the new-wave music crowd, hip-hop and the art scene, which is something that doesn't happen so much now. People are far more like, 'I'm involved in this...'; there isn't that kind of mix-up, which is a shame.

"But back then, you'd have events in which all of those things would be involved. You'd have hip-hop acts like the Soul Sonic Force on the same bill at Danceteria as a new wave band. It was more about new wave than punk rock by that time."

Blondie's 1981 hit 'Rapture' might have been the first mainstream single featuring rap, but hip-hop had been thriving beneath the surface in New York City since the mid-Seventies, with Grandmaster Flash, Afrika Bambaataa and DJ Kool Herc at the helm. After hanging out in New York watching black and Hispanic DJs on street corners, The Slits started to experiment with the genre during 1980. Neneh Cherry, who accompanied them on both of their US tours, was already into hip-hop and funk, but The Slits were making the most of their own chance to hear it and process it first-hand, and these urban influences would be displayed on their final Peel Session. Hip-hop had strong connections to punk in ethos and attitude, and The Slits embraced it with typical all-encompassing gusto. And it wasn't just the music, it was the whole culture that fascinated them, and they had an instant in with some key figures on the scene thanks to Don Letts and Neneh.

"I remember certain graffiti artists like Fab Five Freddy and Futura 2000," says Tessa. "They were friends of Don's. There was a lot of break-dancing, I was fascinated to see that, and the double-dutch skipping, girls with two skipping ropes doing all these different jumps. Break-dancing and that went together, it probably started in the schoolyard and then became hip.

"We'd also get into the music through radio stations like WBLS. Ari used to make cassettes of the radio, and still does to this day, because the radio in New York and America is so good. It was just the most interesting music of that time after punk. In England, the music was going squeaky clean. I lost interest. America was more interesting to me then."

"The Slits were very brave," adds Adrian Sherwood. "They weren't just going for money, they had aspirations to get involved in what was healthy from around the world at the time. The Slits were trying even then to take what was wonderful music – reggae, jazz, hip-hop – and do something with it. Ari was and still is very on the edge of what's new in Jamaica and New York."

Ari, who now has homes in Brooklyn and Jamaica, remembers seeing the connection between punk, reggae and hip-hop straight away, although she feels it has taken a while for the hip-hop scene to recognise its intrinsic link with old school punk.

"It was a trilogy – birth of reggae, birth of punk, birth of hip-hop, Jamaica, London and New York," she explains. "You can see how punk people mixed with reggae and hip-hop from an early time. The Clash got really into the New York thing, rapping, Blondie got into it early, there's a strong connection.

"Just now, it's funny, they're just catching up with it. The hip-hop people are getting interested in punk origins, and because of that, they're getting into punk instead of what they considered rock – it was always just corny heavy metal stuff, that's all they could relate to from the rock scene. But they're realising the real shit is really from our time.

"I went into a hip-hop store recently in Brooklyn, and I saw a top that said: 'Punk is the real thing'. It was a T-shirt with layers so it looked very punk. Hip-hop culture is paying its dues to punk."

Chapter 17

"Everything is going to the beat – it's the beat generation, it be-at, it's the beat to keep, it's the beat of the heart, it's being beat and down in the world and like oldtime lowdown and like in the ancient civilisations, the slave boatmen rowing galleys to a beat and servants spinning pottery to a beat ..."
– Jack Kerouac

The Slits were back in England with fresh plans for the future. While their relationship with Island had come to an end, it did offer an opportunity to move forward and seek out something equally appropriate for them.

The Pop Group had also parted ways with their label, Radar, after discovering it had links with arms dealers. The two bands were like a family, and they still shared the same management and, of course, the same drummer. The Slits had had time to muse over their change in circumstances while on the road, and it made sense to go in with Dick O'Dell and The Pop Group and, punk-style, do it themselves.

O'Dell launched his independent label, Y, named after The Pop Group album of the same name, early in 1980 and The Slits would enjoy a brief but productive period of time on its roster.

"It was very natural for them to be with Y," says Dick. "There was Rough Trade, Mute records, it was a really exciting time for the independents. It was about having a sense of freedom and not always being under the record company's cosh.

"These days it's different. Labels will take on board innovation and creativity. But back then those early independents did help to create a situation where that could come about."

In March, Y Records released the famous Pop Group and Slits double A-side. The Slits displayed their new-found love of rap and funk in the bouncing, sparkling 'In The Beginning There Was Rhythm', against The Pop Group's tribal 'Where There's A Will', produced by Dennis Bovell and the engineer Arun Chakraverty. This release was a symbol of the two groups' unity, but also a celebration of their differences, a sonic echo of the joint Pop Group / *Slits Pictures* short films that had been produced the year before by Don Letts and Mick Calvert, displaying the dancey polyrhythmic playfulness of The Slits and the earnest quality and tangled, dissonant funk of The Pop Group. The Slits' 'In The Beginning' was described by *Melody Maker*'s Chris Bohn as "an awesome funk workout of mammoth length".

Dick remembers, "It was a really great period – the whole tribal theme, mixing up the genres. But they were very different bands, they both kept a very strong identity and they would never have allowed it to be any different, believe me."

There was a notable mystical element regarding the concept of rhythms and cycles coming into play for The Slits by now too. The idea of the rhythm of the earth, the human heart, sex and simply the way we live became a fascination that tied in with Ari's growing interest in Rastafarianism. Ari had even described feeling that she was "sitting next to God" in an interview, during a typically free-form answer to a question that possibly hadn't even been asked, but probably would have been more interesting anyway.

"I see a camera on us, and it's like what people call God," Ari had said. "It's being aware, not of yourself but of life patterns, space. But it seems I'm right in it, more than anyone else probably, underneath I feel I could just be sitting beside God."

The Slits and The Pop Group followed up the release of their joint single with a run of dates in Scotland and then across Europe, playing Holland, Belgium, Italy and Finland, and hooking up at times with new wave group the Delta 5, a band reminiscent of Gang of Four and The Slits themselves. The schedule was so packed and the gigs played in such quick succession that The Slits can barely remember anything about them, other than having to get up early every day to move on to the next venue. And of course, Bruce Smith would be playing drums for both sets every night.

While the groups were out on the road, Y Records had put out *Retrospective* – The Slits' ten-track 'official bootleg' – through Rough Trade. This was a collection of acoustic demos, scratchy home recordings and, of course, live cuts straight from the sound desk, and for some, would become a favourite Slits release. The record boasted a home-made-looking design covered in scribbled-on track titles under a big red crayonny 'Y', and included early tracks such as 'Slime', 'A Boring Life', 'Let's Do The Split', 'Face Place' and 'Or What Is It?' (the latter two to appear re-recorded and polished-up on their final album, with 'Or What Is It?' incorrectly listed on the artwork as 'Or What It Is?'), and 'Bongos On The Lawn', which was, basically, The Slits playing the bongos on the lawn, singing, improvising, and being a bit cheeky. Rough Trade sold the record for £2.50, and it ended up being a favourite of Dick's and Steve Beresford's – although Steve at first was slightly non-plussed.

"The live stuff from the US tour when they bootlegged themselves – I never understood why they did that, nobody told me why," says Steve. "In fact nobody told me anything.

"But they had really good tapes from that tour, which I think was definitely the best stuff I did with them. It's very loose, lots of unexpected things happen. The interplay in the whole group was very strong, it was very spontaneous and interesting."

Dick, perhaps not surprisingly, agrees: "I felt it was the best album, the one we did on Y Records. That period, live, was the best for The Slits, without a shadow of a doubt. They were absolutely stonking. *Cut* was like a bit of a transition between punk and the more elegant dub, it suited them all – Viv became more musical, Tess became a better reggae bass player, she was always good – and Ari always wanted to be throwing her locks about!

"Bruce on drums, well, he's really a fucking good reggae drummer. It wasn't reggae music per se, it was a fusion of great Slits songs, and there were songs that were delicate, especially Viv's more creative stuff, so that really worked well live with these amazing reggae grooves."

The beginning of the Eighties was proving to be a creatively intense time that would see The Slits working harder than ever, but also continuing to find their own interests away from the group. Viv was becoming particularly interested in contemporary dance, while Ari would join Adrian Sherwood on his new project, The New Age Steppers, a collective that would feature Pop Group singer Mark Stewart and writer Vivien Goldman, who cut the tracks 'Private Armies' and 'Launderette' with Adrian, the latter featuring Steve Beresford and Robert Wyatt on percussion.

'Man Next Door', recorded the year before, was released on June 13, with a dub version on the B-side. The collaboration between Sherwood and The Slits was such a success that there was no question they would record more together as soon as the chance arose. So, during a break in touring, Adrian, while recording a string of New Age Steppers tracks, laid down two tracks with Ari – The Slits' own song 'Animal Space' and the Junior Byles classic 'Fade Away'.

"We went into a studio for two days and cut ten songs," remembers Adrian, "including 'Animal Space', 'Private Armies', 'Launderette', 'Fade Away' and 'Love Forever' with Mark Stewart singing, that was the beginning of On-U Sound and the end of HitRun."

It was a time of conclusions and new beginnings for everyone, it seemed. Life within The Pop Group was tense, and it was agreed that, after internal struggles and differences of opinion, they had to split. According to their manager Dick, Mark Stewart and Gareth Sager were the driving forces of the group, but they were too different as individuals to make it work at this stage – Mark being "political and paranoid" while Gareth was a more "joyous" character, in Dick's words.

The Pop Group decided to play one final gig in October 1980 at a CND rally in Trafalgar Square with the industrial post-punkers Killing Joke. The Pop Group's bassist, Simon Underwood, had left to form Pigbag, and Gareth Sager had already spotted the perfect replacement for Simon, and it was someone he knew he wanted to work with post-Pop Group too.

"Gareth saw Sean Oliver busking on the Underground," explains Tessa. "He was so impressed he invited him to play with them in Trafalgar Square. I slowly got to know him."

Gareth and Bruce formed the vibrant, Roland Kirk-inspired Rip, Rig And Panic a year after the dissolution of The Pop Group, and Sean was the obvious choice of bass player. Sean's sister, Andrea Oliver, would also sing with the group, as would Neneh Cherry. For The Slits it was like an extension of the Slits / Pop Group family. But it was when near-disaster struck that Tessa and Sean got to know each other properly.

"They had had this quite horrific car crash, Gareth, Sean and a painter called Dexter, and I remember going in to visit him in hospital. Sean had to have this pin put into his leg. I had met him originally through Bruce, but that was when I started getting close to Sean."

Sean and Tessa became an item, and would have a daughter, Phoebe, but Sean tragically passed away in 1990 after complications from sickle cell anaemia.

By the end of 1980, The Pop Group were no more, Adrian Sherwood was soaring off into new directions and The Slits were in a state of healthy unrest with Y Records, content with their output but requiring more stability and better promotion. Apart from anything else, Y Records didn't have the funds to do that.

Dick would remain on the scene with The Slits, and would produce several tracks on their next album, but their relationship with Y had reached a natural conclusion. Dick himself admits it had always been "precarious" financially, and the group also wanted to be successful in their own right. They'd been lumped in with the now defunct Pop Group for long enough and, positive as this had been, everyone was moving on.

Steve Beresford, who composed and performed with various different groups, maintained a relationship with Y Records. His collaboration with cellist Tristan Honsinger, *Double Indemnity,* came out on the label in 1980, and *Imitation Of Life* – another improvised work, alive with brass, woodwind, toys, sirens and rattles, was released the following year. The Promenaders, featuring Beresford, drummer Terry Day and David Toop on 'one-string violin', were also embraced by Y. They were perfectly in keeping in that they were not in keeping with anything, and they celebrated that fact.

"We'd play waltzes for people on Brighton beach," says Steve, who sang and played euphonium in The Promenaders. "We had a PA that was an old RAF microphone and a five-watt amplifier, and we busked our way through 'Worker's Playtime' and the 'Blue Danube'." They released their eponymous LP on Y in 1982, the same year the company also put out Sun Ra's *Nuclear War* album.

While Y may have been appropriate in some ways for The Slits, they were keen to join a more established label again, and between themselves and Christine they set about arranging some meetings. While it was easy for The Slits to get seen by major labels, it wasn't so straightforward to get signed. After moving on from Y, they released 'Animal Space' on Human Records on November 7, 1980, with the dub version, 'Animal Spacier', on the B-side. But this was a one-off.

The Slits, in the main, felt they needed the profile and financial security that only a bigger label could provide – and it didn't get much bigger than CBS. The fact that The Clash had their artistic control undermined several years earlier by the label when it released (ironically) 'Remote Control' without discussing it with them, wasn't going to put them off. Plus The Slits had been around the block a few times with labels by now, and knew what to expect and look out for. They had also been working hard on material for their second album, and had recorded some tracks already with Adrian and Dennis Bovell, footing the bill themselves. This made them an even more attractive package.

"People in the business were always so interested in The Slits," says Christine. "They might not fund them, but you could get in to see anybody. Richard Branson turned them down, but they signed with CBS in 1980, and they were right into them."

Viv adds, "We always wanted to be more mainstream, foolishly. We never managed it because everything we did and said went against that, but we didn't want to be underground or get swallowed up. We felt we had a message that had to be got across."

After signing to CBS in the winter of 1980, The Slits went straight back on tour across America, with Neneh as a backing singer and dancer and, of course, Bruce and Steve.

"Viv Albertine was very disappointed when she saw me as I'd had a shave," remembers Steve. "She didn't like the idea of anyone shaving hair off any part of their body. She was quite strict about it. But then it turned out that she bleached the hair on her legs, which I thought was cheating."

Body hair issues aside, their second visit to the States reflected how hard they had worked, and how far they had progressed musically, but it also reflected the fact that they were getting increasingly exhausted. One listen to their interview with the college radio station WORT FM in Madison, Wisconsin, lovingly captured and released as a 7" with their second album, *Return Of The Giant Slits*, the following year, shows that some of the excitement the group felt on their first trip to America had worn off, to say the least. Callers would ring up to put their burning questions to The Slits, and in response they would shriek and cackle down the line, play cassette recordings of trains (The Slits were always making recordings of unlikely sounds, moments and snippets of conversation for occasions such as these), sing, demand tea and generally terrorise the listeners and the DJ.

It went something like this:

DJ: The Slits have just walked into the studio – you're a lucky bunch out there if you're huddled to your radio (*peals of laughter from The Slits*)... let's see if we can get this interview off the ground. With me in the studio are Ari Up, Viv and Tessa, am I pronouncing that right, 'Ari Up' is it?
Ari: No, no. 'Tashi'.
DJ: Tashi. OK ... So you just drove in from Chicago?
All: Yes.
DJ: And you're very tired?
All: Yes. (*All affect big yawns and snoring sounds)*
Ari: Could I have a tea with lemon please? (*Tape of train sound effect gets switched on. Giggling. Train sounds get louder.)*
Caller 1: Hello, I want to know about The Slits!
DJ: Well, ask them, who would you like to talk to?
Viv: You'd better have good questions though.
Caller 1: Are you going to give it your best tonight?

Viv: Best what? (*Train tape gets switched on again, accompanied by screams and whoops from The Slits.)* Next caller.
Caller 2: Do you know Nina Hagen?
All: *(Groan) More train noises, yelling and screaming.*
Viv: Next question.
DJ: (*Sounding weary)* WORT, you're on the air …
Caller 3: Who does your hair?
Ari: (*Affecting American accent)* Oh the hairdressers, you know, they have a new way of uncombing hair.
Viv: We comb it backwards.
Ari: We're very backward over in Europe. *Tape starts again, Slits start talking in gibberish in very high voices.*
Ari: Where's my tea with lemon?
DJ: WORT, you're on the air … forget it, they hung up. Talk to The Slits and they'll … be primitive for you. What kind of music do you listen to when you're on the road?
Ari: Oh Jesus. Quick, next phone call … Being in a cage all day is worse than not being in America …
DJ: America…is like a cage?
Ari: It is a bit, very much so.
DJ: What do you think of Ronald Reagan?
All: Boring.
Ari: Full of shit.
DJ: WORT, you're on the air.
Caller 4: It's silly and you're an asshole!
DJ: Goodbye. WORT, you're on the air.
Caller 5: … Er, I don't wanna be on the air. *(Much hilarity)*
Caller 6: (*Strong Midwest accent*) Do you Slits play any good country?
Ari: Country?

And so on. But as Don Letts explained as he reminisced about the White Riot tour back in 1977, The Slits didn't just save their cheeky, funny and sometimes infuriating side for times like these – they were like this all the time, it wasn't an act. Unfortunately it could hold them back at the most inopportune moments. After arriving in Los Angeles, fatigued and starving, The Slits had finally managed to find an appropriate restaurant when all hell broke loose.

"When you're touring, eating is such an important thing," sighs Christine. "Ari's unpredictability could be a pain in the arse because I'd have to clear up the mess. The worst thing happened in this posh part of LA. We had just got there and we were going out for something to eat at this lovely health food restaurant. They were already the centre of attention because of the bizarre dress and Ari had started growing the dreadlocks. We were all starving and we just had to eat, so we sat in this restaurant and we were waiting a little while for the waitress to come, she was probably a bit scared. And then Ari starts.

"She goes at the top of her voice, 'You're using Mexican slaves in the kitchen!' Which was quite true, that's exactly how LA was run, 'You American people, you're disgusting, you're no better than slavemasters!' Everyone's going, 'Shut up, Ari, shut up, we want to eat!' Then the waitress comes over and says, 'Madam, would you lower your voice, you're upsetting the customers,' and she yells, 'I don't care!' and is standing on the table and all the rest of it, and we were all thinking, 'We're not going to eat tonight.'

"Then it got worse. The manager came out, a really uptight American woman, 'You'll have to leave my restaurant!' and Ari's going 'You are a slavemaster! You are exploiting slaves,' and then she spat on her."

The outraged manageress promptly called the police, claiming she had been assaulted. The Slits had started to make their way out of the restaurant, but the police were already outside, waiting to arrest Ari. She was frisked, cuffed and bundled into the car. "It was proper stuff," says Christine. "They were brutal, as they were."

Ari was taken to the station with Christine. The manager of the restaurant pressed charges, and Ari had to be bailed, although the money – the equivalent of £1,000 – was not readily available. Christine: "I had to phone the bank in England and they had to wire the money to a named bank in LA and we had to go in with two forms of ID to pick it up. But they were quite good, it happened quite quickly."

This tour, from Christmas 1980 to January 1981, felt far more fraught than their last. They were all at the end of their rope. They'd been travelling, writing and recording non-stop all year and it was taking its toll. The group remained strong at its core, but they seriously needed a break.

Steve: "It's hard for me to evaluate the vibe on that tour, I was just kind of trying to stay sane! I think I had to block out a lot. It was like, 'No, this is too painful, I can't deal with this. There's somebody here who is the manager so I'm going to leave it to her'."

Luckily for everyone, it was the uber-capable, loyal – and patient – Christine. Steve had enough to worry about trying to keep track of his ever-growing collection of instruments, hoping none of the roadies were going to crush his euphonium or decimate his toy pianos accidentally in a misguided gear-loading incident. Those hopes were in vain.

"My euphonium got flattened on one of the journeys," he recalls. "These things happen. It wasn't a very good euphonium, I'd have been more upset if it was. I had a lot of instruments, I had a flugelhorn, euphonium, guitar, couple of keyboards, toy pianos, little percussion instruments, so I had a lot of stuff. The roadies could never quite understand what that was about.

"Roadies traditionally are big heaving guys with black T-shirts, but these guys were nice, middle-class boys. But even so I was desperately worried that someone was going to tread on my trumpet at any moment."

Chapter 18

"We were child stars, ignored child stars, forgotten child stars!" – Ari Up

Creating the second album, *Return Of The Giant Slits*, was taking time. Unlike with *Cut*, tracks were being recorded separately in different places with different producers. The idea was to be able to give each track individual attention and its own feel, but as a result the album, as far as The Slits were concerned, seemed less cohesive and whole, and the process of making it felt never-ending. Some tracks had already been recorded, but the album was finished after CBS signed them and they had more money. But the fact remains that *Return Of The Giant Slits,* while totally different from *Cut,* has a magical but more mature, contemplative quality, still with a liberal sprinkling of Slits madness.

Dennis Bovell would produce some of the tracks, as would Dick O'Dell, Adrian Sherwood and Nick Launay, a producer who had worked with PiL. They recorded partly at Studio 80, Dennis' own studio at Southwark Bridge; partly at Gooseberry in Gerrard Street, London's Chinatown, and partly in Berry Street, near the East End.

Even though The Slits themselves admitted at the time that it felt like they'd been working on the album for years, the time they gave themselves to approach their own songs in a more considered way seemed to be paying off when it came to the ideas being expressed.

"I felt really good for them," says Dennis. "They'd progressed, their writing skills had moved on and their love of merging different types of rhythms had multiplied. It was real progress. I love them girls, so anything that was good for them, you know?"

The themes on the second album were the same as before but with added eco-mysticism in the mesmeric 'Earthbeat', 'Walkabout', a percussion-packed track with funk-driven bass and guitar, the timeless 'Animal Space' and 'Life On Earth', which was rather spooky. They were still exploring the complications of love in the hypnotic, twinkling 'Or What Is It?', the increasingly tiresome difficulties of simply leaving the house and getting on the Tube while dressed like, well, a Slit in 'Improperly Dressed', a spiky, funny song full of vocal rounds and an idiosyncratic bass line that seems to dance along independently from the rest of the instrumentals. 'Face Place', written by Tessa, originates from before *Cut* but was kept back, and it explores issues similar to those in 'Typical Girls', the vanities girls can so easily slip into. 'Face Place' is like several songs in one, and on *Return* it was whipped into a fascinating combination of *Play School*-like toy instruments, ominous silent movie music, brass and jazz influences all laced with The Slits' chanting group vocals and Ari's octave-busting, almost operatic voice, which, on this album, is on top form and has an almost jewel-like clarity.

Steve Beresford: "I loved Tessa and Viv's playing, and now I appreciate Ari's singing more than I did. Maybe because Björk ripped her off so shamelessly! Wow! The first time I heard Björk I thought she sounds exactly like Ari. I listen to that music now and I think, 'Actually, Ari's really good at this."

Tessa had sung 'Adventures Close To Home' on the previous album, and this time it was Viv's turn to take the mic. While Viv feels dubious about the track 'Life On Earth', her vocals have a high, quavering fragility and sound like an instrument, tangling up with the ticking sound of the woodblock and hi-hat drum part and her chiming guitar, lending the song an almost oriental quality before it descends into animal sounds and percussion. Viv sums up the track concisely: "My go at singing was pathetic. But it used to work brilliantly live. It was all about the planet and jungle and animals."

The concepts assembled in *Return* reflected the developing interests of The Slits, which were growing slightly apart. Ari spent every night she could at the Bali Hai in Streatham to catch Moa Anbessa sound system, and she was simultaneously becoming less and less interested in guitar-based music. Tessa's leaning towards what was happening musically in New York pushed her towards funk, and Viv's lyrics became more questioning and intense. She was keen to keep their output about songs and stories, while Ari was getting more deeply entrenched in reggae.

"It was more beat-oriented rather than song," Viv says of the album. "Ari's gone very much that way now, whereas I love songs. I think it moved away from song and towards rhythm, we were getting into ethnic music, jazz and improvisation, reggae. There were so many things coming at us and as you move on, you want to incorporate what you're hearing."

The Slits were learning more about jazz chords and different time signatures, and in Viv's opinion, they started to complicate their music at this point – whereas it was the relative simplicity of their previous work that was so charming. But this was an opportunity to try new things, and the result would be mind-boggling at times. Also, their relationship with each other was changing, the bond was still strong but they were all growing up, and were at different levels of development personally.

"We were feeling darker," explains Viv. "We'd now been through the music business and we'd been shafted, we'd been hit on, tricked, everything, we were very different people, and sick of each other at this stage as well probably!

"It was still a family, but we were interested in other people, and Ari had totally grown up from being a child of 14 at the beginning, so she found herself and different types of people she was into. She started dating, all those things she wasn't doing at the beginning. It was a huge curve she went through."

Bruce Smith remembers feeling that the songs on the album were revealing vignettes that provided a view into the group themselves, from their feelings to their musical process. Their time in the music industry had not hardened them up to the point that they were going to start writing formulaically, and fortunately CBS did not expect that of them. "No question, that album absolutely reflected what was going on for the three of them," he says.

"But in some ways second records are not quite as strong as the first, because the people making them don't really have enough time to gather the same sort of creative ideas and focus. With a little more time to develop it, who knows what might have happened?"

Although plenty of time had been taken, what The Slits may have needed was to hole up for one chunk of time in one place where they could make the album grow organically as a whole, as they did with *Cut*. But it can't be denied that the eventual release is a unique, brave and colourful album that demands full concentration and patience, and is well worth the effort. From the listener's point of view, there is a sense of almost learning another language, but once the code is cracked the results are magical and rewarding.

"It's mentally good," says Adrian Sherwood. "Dennis will always say they are among his favourite records he's ever done. Both *Cut* and *Return* have a unique character. It's very hard for women in the business anyway, they don't get the credit. Everybody goes, 'Oh, it's got to be Dennis Bovell, it's got to be Adrian Sherwood,' the fact is, it's bollocks.

"Ari is a great producer, she's a visionary and has been since she's been about 13, 14; that is a woman who is absolutely unique. And as a band, if you go and see The Slits, don't take the piss because they'll eat you up! You can see the power coming off them. They could have done a lot better. Circumstances are the only reason they didn't crack on, plus the fact that they're all a bit bonkers.

"But if people say, 'What did you do?', The Slits can hold up those records and say, 'We did this. What the fuck have you done?'"

Viv was, by now, very much pushing the group forward and organising everything, which didn't always go down well, but it was a question of getting everything done or not. As usual they had been very much left to their own devices, but this also gave them the freedom to shape the product from the songs to the artwork themselves. Graphic designer Neville Brody was in charge of putting together the artwork, which featured dramatic paintings of Tessa's.

Viv: "It was a good package. We were always very concerned with how things looked, a lot of effort went into that. It was kind of a punk ethos. Not many groups did it, but we really did, we cared very much. Things had to look right, the attitude was right, the merchandise was right, the songs, everything had to be in the right vein.

"We had to change the artwork because instead of saying 'Return Of

The Giant Slits' it said 'Giant Return of The Slits'! It was on the merchandise, on the T-shirts. I said, 'No, it's a totally different thing, to make the return giant or The Slits giant! It's not a B-movie joke.' I was the one on top of everything back then and it exhausted me."

Dick O'Dell saw from the word go that a lot of pressure was on Viv to keep things moving in the group. "I always felt a bit sorry for Viv," he says. "She had the whole thing on her shoulders. Ari couldn't keep the band together on her own – and Tess, well, at that time, God bless her, forget it. It was Viv who ran that band, and I mean that 100 per cent. No Viv, no band."

Dick was to work with The Slits one final time after the album, travelling to New York with them in June to support The Clash at Bond's in Times Square, alongside Bad Brains. This would also be the last time that The Slits would see The Clash for a long time. There seemed to be a sense of finality wherever they looked: Mick Jones and Joe Strummer were struggling to communicate – the creative tension that was always there had started to boil over into something less constructive – The Slits themselves were fraying at the edges due to sheer exhaustion apart from anything else, and Viv would see her old mentor Keith Levene, living in New York and at a particularly low point with his addiction, for the last time in more than 25 years.

"Keith Levene was around, but he was already a casualty," says Dick. "Great fucking guitarist. We really did try to help him, but it was no use. When people get into smack, it's fucking hard to get them out of it. I've got no time for it."

Keith remembers, "I bumped into them in New York, we were in a dressing room, Dick was there. It was like Dick had the band now, and I was a bit like, 'Grr, yer cunt!' but I was also like, 'Good, you're taking them where they need to go.'

"After we left that dressing room that was the last time I saw any of them for ages, although Ari ended up in my front room in New York with my first wife and my kid, and Ari was there with her kids and dread boyfriend in '84, '85. She was going, 'Oh Keith, it's so funny to see you all domesticated!' and I was thinking, 'Domesticated, my fucking arse!'"

Once The Slits returned to the UK, the group were keen to take some time out of the city and relax, rehearse material for their promotional tour of *Return*, and write new songs for what they hoped would be their third album. They felt like they hadn't stopped up to this point, and needed to slow things down.

In a bid to relive the Ridge Farm experience, Ari, Viv, Tessa, Christine, Bruce and Neneh escaped to spend the late summer and early autumn months in a remote cottage surrounded by fields in Wales. "We went to write and get out of London, have some peace," explains Tessa. "We'd done a hell of a lot of travelling, sometimes you need to look back, observe and take another view.

"I remember going to the fields and it was mushroom season, I was picking thousands of mushrooms and hanging them up to dry for my cooking. Neneh was there, I remember while we were rehearsing in the rehearsal room she was sitting there doing her knitting!"

Because Christine was – and continues to be – a skilled film-maker, The Slits decided to use the time and woodland surroundings to make a video for the Viv and Tessa-penned 'Earthbeat', which was released as a single that August.

"We did a beautiful video with Neneh Cherry, we were riding horses," says Ari. "We're galloping around, it should be seen. Viv walked with hers, but me and Tessa are horse people, we grew up riding horses. I remember riding racehorses when I was a little kid, it was great! I felt like I was flying."

"Neneh does African dancing in the video," adds Tessa. "She was like another Slit towards the end, and added another element to the group – her African experiences. Her real father was an African drummer and she'd been to Sierra Leone recently, so she brought a different influence into the group.

"She taught us a couple of traditional songs that we used on stage, like a traditional wedding song. She had a bit of input into what we were doing, and she danced really well."

The Slits' new writing was going ever more down the 'world-beat' route, and CBS was excited to hear what they were coming up with, agreeing to organise recording sessions in South America with a local jazz producer for their next album. They were also in the throes of planning gigs in Japan and Australia, further afield than The Slits had ever been, but it wasn't to be.

As the group's time in Wales was coming to an end, and they prepared to head back to London for the release of *Return* and a Peel Session, some stunning news was heading Ari's way. "That was the exact time she found that she was pregnant with twins, right towards the end," says Tessa. This wouldn't stop Ari from touring, doing interviews and giving her all on stage, but it was tiring and tense. "She didn't have an easy pregnancy," Tessa explains.

On October 12, just before the album release, The Slits recorded what would be their final Peel Session, recording a beautiful version of 'Difficult Fun'; more beautiful than on the album thanks to the use of piano instead of "nasty synth", in Steve's words, sprinklings of echo and effects and pure reggae bass and drums. Sean Oliver and Neneh featured on the joyous funky rap marathon 'In The Beginning', and 'Earthbeat' also featured, augmented by tumbling percussion and segueing into Neneh's haunting African 'Wedding Song'.

Anyone who tuned in to that session could hear that The Slits were going into exciting new areas that were a million miles from the glossy pop that was normally on the radio, but again, their new album proved to be an acquired taste.

"It was not well received because it was so different," says Christine. "Not that it really bothered CBS, because they were into them for the long term, and they had already chosen a South American jazz producer for their next recording.

"The direction they were going in just before they split up was a whole new thing again. They were writing a new female music at the time, and it didn't have reference points. And of course the media and the public need reference points. Look at today, you go into MySpace and you've got to put yourself into genres. What if you don't fit into a genre? Or if you fit into more than one?"

Tessa admits she wasn't bothered that the album wasn't a hit in the conventional sense. The only problem was, due to the comparative lack of outlets at that time, if a record wasn't a commercial success, it ultimately just wouldn't get heard. "You want as many people as possible to hear your music," she says. "We didn't have computers then, it was only going to be the people who heard it on the radio or who bought the record if they could get it in that country. Now it's completely different of course.

"To me it was more of a creative endeavour, to break new ground in what you're doing. But we all felt a bit disappointed that we weren't more successful or recognised, and that we'd be virtually written out of the history books – or her-story books!

"They released the album here, and re-released it in Japan. What's funny about the Japanese import is that they've written the lyrics down all wrong! They've just listened to the record and totally misheard what the lyrics are. Completely different meanings of the songs, just abstract lyrics. So funny."

CBS stumped up some tour support for The Slits to head off around the UK that winter, a tour that would culminate in a homecoming gig at Hammersmith Palais just before Christmas. CBS weren't as generous as Island in this respect, but at least this meant that the group played more realistically sized venues in the regions, and instead of flying jazz stars or reggae artists with extravagant tastes over for the tour, they had an avant-garde female dance troupe called The Carpets to open the shows, and Adrian Sherwood mixing the sound. Financially the tour was a success, certainly in comparison with the Simply What's Happening tour for *Cut*.

However, Ari was starting to become unwell and anxious during her pregnancy. Viv recalls her pulling out her eyebrows on the tour bus until she literally had none left by the time they got to the gig. Travelling together soon became difficult and Christine took Ari under her wing. But The Slits didn't realise that Christine had also become pregnant, she just didn't want to tell anyone yet.

"I was in a relationship and thought I'd have the baby, fuck it," says Christine. "I'd carry on working and then tell them. But Ari was very sick with it from the word go. I think once you've had kids you can understand a bad pregnancy, but you can't if you haven't and you're trying to make a career of something. This put huge stress on everything.

"In the end, I just got a hire car and drove her. When it came to being on stage Ari was always Ari, and the performances were always fine, but at the end of the tour everybody was really pleased to not see each other for a while."

The Hammersmith Palais gig was a success, and the London Contemporary Dance Theatre also performed as part of the show. "They used great music," remembers Viv. "The lead guy had locks, they were great dancers, really cool." Nobody knew this would be the final Slits gig, but as far as Viv was concerned, the end was nigh.

"Viv was banking her life on this," says Christine. "She was 26, not that that should matter, but she still didn't have any money in her pocket. She had all the fame but none of the benefits and she was unhappy.

"Another thing that had led up to this, [was the fact that] because Ari had been ill, there was a really important demo recording for CBS and, as Ari wasn't there, Neneh had to sing on it. It had become difficult to carry on.

"On top of this, Tessa by now had a drug problem. I had no idea, I just thought she did a lot of weed. I wasn't averse to a bit of that myself, but I'd got no experience of heroin. Anyway, at that point, all the responsibilities had come down to Viv. She didn't mind driving things, but I think she became burdened towards the end."

After the Hammersmith gig, The Slits individually had a chance for a rest and some time to think before reconvening in the New Year of 1982. Tessa admits she was ready to put music down for a while, she'd been going through her own difficulties, and Viv, responsibilities aside, had started to feel that musically they were all starting to pull in very different directions. Not only that, but simply the life of being a Slit, years of being attacked and hit on, had toughened her up to the point that she didn't recognise herself.

Viv remembers, "It got to the stage in the Eighties where I felt, 'Can I go out of my front door again, dressed like this, and take what I'm going to have to take all day long?' Every step there'd be staring, comments, swearing, physical stuff, on the Tube it was the same. My face got so hard. I walked past a window in Knightsbridge and I caught sight of this hard blonde woman, and, my God, it was me.

"I thought, 'Oh no, that's it.' Years of feeling: 'Don't you dare look at me, or say one thing or I'll give it back to you.' When I saw that though, I just didn't recognise myself. I had to work on my expression, I had to consciously soften my face, change my hair just not to court attention. I just didn't want to be the person I caught sight of.

"It was so difficult. Ari didn't want the group to split, but apart from anything else, after that last album, we had musically run our course. It sounds corny to say musical differences, it's great to come from different places musically because together you make a bigger whole, but there has to be a crossing over."

Tessa also observed that Ari had started to become unhappy living in England, she found the weather dreary and it no longer suited her. They were all keen to have a break. "Ari had had enough, she couldn't take the climate any more," explains Tessa. "I was quite happy with us finishing at that point. I actually wanted and needed to do something else, so I was quite relieved.

"We'd been so close from Ari being 14, me being 17, and it's like you've missed out on a certain side of life, your own personal journey. You're a group, but you need to discover things about your own personal self, so that to me wasn't a bad thing."

Just after New Year, The Slits called a meeting with CBS executive Howard Thomson at a café in Covent Garden. Christine was oblivious to the fact the group were actually going to split, and decided that now would be a good time to announce her happy news. "I told them I was pregnant and explained I could carry on and work through it, but then Viv came forward and said, 'I don't want the band to continue.'

"The only part I played in that meeting was that I said, 'Are you really sure? Why don't you take a year off and do something else for a bit and then go back to it? Just take a break. Just arrange things for South America and then sort everything out there,' but it was too much for Viv. I'm not sure how Tess felt."

Viv: "Howard wasn't surprised we were going to split, and it was no loss to CBS I'm sure. We went our separate ways. I started to work towards going back to art school, making short films."

After the split, Viv couldn't listen to any music for several years, listening only to LBC or BBC Radio 4. She equated the end of The Slits to the end of a love affair, and duly went through a process akin to post-traumatic stress. Ari, conversely, never stopped making music, and after having her twins (with Tessa at her bedside), she travelled to the jungles of Belize and Borneo, before settling in Jamaica. Tessa, however, while glad of the breathing space, found her addiction deepened immediately after the split. There was a hole in her life where The Slits used to be, the excitement of getting up on stage, life on the road, the family atmosphere of the group, all of this had gone and heroin became even more of a crutch.

"I just had that gap in my life," she explains. "I felt a bit lost and I fell into the trap of heroin addiction. I didn't have as bad a habit as some people, but it did affect me really badly for about five years on and off. I just treat it as an education."

Tessa knew she needed an adventure to take her out of herself, and travelled to Sudan with a friend. "It was an incredible experience, I don't think you could travel there in that way now, but my friend had been before to that part of the world and spoke fluent Arabic. We stayed there for two months and then I went to Ethiopia for two weeks.

"But really, the group never ended because we're back in a new chapter now."

In 2006, more than two decades after parting ways, Ari and Tessa decided to revive The Slits. Viv chose not to be involved, feeling that The Slits, as a concept, very much belonged to a moment in time, and she was reluctant to take a step backwards. But Tessa found that it was exactly what she needed at the time. "It's quite uncanny because just before Ari contacted me about it, we were both thinking the same thing separately. I went to Sean's gravestone, and I was feeling a bit low, and I was saying, 'Help me, I just feel really lost at the moment,' and it just came to me that we should get back together when I was sitting by the gravestone.

"And then I met Ari a couple of months later and she'd been thinking the same thing. A friend of mine had also said, 'Why don't you get The Slits back together?' All the signs were there."

Ari, based in Kingston, Jamaica, had become a dancehall star known as Madussa, also living and working in Brooklyn, New York, touring and recording with her backing group, The True Warriors. Tessa, meanwhile, had been exploring martial arts and Chinese medicine, and had continued to draw and paint. The pair assembled a sort of punk era supergroup, featuring Adam & The Ants guitarist Marco Pirroni, Sex Pistols drummer Paul Cook, with Tessa's daughter Phoebe and Paul's daughter Hollie on backing vocals. They released an EP – 'Revenge Of The Killer Slits' – before creating a new line-up featuring two new female guitarists, No and Adele Wilson, and drummer Anna Schulte. They performed in 2006 with The New York Dolls and Buzzcocks at Selfridges' 'Future Punk' event, as part of the department store's celebration of the 30th anniversary of punk. The basement was decorated to recreate Soho's notorious drinking den the Colony Room, Don Letts appeared as star DJ and Ari jokingly urged the crowd, which included unlikely punk fan Jude Law, to raid Selfridges in the true spirit of 'Shoplifting'.

Viv Albertine, who had been working as a TV director and film maker, joined them for two gigs in 2008, one at a Spanish festival, and the other at Manchester's Ladyfest, but while they were successful, these dates confirmed Viv's inner feelings about reforming. At the time of writing The Slits are recording a new album. Viv is also working on a solo album.

Whatever the future might bring it is The Slits' first album, *Cut,* which has sealed their place in history, and remains an inspiring legacy. The Slits left the door wide open for women to become musicians – or indeed become any kind of artist – without feeling the need to compromise. "The great thing is that there are so many more women playing instruments," says Tessa. "There are women drummers, women horn-players, it really has moved on. It's not just a woman with a guitar singing folk. I think what we did had an effect."

The Slits' importance goes far beyond gender issues alone, however. Artistically they were brave and innovative against all odds. They tried anything and everything, nothing was off-limits if it was interesting enough. They were pioneers exploring uncharted territory, and their tireless experimenting and forward-looking stance remind us to strive for originality, to make that effort.

Budgie admits that, from many people's point of view, it was his work on *Cut* that caught the imagination. "I was doing some rehearsing when the Banshees had stopped, and I was putting The Creatures' stuff together. I went into this rehearsal room in London and the guys from Elastica were there.

"When I walked in they all went like this (worshipping motion), and I was like, 'What's going on? They're taking the piss, right?' And they were going: 'The Slits! *Cut*, man, it's God!'"

"It's important they've got a 30th anniversary of *Cut,*" adds Keith Levene. "It happened, read about it, write about it, look at the fucking pictures. And look at them now! They're a lot better than a lot of these male bands, debauched wankers, balding gits. It's not an issue about age, it's an issue about handling your life. They must have done something right, as far as I'm concerned."

Discography

7" Singles

Typical Girls / I Heard It Through The Grapevine
Island WIP 65-5 September 1979

In The Beginning There Was Rhythm / Where There's A Will (by The Pop Group)
Rough Trade / Y Records RT 039/Y-1 March 1980

Man Next Door / Man Next Door (Version)
Rough Trade / Y RT 044/Y-4 June 1980

Animal Space / Animal Spacier
Human Records HUM 4 November 1980

Earthbeat / Begin Again Rhythm
CBS A 1498 August 1981

American Radio Interview / Face Dub
(Released with album *Return Of The Giant Slits*) CBS 85269 October 1981

12" Singles

Typical Girls (Brink Style) / I Heard It Through The Grapevine and Liebe And Romanze
Island 12WIP 6505 September 1979

Earthbeat / Earthdub and Begin Again Rhythm
CBS A 131498 August 1981

Albums

CUT
Instant Hit/So Tough/Spend, Spend, Spend/Shoplifting/FM/New Town/Ping Pong Affair/Love Und Romance/Typical Girls/Adventures Close To Home
Island ILPS 9573 September 1979
Reissued in the UK in 1990, with the inclusion of I Heard It Through The Grapevine and Liebe And Romanze
Island IMCD 89 April 1990

BOOTLEG RETROSPECTIVE
Number One Enemy/Slime/A Boring Life/Or What It Is?/Face Place/Once Upon A Time In A Living Room/Mosquitoes/(Vindictive) Let's Do The Split/Vaseline/Bongos On The Lawn/No More Rock And Roll For You
Rough Trade YY3 May 1980

RETURN OF THE GIANT SLITS
Earthbeat/Or What It Is?/Face Place/Walk About/Difficult Fun/Animal Space –Spacier/Improperly Dressed/Life On Earth
CBS 85269 October 1981
Reissued in Japan by Sony Japan MHCP208 April 2004, with Earthbeat (Japanese Version)
Reissued in the UK on Blast First Petite PTYT08 October 2007, with dub versions and American Radio Interview

(Mini album) THE PEEL SESSIONS (First and second sessions)
Vindictive/Love And Romance/New Town/Shoplifting/So Tough/Instant Hit/FM
Strange Fruit SMPA November 1988
Strange Fruit SMFPACD 207 (CD) November 1988
Reissued 1989 SFPSO21 with the tracks Difficult Fun/In The Beginning There Was Rhythm/ Earthbeat/Wedding Song

IN THE BEGINNING: A LIVE ANTHOLOGY 1977-1981
Vindictive/A Boring Life/Slime/New Town/Love And Romance/Shoplifting/Number One Enemy/Number One Enemy/In The Beginning/New Town/Man Next Door/ Grapevine/Typical Girls/Fade Away / In The Beginning
Jungle FREUD DD 057 October 1997

LIVE AT THE GIBUS CLUB
Split/Vaseline/So Tough/New Town/Instant Hit/Un Homme et Une Slit/Love And Romance/Femme Fatale/Shoplifting/Enemy Numero Uno/Split (Encore)/Shoplifting (Encore)
Castle Music CMQCD 1058 February 2005

EPs

THE PEEL SESSION 19.9.77
Vindictive/Love And Romance/New Town/Shoplifting
Strange Fruit SFPS 021 January 1987

REVENGE OF THE KILLER SLITS
Slits Tradition/Number One Enemy/Kill Em With Love
Saf Records SAF-14 October 2006

Solo releases

DREAD MORE DAN DEAD – Ari Up
Baby Mother/True Warrior/Exterminator/Me Done/Young Boy/Bashment feat.LA Lewis/Kill Em With Love/Allergic feat. Terranova/Can't Share/Can't Trust The Majority Mass/Baby Mother/Me Done (vocal)/Bonus: CD Video
Collision Cause Of Chapter CCT3002-2 July 2005

Bibliography

Gardner, Ken. *In Session Tonight* (BBC Books, 1993)
Gilbert, Pat. *Passion Is A Fashion* (Aurum Press, 2005)
Letts, Don. *Culture Clash* (SAF Publishing, 2006)
Lydon, John. *Rotten – No Irish, No Blacks, No Dogs* (Picador, 1995)
Peel, John. *Margrave Of The Marshes* (Bantam Press, 2005)
Reynolds, Simon. *Rip It Up And Start Again* (Faber & Faber, 2005)
Savage, John. *England's Dreaming* (Faber & Faber, 1991)

Online:
3am Magazine – http://www.3ammagazine.com/3am/
Perfect Sound Forever – http://www.furious.com/perfect/
Black Market Clash – http://homepage.mac.com/blackmarketclash/
Rock's Back Pages – http://www.rocksbackpages.com/

Journals:
Thanks to the British Library, and also the *NME* archives, I have spent many happy hours leafing (very carefully) through thousands of original *Melody Makers*, *NME*s and *Sounds.* I would have been quite happy to move in.